THE HANDBOOK OF RECOVERY CAPITAL

Understanding the Science and Practice

Edited by
David Best and Emily A. Hennessy

With a Foreword by
William White

First published in Great Britain in 2025 by

Bristol University Press
University of Bristol
1–9 Old Park Hill
Bristol
BS2 8BB
UK
t: +44 (0)117 374 6645
e: bup-info@bristol.ac.uk

Details of international sales and distribution partners are available at bristoluniversitypress.co.uk

© Bristol University Press 2025

British Library Cataloguing in Publication Data
A catalogue record for this book is available from the British Library

ISBN 978-1-5292-4027-6 hardcover
ISBN 978-1-5292-4028-3 paperback
ISBN 978-1-5292-4029-0 ePub
ISBN 978-1-5292-4030-6 ePdf

The right of David Best and Emily A. Hennessy to be identified as editors of this work has been asserted by them in accordance with the Copyright, Designs and Patents Act 1988.

All rights reserved: no part of this publication may be reproduced, stored in a retrieval system, or transmitted in any form or by any means, electronic, mechanical, photocopying, recording, or otherwise without the prior permission of Bristol University Press.

Every reasonable effort has been made to obtain permission to reproduce copyrighted material. If, however, anyone knows of an oversight, please contact the publisher.

The statements and opinions contained within this publication are solely those of the editors and contributors and not of the University of Bristol or Bristol University Press. The University of Bristol and Bristol University Press disclaim responsibility for any injury to persons or property resulting from any material published in this publication.

Bristol University Press works to counter discrimination on grounds of gender, race, disability, age and sexuality.

Cover design: Lyn Davies Design
Front cover image: Stocksy/Single Fin Photo

To my beautiful wife Jessica and my wonderful children, Billy and Skye, who inspire so much of what I do

David

To Gary, my best friend and greatest supporter, and to my children, Saoirse and Caoimhe, who always put a smile on my face

Emily

Contents

List of Figures, Tables, and Boxes		vii
Notes on Contributors		ix
Foreword by William White		xiv
1	Introduction to the Handbook of Recovery Capital *David Best and Emily A. Hennessy*	1
2	Inception to Integration: The Theoretical Roots and Institutional Growth of Recovery Capital *Robert Granfield and William Cloud*	10
3	Reflections on Initial Attempts at the Quantification of Recovery Capital *David Best, William White, and Lauren A. Hoffman*	33
4	The Evolution of Approaches to Measure Recovery Capital *Adela Bunaciu, Matthew J. Belanger, Ana-Maria Bliuc, and Arun Sondhi*	50
5	Recovery Capital as an Explanatory Model for Change and Growth *Emily A. Hennessy, Rebecca L. Smith, and Corrie L. Vilsaint*	75
6	Conceptualizing Recovery Capital: Domains and Critical Perspectives *Elizabeth Bowen and Emily A. Hennessy*	97
7	Community Recovery Capital and How it Contributes to Building Recovery Capital at an Individual Level *David Best, Beth Collinson, and David Patton*	120
8	A Realist Perspective on Recovery Capital: Agents, Structures, Contexts, and Mechanisms *Tim Leighton*	142
9	The Role of Specialist Substance Use and Addiction Treatment in Building Recovery Capital *Wouter Vanderplasschen, Florian De Meyer, Clara De Ruysscher, Aline Pouille, and Deborah Louise Sinclair*	169
10	Recovery Capital Applications in Policy and Practice *Reed Yearwood, Amy Mericle, and Jessica Best*	193

| 11 | Justice Capital: Delivering Equitable Outcomes for Indigenous Children in State Care
Sharynne Hamilton and Lorana Bartels | 211 |
| 12 | Conclusion: Generating a Robust Science of Applied Recovery Capital
David Best, Maike Klein, and Phil Hodgson | 231 |

Index — 240

List of Figures, Tables, and Boxes

Figures

3.1	Recovery capital/Problem severity matrix	35
4.1	Recovery capital domains identified in the available questionnaires	63
5.1	G-CHIME and the vehicle of recovery	78
5.2	Visualization of the potential within-person heterogeneity in recovery capital	87
6.1	Recovery capital domains across ecological levels	99
6.2	Different ways to conceptualize positive and negative dimensions of recovery capital	100
7.1	Three key components of the assertive linkage process	128
7.2	Stages 1–4 of the Asset Based Community Engagement framework	130
10.1	REC-CAP assessment summary results screen: Data visualization of the recovery capital indices	198
10.2	VARR network admissions (by ethnicity) (ROI, 2019)	200
10.3	Admissions diversity by per cent (%) VARR network providers (ROI, 2023)	200
10.4	REC-CAP discovery map (ROI, 2023)	206

Tables

4.1	Names of the reviewed recovery capital questionnaires	51
5.1	Purpose of recovery capital metric by key stakeholder	77
5.2	Recovery definitions and implications for recovery capital as a model of growth and change	90
7.1	Three conditions for assertive linkage (Manning et al, 2012)	128
8.1	Archer's modes of reflexivity and their relation to recovery capital	154
11.1	Examples of negative and positive justice capital	216

| 11.2 | Justice Capital Assets Scale | 219 |
| 11.3 | Elements of negative and positive institutional justice capital that support personal justice capital | 222 |

Box

| 7.1 | Key findings from ABCE in practice (Collinson, 2021) | 132 |

Notes on Contributors

Lorana Bartels, PhD, is Professor of Criminology at the Australian National University and Adjunct Professor of Law at the University of Canberra and University of Tasmania in Australia. Her research focuses on improving criminal justice and other system responses to the needs of Aboriginal and Torres Strait Islander peoples, young people, women, and people with disabilities.

Matthew J. Belanger, PhD, is a lecturer at the University of Stirling in the UK. His research primarily focuses on the influence of conditioned environmental cues on drug seeking or consumption behaviours. He is also interested in recovery capital growth and how it affects recovery outcomes.

David Best, PhD, is the Director of the Centre for Addiction Recovery Research at Leeds Trinity University in the UK. He is a founding member of the College of Lived Experience Recovery Organisations (CLERO) and of Inclusive Recovery Cities. He holds affiliate positions at the Australian National University, Monash University (Melbourne, Australia), and the Public Health Institute in California. He has studied and written about addiction recovery for many years.

Jessica Best is the Executive Director for Recovery Outcomes Institute, Inc., in Florida.

Ana-Maria Bliuc, PhD, is an associate professor at the University of Dundee in the UK.

Elizabeth Bowen, PhD, is an associate professor at the University at Buffalo School of Social Work in the US. Informed by her social work practice experience, Bowen's research addresses homelessness and socioeconomic status as social determinants of health, with a focus on addiction recovery. She led a research team in developing the Multidimensional Inventory of Recovery Capital, a free tool that measures recovery capital including social, physical, human, and cultural/community domains.

Adela Bunaciu is a postgraduate student at the University of Dundee in the UK. Her research interests are in the field of addiction recovery, and her PhD work focuses on the measurement of recovery capital.

William Cloud, PhD, is a professor emeritus in the School of Social Work at the University of Denver in the US.

Beth Collinson, PhD, is the Director of Research at The Phoenix, a US-based non-profit offering free, meaningful activities to individuals impacted by substance use. Her research explores the power of community engagement in recovery, building on her earlier work developing the Asset-Based Community Engagement framework, which maps community resources and assertively links individuals to support. This approach is brought to life in her work at The Phoenix, where their digital platform links members not only to The Phoenix community but also to a broader ecosystem of recovery resources. She also coordinates an addiction recovery public and patient involvement panel.

Florian De Meyer is a PhD student in the Department of Special Needs Education at Ghent University in Belgium. Florian's PhD focuses on natural recovery in adults, and he examines the extent of the phenomenon in the Belgian context.

Clara De Ruysscher is at Ghent University in Belgium.

Robert Granfield, PhD, is the Vice Provost for Faculty Affairs and a professor in the Department of Sociology at the University at Buffalo in the US.

Sharynne Hamilton, PhD, is an Aboriginal woman whose ancestral links are to Ngunnawal Country in Canberra, Australia. Sharynne is a senior research fellow with The Kids Research Institute Australia and adjunct professor at the University of Canberra in Australia. Her research interests and work focus on Elder and community priorities and led research that promotes equitable, inclusive, and culturally secure access to systems and information for Aboriginal and Torres Strait Islander children and families involved with state child protection and criminal justice systems.

Emily A. Hennessy, PhD, is the Director of Biostatistics and Associate Director at the Recovery Research Institute and the Associate Director of the National Center on Youth Prevention, Treatment, and Recovery at Massachusetts General Hospital in the US. She is also an Assistant Professor in Psychiatry at Harvard Medical School. Dr Hennessy was a US–Norway Fulbright Scholar where she completed an MPhil in Health Promotion and focused on adolescent development and well-being. She completed her PhD at Vanderbilt University and her postdoctoral fellowship at the University of Connecticut. Her research focuses on examining adolescent and emerging adult recovery capital.

Phil Hodgson, PhD, is Professor and Dean of Social and Health Sciences at Leeds Trinity University in the UK.

Lauren A. Hoffman, PhD, is a research scientist at the Recovery Research Institute within Massachusetts General Hospital, as well as an assistant professor in psychiatry at Harvard Medical School in the US. Dr Hoffman's programme of research seeks to elucidate the biopsychosocial correlates of successful substance use disorder treatment and recovery, with an emphasis on opioid use disorder and translation to real-world populations. The ultimate goal of her research is to leverage identified biological and psychosocial correlates to develop and test novel interventions that more effectively address barriers to successful treatment and sustained recovery.

Maike Klein, PhD, is Lecturer in Clinical Psychology in the Division of Health Research at Lancaster University in the UK.

Tim Leighton, PhD, is currently an independent consultant in addiction recovery research, staff team and programme development, practitioner training and clinical supervision, and professional education. He led professional education courses and degrees in the field of addiction for over 30 years. He has worked as practitioner, supervisor, programme designer and consultant, researcher, and educator in the charity sector and the NHS. Tim was a UKCP registered Cognitive Analytic (CAT) Psychotherapist from 1994 to 2022 (moved to retired status) and is an accredited trainer and supervisor. His research interests are addictions counselling as a social practice, theory-based evaluation of treatment programmes, the development of social identities in recovery from addiction and the ecology of recovering communities. His PhD was a critical realist study of mechanisms of change in alcohol and drug rehabilitation programmes. For more information, see ORCID: https://orcid.org/0000-0002-1806-3849

Amy Mericle, PhD, is a scientist in the Alcohol Research Group at the Public Health Institute in California, US.

David Patton, PhD, is an associate professor in Criminology at the University of Derby in the UK. Dr Patton's research centres on the lived experiences of individuals recovering from addiction and criminal histories, using their often-marginalized voices to cocreate visions for transforming recovery, the criminal justice system, and society to support human flourishing. His published work includes 'The power, capacity, and resiliency of women in substance use disorder recovery to overcome multiple and complex housing transitions' (2024; *Social Sciences* 13(4): 206) and, with D. Best, P. Pula and Y. Hallandy 'The culture of recovery: An antidote to coloniality' (2023; *Addiction & Criminology* 6(5): 166).

Aline Pouille is at Ghent University in Belgium.

Deborah Louise Sinclair, PhD, is a postdoctoral fellow at the University of the Western Cape and a member of the Recovery and Addiction Research Cluster at Ghent University. Her research interests include recovery in individuals experiencing gambling problems, recovery from substance use disorders, and substitute addictions.

Rebecca L. Smith, PhD, MSW, is an instructor and Program Manager of Undergraduate Research for the Institute for Research on Behavioral and Emotional Health in the School of Social Work at Virginia Commonwealth University in the US. Her research explores the social, environmental, and genetic factors that influence behavioural health disorders and recovery among young adults and people who are justice-involved.

Arun Sondhi, PhD, is a research manager at Therapeutic Solutions (Addictions) Ltd and the deputy director at the Centre for Addiction Recovery Research at Leeds Trinity University in the UK.

Wouter Vanderplasschen, PhD, is Professor and Head of the Department of Special Needs Education at Ghent University (Belgium). He is a senior researcher in the field of substance abuse treatment and recovery and coordinates the Addiction & Recovery research group at Ghent University. For the past 25 years, he has studied the accessibility, effectiveness and quality of care in substance use treatment and addiction recovery in general. Recent projects focused on recovery pathways of persons who use drugs, natural recovery and patient-reported outcomes and experiences.

Corrie L. Vilsaint, PhD, serves as Associate Director of Recovery Health Equity for the Recovery Research Institute at Massachusetts General Hospital, and Instructor in Psychiatry at Harvard Medical School in the US. As a community psychologist her science focuses on racial differences in recovery, eliminating recovery-related discrimination, and the effectiveness of recovery support services. Dr Vilsaint developed the Brief Assessment of Recovery Capital.

William White, PhD, is an emeritus senior research consultant at Chestnut Health Systems in the US.

NOTES ON CONTRIBUTORS

Reed Yearwood is the owner of Holistic Addictions Recovery and peer recovery coordinator at Radford University in the US. His research interests stress applied sociology to enhance approaches toward civil transformation. Reed is a person in long-term recovery from severe substance use disorder. He would like to dedicate this work to recovering individuals everywhere, may this handbook be an offering to inspire wellness exploration and further recovery capital integration. *To my mama, hero of a father, and to my dearest Ashlea Marie, anything worth meaning I learned from you.*

Foreword: The History of Recovery Capital

*William White, MA, Emeritus Senior
Research Consultant, Chestnut Health Systems*

Recovery capital as a transformative concept

The injection of a compelling, actionable, and timely new idea can overturn prevailing principles and practices within well-established fields of endeavour. Such is the case with Granfield and Cloud's introduction of the concept of *recovery capital* into the alcohol and other drug (AOD) problems arena. Since the publication of their original 1994 paper, the term 'recovery capital' has appeared in the titles of more than 90 peer-reviewed scientific and medical articles and exerted a profound influence at policy, service practice, and personal recovery levels.

The AOD problems field, and more specifically the specialized addiction treatment industry, has historically featured a distinct pathology focus. This is exemplified by its preoccupation with drug psychopharmacology, medical and social harms of drug use, its alarmist portrayal of drug use trends, problem-focused studies of the aetiology/patterns/course of substance use disorders (SUDs), elegant schemes of clinical classification, methods of brief clinical intervention, and a fear-infused fixation on post-treatment relapse risk. The introduction of recovery capital into the field's discourse was part of the larger shift toward a recovery paradigm. This shift extended the field's vision and focus toward the successful, *long-term* resolution of AOD problems at personal, family, community, and cultural levels. Recovery capital writ large expanded the field's understanding of the prevalence, pathways/styles, stages, processes, and personal and social contributions related to AOD problem resolution. It is questionable whether we would have seen the rise of new grassroots recovery community organizations, international recovery-focused policy initiatives, and a dramatically expanded investment in recovery-focused research without this more solution-focused shift seeded by the concept of recovery capital.

Traditionally, addiction recovery has been viewed as a process of subtraction – deleting AOD use and its progeny of allied problems – with success measured by disordered individuals achieving a state of remission solely based on the cessation of drug use (now assessed as no longer meeting substance-specific diagnostic criteria for a substance use disorder in the past 12 months). In contrast, recovery capital proponents place great emphasis on recovery as processes of addition and multiplication – the acquisition of new assets, the achievement of global health and functioning, and the potential to thrive and flourish, to get 'better than well'. The concept of recovery capital suggested that the evaluation of addiction treatment and non-clinical recovery support services evolve from a singular focus on the subtraction of destructive drug use to a more holistic evaluation, including such dimensions as quality of life, citizenship (social contribution), and life meaning and purpose.

For more than two centuries, the prevailing cultural and professional portrayal of the course of addiction was one of self-accelerating severity, insanity, and death, with successful treatment and recovery being the 'exception to the rule' of 'once an addict, always an addict'. Recovery capital challenged this conception by suggesting that recovery from addiction was the norm, not the exception, and that most people resolved significant AOD problems drawing on both internal and external supports without involvement in either formal addiction treatment or lifelong participation in a recovery mutual aid organization. Granfield and Cloud's work on the concept of recovery capital raised significant questions about the prevalence and diversity of recovery experiences – questions that have been explored in a continuing series of landmark recovery prevalence and life in recovery research surveys. These survey findings have served as the core of subsequent addiction/treatment/recovery anti-stigma campaigns. It should also be evident that this shift in emphasis from human pathology to human potential exerted a liberating effect on individuals and families seeking recovery who through the lens of recovery capital were encouraged to shift their self-understanding from a focus on cataloguing pain and problems to an inventory of assets, hopes, and aspirations for the future.

Since its inception in the mid-19th century, the specialty field of addiction treatment has based its understanding of addiction upon the clinical experience of treating people with the most severe, complex, and prolonged addiction histories and severely depleted recovery capital. It then applied its derived 'truths' from that knowledge to the larger landscape of AOD problems. Recovery capital proponents, in contrast, suggested that AOD problems existed on a spectrum of severity, complexity, and chronicity as well as variable recovery assets and that the course and resolution strategies of these problems differed dramatically across these continua. They further posited that recovery outcomes were determined as much by internal and external assets as by traditionally assessed intrapersonal deficits and vulnerabilities. This shift in perspective exerted a significant influence on processes of clinical screening and assessment in addiction treatment, particularly on decisions on the need for professional interventions; the intensity and duration of such treatment; level of care placement and transition decisions; and the scope and duration of post-treatment monitoring and support. Increased recognition of the import of recovery capital on treatment outcomes sparked growing interest in the development and refinement of recovery capital measurement instruments.

Professional and public responses to AOD problems have had throughout history a distinctly intrapersonal focus – both in the understanding of the aetiology of addiction and on the targets of intervention. Recovery capital expanded this focus by exploring the *physical and social ecology of addiction recovery*. Recovery capital, and particularly the notion of *community recovery capital*, expanded strategies of mobilizing community resources (forging *recovery spaces/landscapes* and shaping *recovery-friendly communities*). Recovery capital conceptually seeded the birth of new recovery support institutions (for example, recovery community centres, recovery residences, recovery high schools and collegiate recovery programmes, recovery cafes, recovery ministries, recovery art and music festivals, and so on). Community recovery capital implied that recovery was contagious – could be socially transmitted, and that this contagion could be accelerated if the correct conditions were established. Recovery capital proponents argued that the prevalence of recovery within local communities could be elevated by increasing the density of *recovery carriers/champions* (people in recovery who made recovery attractive via the visibility and power of their stories and character). The contention that 'recovery is contagious' offered the potential of *recovery cascades* – dramatic surges in recovery initiation and overall prevalence at neighbourhood, community, and cultural levels. The concept of recovery capital exerted a significant influence on the growth of recovery advocacy organizations, a larger new recovery advocacy movement, and new recovery support roles (*recovery coaches* and other *peer recovery support specialists*) working in addiction treatment and allied health settings and in other community outreach settings. Recovery capital also provided a rationale for the birth and spread of an ecumenical (multiple pathway) *culture of recovery*. This spurred recovery cultural production in such arenas as language, literature, history, art, music, film, theatre, public storytelling, sport, leisure, and public recovery celebration events.

From its inception, addiction treatment has been characterized by competing professional silos, most advocating a single pathway model of recovery – one cause, one course, one viable treatment method, one successful style of recovery maintenance. Since Granfield and Cloud's introduction of the concept of recovery capital, its proponents have illuminated the varieties of recovery experience and celebrated multiple pathways and styles of recovery, including patterns of AOD problem resolution of people who do not consciously embrace a *recovery identity* or a recovery-dominated social network. Recovery capital proponents also acknowledged people with mild to moderate AOD problems and high levels of recovery capital whose resolution pattern may involve deceleration rather than cessation of AOD use.

Given these profound influences, it is with great pleasure that we welcome the first comprehensive collection of papers authored by those who have worked on the conceptual refinement, measurement, and practical applications of the concept of recovery capital. It is our collective hope that this landmark text providing both a look back and a look forward for the future of recovery capital research and practice will spur a deeper understanding of the resolution of AOD and related problems.

1

Introduction to the Handbook of Recovery Capital

David Best and Emily A. Hennessy

Transition to a strengths-based model

This book is a testament to the growing evidence base around recovery and recovery capital that has emerged globally and particularly in the English-speaking world over the course of the last 25 years. It is also part of a wider movement away from deficit management and symptom reduction to a strengths-based approach not only in the addictions field but across the behavioural sciences. This is seen in such disparate fields as positive psychology, restorative justice, therapeutic jurisprudence, and the mental health recovery movement.

This transition involves six key actions that are briefly outlined here, which have significant resonance for the content of this book:

1. The transition from measuring deficits to measuring and attempting to build strengths, which is at the heart of the 'recovery capital' model. Essentially the model is predicated on the assertion by White and Cloud (2008) that long-term recovery is better predicted on the accumulation of strengths rather than on the amelioration of symptoms. This has implications for what we measure and how we measure it, and for our assumptions about goals and end points. If our aim is strengths building then success is not a homeostatic zero, but to measure being 'better than well' (Valentine, 2011).
2. Transition from an expert–patient to a partnership model: one of the challenges of moving to a strengths-based approach is that it challenges the 'expert' status of professionals, diminishing the power disparities between parties, in favour of a partnership approach. For research, this

means a switch to a coproduction approach in which the recovery research participant is an active player in the ownership of the process of measuring recovery capital and in having control over the resulting data.
3. Shifting to a strengths-based model also moves our focus from the individual (the body and the brain) as the 'problem' and locus of change to the social. This is a fundamental shift in the conceptualization of recovery where both the location of activity and the area for study is inter-personal as much as it is intra-personal. Recovery is seen as a fundamentally social process that happens between people and so all kinds of social networks and social activities are essential to our understanding of recovery and recovery capital (Best et al, 2016).
4. Point 3 implies that there must be a transfer of the locus of change from the specialist clinic or treatment setting to the community, and so this is where recovery resources and efforts should be directed. It is crucial that we not only consider social networks in reviewing recovery capital but the setting itself as a significant influence on the likelihood and trajectory of capital growth. In a recovery capital model, it is essential to understand the context both as a source of recovery resources but also as the locus for interventions with community-building an essential component of creating the conditions for growing each individual's recovery capital.
5. With the shift from the individual to the communal, and from the clinic to the community, there is a necessary refocus on social contagion and on the prominence of peers in recovery science and recovery capital (White, 2009; Humphreys and Lembke, 2013). The presence of visible recovery icons and champions is thus an essential element of social and community recovery capital. We also assume that visible and successful peers are a fundamental source of recovery capital through role modelling, mentoring, and championing of recovery causes.
6. These changes also have implications for research in that we cannot assume that the traditional principle of replicability can or should apply. If the resources in the community are an intrinsic component of recovery capital, we should not then assume that it is possible to replicate gains in one location to another setting without adequately mapping the consistency of assets across the two settings. This makes a science of recovery and recovery capital more complex as it requires mapping individual growth and change against aspects of social networks and community resources and barriers.

The conclusion from this overview is that a recovery model of research and science involves a fundamental paradigm shift in research, policy, and practice that captures a new way of conceptualizing addiction and its resolution, which has profound implications for what we (academics, community-members, policy makers, practitioners, researchers) do. As Best and Hennessy (2022) posited, these shifts create four primary areas for scientific review and development:

(i) Conceptual development (for example, how recovery capital domains are unique, but interrelated entities; valence of recovery capital) and how we address concepts such as negative recovery capital;
(ii) empirical testing, and examining the adequacy of measurement and analysis, through rigorous research, synthesis, and partnerships;
(iii) directions for novel application in treatment and recovery settings, and applications to a range of diverse populations;
(iv) dissemination and communication to policy, practice, and lived experience groups.

The authors concluded, 'to move RC forward as a conceptual model in an empirically driven and culturally appropriate manner, that a formal collaboration between scholars, practitioners and individuals in recovery worldwide working on this issue be established' (Best and Hennessy, 2022, 6). In this book, we have attempted to provide a range of diverse perspectives on where we are on this journey and what innovations and progress have been made. However, before doing this it is worth briefly examining the history of 'capital' as a framework for considering strengths-based approaches.

What do we mean by capital?

The originating concept here is social capital, with both European and American traditions framing this concept. For Bourdieu (1985), social capital involves the social networks, histories, and cultural affordances that can generate a sense of belonging but also provide access to a range of resources, including social support and social identity. However, it is important to note that, within this framework, Coleman (1988) has argued that the poor structures of our communities mean that accessing social capital is difficult, particularly for those who are marginalized or excluded. Furthermore, Bourdieu's concepts of habitus and field create significant challenges around both the definition and measurement of cultural capital, a challenge that we will return to throughout this book.

In his book *Bowling Alone,* Putnam (2000) refers to social capital both as a resource that individuals can draw upon but also as a commitment to the group, creating a mutual bind. For Putnam, there are three domains of social capital:

- 'Bonding' capital which refers to the strength of links within established groups;

- 'bridging' capital which refers to the links and associations between individuals at different levels or an organization or group; and
- 'linking' capital which refers to the ties across different groups and networks.

Social scientist John Braithwaite later articulated:

> Social capital, human capital, recovery capital and restorative capital are unlike financial capital in that they are not depleted through use. When you spend your money from the bank, you deplete your capital. When you trust someone, you do not deplete trust: trust tends to be reciprocated and this engenders virtuous circles of trust-building. A politics of hope is likewise redemptive as we face adversity; it is infectious. (Braithwaite, 2022, 363)

This suggests that capital is a resource but not one that is linked to finance; the use of the same label for 'recovery capital' should not imply similar dynamics and has important implications for how we consider recovery capital development and growth in communities.

For Bourdieu and Putnam, social capital was intangible but crucially important not only for individuals but also for communities. It is here that we need to consider recovery capital within this broader framework of something that has implications for individuals, for the groups they belong to as well as for the broader communities and societies that are the settings for recovery attempts and recovery journeys (Best and Ivers, 2022). This concept has been particularly well articulated by Hamilton and colleagues (2020) when introducing the concept of justice capital. Justice capital, developed further in the Hamilton and Bartels chapter in this volume (Chapter 11), brings to focus a binary that is an inevitable conclusion of the paradigm shift outlined earlier: if we are serious about measuring recovery capital, it cannot only be through the lens of its individual beneficiaries. The next key area for measuring recovery capital must address and account for the context in which recovery (or justice) occurs. In other words, recovery capital adheres not only to individuals' capacities to advance in their recovery journeys but also to institutions (families, workplaces, treatment and recovery services, prisons, and other justice locations) that have the capacity to create the conditions that maximize the chances of individual growth.

For Hamilton and colleagues, justice capital is as much about the setting as about the individual who is located there, in this case the youth detention centre in Western Australia that predominantly houses young Aboriginal men. The question they ask of a capital model is whether it can provide an understanding of the location in which change can take place, the extent to which a detention centre, set up for control and reform, can still create conditions for individual flourishing or thriving to occur. This is a crucial issue for the theory of recovery capital as it inevitably blends the personal with the social and the community to create a nuanced model of well-being and growth.

The second issue that has plagued the field has been around the concept of negative recovery capital and whether such a term should be embedded within a strengths-based model (discussed in more detail in Chapter 6 by Bowen and Hennessy). The origin of this term is a 2008 paper by Cloud and Granfield where it is framed in the context of factors that can restrict or diminish the growth of recovery capital. The authors suggested four such factors – older age, female gender, a history of incarceration, and a history of serious mental health problems. While this supposition has provoked debate about the specific factors involved, the broader question of the transition to a balance of negative and positive factors represents a challenge to the idea that there is something unique about a recovery capital approach. This compromise is also reflected in the resulting measures (see Chapter 4 by Bunaciu and colleagues) in which barriers to recovery are included in several recovery capital measures.

The questions for us are about *how* we measure and *what* we measure in a science of recovery as well as questions around to what end. But this book is not only about science it is also about policy and practice, and in developing this handbook, we have solicited a wide range of experience and expertise to shed light on some of the challenges that we outlined in our 2022 paper (Best and Hennessy, 2022).

Aims of the handbook

Our goal with this book is to provide a comprehensive overview of the concept of recovery capital, advances in research and science around this topic, and what this has meant for policy and practice. The emergence of many recovery capital measures has provided us with a mechanism for testing core ideas around recovery pathways and variations in recovery growth across individuals and communities, offering a series of metrics through which scientific precision can be brought to bear. However, the term 'recovery capital' has now entered the popular lexicon of providers of recovery support services and their clients, and so has created a framework for applied action and reflection in practice as well as in policy and a means through which individuals, and their families and loved ones, can track progress on a recovery journey.

For that reason, we have attempted to bring together a diverse range of authors, including some of the most eminent figures who have been thought leaders in articulating and developing the concept and theory of recovery capital, as well as emerging academics and researchers who have pushed the idea in a range of different directions. However, we also attempt to shift emphasis to assess how these concepts have been applied both in the context of measurement and the impact this has had in the field on bringing recovery capital to bear in a range of applied settings, particularly recovery residences in the US where the model has been used as a central part of outcome monitoring and individual client management.

We are not attempting to create an orthodoxy around recovery capital conceptualization or operationalization, and we have encouraged a range of voices to provide as personal and individual a story as possible. Particularly in the context of the history of the evolution of recovery capital, we have encouraged our authors to tell their own stories to provide insights about the history and the development of the ideas and concepts foundational to our understanding of recovery capital. What this means is a pluralistic and diverse array of voices captured under an overall umbrella of support and enthusiasm that recovery capital can be a transformational model for recovery science and that this plurality and diversity will actively promote meaningful growth in the science and practice of recovery capital. With this book, we hope that you the reader – researcher, academic, practitioner, politician, person with lived experience – walk away with new ideas for bringing the concept of recovery capital back to your unique space and novel ways of understanding its key role in building healthier and more connected communities.

Overview of the content

We are delighted that the foreword has been provided by William White, the leading researcher, historian, and advocate for the recovery movement over the course of the last 50 years. This provides a contextualization of the debate about recovery capital and its role in building recovery science and creating an application of this process.

In Chapter 2, Robert Granfield and William Cloud give an overview of the origins of the recovery capital concept and its subsequent evolution and growth including its translation into measurement tools. The philosophical foundations of the concept in a study of individuals who had experienced 'natural recovery' without hitting rock bottom are discussed.

In Chapter 3 we return to a developmental and historical approach with William White discussing his role in the evolution and rollout of the recovery capital concept and model, Lauren Hoffman summarizing the role that the Recovery Research Institute has played in this, and David Best describing both the international application and implementation of recovery capital and his role in translating the broad concept into a series of measurement tools and how that measurement process has evolved.

For Chapter 4, Adela Bunaciu, Matthew Belanger, Ana-Maria Bliuc, and Arun Sondhi build on a recent systematic review of recovery capital measurement tools (Bunaciu et al, 2023) and extend their work to update the evidence base and to consider measurement methods other than self-completion questionnaires. They also consider the gradual transition from paper and pencil-based measurement to online completion with the resulting impact on processes of feedback and action based on the results.

Chapter 5 is written by Emily Hennessy, Rebecca Smith, and Corrie Vilsaint, and addresses how recovery capital can be used as an explanatory framework for individual and community growth and change. They discuss this from both researcher and practitioner lenses, providing examples of how the construct of recovery capital is flexible to meet the needs of a variety of stakeholders.

In Chapter 6, Elizabeth Bowen and Emily Hennessy review the major conceptualizations of recovery capital, address critical inquiries about the relative importance of different recovery capital domains and the issue of negative recovery capital, and review the importance of applying an intersectional lens when trying to understand recovery capital among specific populations.

Chapter 7 focuses on a specific component of recovery capital, community recovery capital, and is a plea from David Best, Beth Collinson, and David Patton to recognize the importance of contextual and environmental factors in both framing and, in particular, measuring recovery capital. While virtually all the published measures to date have focused on individual change (albeit incorporating elements of setting and context), this chapter describes how the context itself is an important zone of assessment for recovery capital researchers and theorists and that context – at the micro, meso, and macro levels – is a critical determinant of recovery outcomes.

In Chapter 8, Tim Leighton reviews the conceptual framework for recovery capital measurement from a philosophy of science perspective and examines the epistemological foundations for the concept and its applications. This chapter takes a critical approach to the attempts at both conceptual development and implementation of a recovery capital model.

In Chapter 9, Wouter Vanderplasschen, Florian De Meyer, Clara De Ruysscher, Aline Pouille, and Deborah Louise Sinclair provide an overview of recent studies on recovery capital and how these have impacted the field of addiction treatment beyond dedicated recovery support services. This includes an assessment of studies looking at the impact of recovery capital models on individual functioning and treatment outcomes, and more qualitative studies looking at the experiences of both service providers and service users.

In Chapter 10, Reed Yearwood, Amy Mericle, and Jessica Best switch to a more applied approach to the utilization of recovery capital measurement tools based on Virginia, US, as a case study. This chapter involves analysis and interpretation of a series of original interviews with key stakeholders in the implementation of the recovery capital measurement model in recovery residences in Virginia.

Chapter 11 returns to the theme of context by extending the concept of recovery capital to the criminal justice arena, with Sharynne Hamilton and Lorana Bartels' assessment of the evolution of the concept of justice capital and its implementation in practice using a measure that attempts to assess access to resources. Again, this takes the concept of recovery capital and applies it to a very important policy and practice domain.

Chapter 12 provides an overview of the book and identifies key themes that emerge from the collection. David Best, Maike Klein, and Phil Hodgson also identify key areas for conceptual and empirical development and synthesize the key learnings from the book.

References

Best, D. and Hennessy, E. (2022) 'The science of recovery capital: Where do we go from here?', *Addiction*, 117(4): 1139–45.

Best, D. and Ivers, J.H. (2021) 'Inkspots and ice cream cones: A model of recovery contagion and growth', *Addiction Research & Theory*, 30(3): 155–61. https://doi.org/10.1080/16066359.2021.1986699.

Bourdieu, P. (1985) 'The forms of capital', in J.G. Richardson (ed), *Handbook of Theory and Research for the Sociology of Education*, New York: Greenwood.

Braithwaite, J. (2022) *Macrocriminology and Freedom*, Canberra: ANU Press, pp 241–58.

Bunaciu, A., Bliuc, A-M., Best, D., Hennessy, E., Belanger, M., and Benwell, C. (2023) 'Measuring recovery capital for people recovering from alcohol and drug addiction: A systematic review', *Addiction Research & Theory*, 32(3): 225–36.

Cloud, W. and Granfield, R. (2008) 'Conceptualising recovery capital: Expansion of a theoretical construct', *Substance Use and Misuse*, 43(12–13): 1971–86.

Coleman, J. (1988) 'Social capital in the creation of human capital', *The American Journal of Sociology*, 94: S95–S120.

Humphreys, K. and Lembke, A. (2013) 'Recovery-oriented policy and care systems in the United Kingdom and United States', *Drug and Alcohol Review*, 33(1): 13–18.

Putnam, R.D. (2000) *Bowling Alone: The Collapse and Revival of American Community*, London: Simon & Schuster.

Valentine, P. (2011) 'Peer-based recovery support services within a recovery community organization: The CCAR experience', in J. Kelly and W. White (eds) *Addiction Recovery Management*, New York: Humana Press, pp 259–79.

White, W. (2009) *Peer-based Addiction Recovery Support: History, Theory, Practice, and Scientific Evaluation*, Chicago, IL: Great Lakes Addiction Technology Transfer Center and Philadelphia Department of Behavioral Health and Mental Retardation Services.

White, W. and Cloud, W. (2008) 'Recovery capital: A primer for addictions professionals', *Counselor*, 9(5): 22–7.

2

Inception to Integration: The Theoretical Roots and Institutional Growth of Recovery Capital

*Robert Granfield and William Cloud**
*The authors wish to thank Jessica Cooksey and
William White for their contributions to this paper.

Introduction

Scientific concepts have peculiar histories. The history of scientific knowledge, including its production, dissemination, and acceptance, is shaped by broad contextual forces within the social milieu. As Pierre Bourdieu (1991) has argued, scientific knowledge can be best seen through the lens of social construction; that is, scientific knowledge, discovery, advances and so on never emerge as fully developed concepts that are accepted into culture. Rather, the production, dissemination, and acceptance of knowledge is influenced by social, cultural, historical, and even political forces. There are several factors associated with the accumulation and advancement of scientific knowledge, such as the cultural authority of existing institutions or 'fields' that define what acceptable knowledge is, the power and legitimacy of individuals or groups advancing alternative paradigms, the broad historical context of accepted knowledge, the degree of resistance to new ideas by those promulgating what Thomas Kuhn (1962) called, 'normal science', as well as circumstances within the environment that would at first glance seem to be superfluous to the history of ideas.

The discovery of penicillin and its impact on the world is a case in point (Lax, 2005). Alexander Fleming's 1928 discovery of penicillin occurred, in large part, by accident. The Scottish bacteriologist working at St Mary's Hospital in London discovered, after a two-week hiatus from his laboratory, that mould had grown in one of his samples of bacteria. In this sample the bacteria around the mould, a strain of penicillium, were dying while the bacteria further away from the mould were thriving. Fleming reasoned that this mould could be developed to combat bacterial infection.

In 1929, Fleming published his results in the British Journal of Experimental Pathology and while his work received some attention, its full impact would take years to be realized. This was due to several factors, including strong resistance from the medical community that was sceptical of the idea that a substance grown from mould could effectively kill bacteria. There was considerable demand from the established scientific 'field' for independent validation. The conventional wisdom of the time was that sulfa drugs (synthetic antibiotics) were the prescribed method for treating infection. Furthermore, there were problems isolating the substance and producing it in large enough quantities for distribution in collaborative efforts and future clinical trials. The Second World War created a social condition for increasing acceptance of penicillin as an effective treatment of infection and led to increased research funding to develop it on a large scale. In the early 1940s the pharmaceutical company Merck became the first commercial drug company to produce penicillin in large qualities. Post-Second World War commercial production of penicillin along with its demonstrated proven efficacy over sulfa drugs during the war increased the acceptance of the drug by the medical community and the larger global population.

The concept of addiction can be seen as following a similar historical trajectory. In the traditional disease model of addiction, addiction is seen as a chronic, relapsing brain disease that requires medical treatment and ongoing management. This perspective has dominated the field for a significant period of time. Constituencies including medical professionals, addiction treatment providers, support groups like Alcoholics Anonymous, government agencies, and the for-profit treatment industry have played a crucial role in institutionalizing the disease model framework. Indeed, the addiction field, like all 'fields', has developed within a broad social, cultural, historical, and political context.

However, over the past few decades, there has been a growing recognition of the limitations of the disease model that has contributed to the development of recovery-oriented perspectives and the related concept of recovery capital (Ashford et al, 2019). The recovery capital framework emphasizes the strengths, resources, and social connections that individuals possess to support their recovery from addiction. It acknowledges that recovery is a multidimensional process influenced by various personal, social, and environmental factors. It further acknowledges that there are multiple pathways out of addiction. Yet, while this concept has gained considerable acceptance by scholars, community members, addiction treatment professionals, and policy advocates, making the concept 'the emerging international construct for the addiction field' (Best and Hennessy, 2022), its conceptual foundations have been under-analysed.

This chapter charts the development and expansion of the concept of recovery capital. Initially formulated in our qualitative study of self-remitters from addiction (Granfield and Cloud, 1999), the concept of recovery capital has since expanded broadly in the academic literature, within recovery-oriented groups, in treatment organizations, and in government policy circles. This chapter traces the intellectual origins of the recovery capital concept and explores the circulation and growing institutionalization of the concept.

Theoretical foundations

All origin stories are rooted in a narrative that provides the context to explain the beginnings of individuals, places, and concepts. This is no less true for the recovery capital concept. It is perhaps not surprising that the concept of recovery capital emerged at a time when there was a conflagration of critical discourse on the addiction-as-disease paradigm. While there had been critical commentaries on the disease concept of addiction in the academic literature (Levine, 1978; Schneider, 1978), casting addiction as a social construction, books such as Stanton Peele's *Diseasing of America: Addiction Treatment Out of Control* (1989) and William White's *Slaying the Dragon: The History of Addiction Treatment and Recovery in America* (1998) established much of the groundwork for the development of the recovery capital concept.

Much of this emerging literature helped establish the proposition that the concept of addiction as a disease has a distinct genealogy that is rooted more in ideology than in scientific discovery (Reinarman and Granfield, 2015). For much of the 20th century human troubles have been viewed principally through a pathologized lens (Reinarman and Granfield, 2015). Everyday life has been cast in terms of neurochemistry, biological predispositions, and diseases of the will (Rose, 2003). While the 19th century Temperance Movement found the source of addiction in the drug itself, 20th century medical, scientific, and popular understandings of addiction have located its source within the individual body (Room, 2003). An emerging pathologized view of addiction began to take hold within American society, especially after prohibition. While prohibitionist policies defined much of the early 20th century American landscape, best exemplified by the Harrison Narcotics Act of 1914 and by the passage of national prohibition through the 19th Amendment, post-prohibitionist understandings of addiction focused increasingly on a medical paradigm of problematic use.

There was little organized interest in a disease concept of addiction from the end of the 19th century until after prohibition. As the moral crusade against alcohol began to recede after prohibition, new 'medicalized' definitions of addiction became increasingly popular. In part, the shift in the paradigm of addiction from a movement to control the substance to a movement to control the individual coincided with the rise of scientific and medical rationality. Indeed, the example of penicillin discussed earlier is emblematic of the impact of the scientific enterprise of the 20th century. Given the emerging prevalence of science and medicine in everyday life, it is not entirely surprising that conceptions of addiction followed suit.

As many medical historians have pointed out, the emergence of Alcoholics Anonymous (AA) in 1935 was a pivotal moment in the history of the addiction-as-disease concept. The concept of the alcoholic as having a psychological sensitivity and an 'allergy', a view that became the central organizing feature of AA, found wide acceptance during the latter half of the 20th century. Its widespread circulation and eventual acceptance as the reigning view of addiction was aided by the Yale Center for Alcohol Studies, E.M. Jellinek's publications outlining the disease concept of alcoholism, the advocacy of Marty Mann (a prominent actress and socialite who founded the National Council on Alcoholism in 1944 with strong involvement of the medical community), the establishment of the National Institute on Alcohol Abuse and Alcoholism in 1970, and the rise of the for-profit addiction treatment industry. All these factors ultimately led to the institutionalization of the medicalized paradigm of addiction as an irreversible disease requiring professional treatment, perhaps captured best in the words of former director of the National Institute on Drug Abuse, Robert Dunlop: 'Addiction is not self-curing. Left alone, addiction only gets worse, leading to total degradation, to prison, and ultimately to death' (Granfield and Cloud, 1999).

However, this proclamation denied an inconvenient truth; namely, that a sizable proportion of people with substance use-related problems successfully overcome addiction without the assistance of treatment. By the time of Dunlop's declaration, there were already cracks in the addiction-as-disease wall that revealed themselves in the work of scholars using data from small qualitative studies (Winick, 1962; Biernacki, 1986; Waldorf, Reinarman, and Murphy, 1991) to data from larger scale general population studies (Valliant, 1983; Dawson et al, 1995). These studies supported the proposition that large numbers of individuals suffering from addiction can and do overcome their problematic use without the benefit of treatment. Within the addiction literature this phenomenon has been typically referred to as natural recovery or spontaneous remission and it was this literature that formed the broad intellectual foundation for the development of the recovery capital concept.

Developing the recovery capital construct

We both joined the University of Denver in 1989 as assistant professors, William in the School of Social Work and Bob in the Department of

Sociology. We each came to the university with a healthy dose of scepticism regarding the disease conception of addiction and its various components; the biological inevitability of addiction, the irreversible nature of addiction, and the necessity of treatment to overcome addiction. We had both previously taught academic courses related to addiction and drug policy and we each had practical experience working in the areas of treatment and prevention. It was completely by happenstance that we developed a collaboration soon after arriving. As Stanton Peele (1989, viiii) writes in the foreword to our first book, *Coming Clean: Overcoming Addiction Without Treatment* (Granfield and Cloud, 1999):

> Writing a foreword to *Coming Clean* is a bit like being the best man at a wedding between two people you introduced – Bob Granfield and William Cloud were both teaching courses at the University of Denver on drugs. Both were using my book *Diseasing of America*. When William learned this, he immediately contacted Bob – and one of the results is the volume that follows (as well as a strong friendship between the two men and their families).

However, it would not be until ten years after initiating our collaboration that we coined the term 'recovery capital'.

Our early collaborations focused on what could be described as 'paradigmatic' science in the field, focusing on questions of substance abuse prevention especially within marginalized populations. Our federally funded studies, while unrelated to our eventual work on recovery capital, nevertheless established a context for early dialogue on the limitations of the addiction-as-disease construct. These conversations led to our decision to conduct a qualitative investigation of individuals who overcame addiction without treatment. While we were familiar with the literature on natural recovery from addiction, we believed that the concept and the related implications had been largely ignored by professionals and the public.

Having decided to study natural recovery from addiction, we were immediately presented with the dilemma of locating a sample of research subjects willing to participate in extensive life history interviews. As we describe in our book (Granfield and Cloud, 1999, 20).

> Our initial step was to use referral chains developed through the chance meeting of an untreated remitter by one of the authors. This person put us in contact with two others who gave us the names of other untreated remitters they knew and so on. About half of the individuals we interviewed were contacted through these methods. In order to solicit additional interviews, we placed advertisements in local newspapers.

Using these 'snowball' sampling techniques, we were able to conduct elaborate interviews with 46 individuals residing in Denver, Colorado. This sampling procedure evolved over an extensive period of time and although we published early articles derived from our study, by the time we began work on our book, *Coming Clean: Overcoming Addiction without Treatment*, it is fair to say that neither of us had any grand illusions about the importance of our work, developing the concept of recovery capital, or its eventual impact on helping to shift the addiction paradigm away from a treatment-centric orientation and towards a recovery-centric orientation.

Our work sought to elucidate the micro- and macro-components of natural recovery. As we analysed the in-depth life histories and recovery narratives we had collected, our attention was initially drawn to the *processes* through which individuals overcame their addictive behaviours. The basic sociological tenet that 'all behaviors, emotions, beliefs, rules, and objects become meaningful within the broader social context of interaction with others' guided our work (Granfield and Cloud, 1999, 18). Focusing on the process of natural recovery, we developed a 'conversion' model of recovery that identified stages and strategies used by our subjects. The common patterns included the experience of individual strain associated with addiction such as health problems, family conflict and dissolution, career challenges and disruption, and legal entanglements. All our respondents experienced a profound 'turning point' that often followed a dramatic event in their lives. These turning points led our subjects to take direct action and implement cessation strategies that promoted cessation and helped maintain it. The final stage of the personal transformation was the realization and appreciation of the rewards associated with their new-found recovered status.

Additionally, our work focused on the question of personal meaning and identity construction in relation to addiction and natural recovery. We explored the question of why individuals avoided formal treatment and self-help groups. Using a concept drawn from Foucault known as 'technologies of the self' (Martin et al, 1988), we described how our subjects resisted the subjectivities imposed upon them from the disease concept of addiction that emphasized powerlessness over addiction, flawed biology, and treatment mandates. The focus on identity construction led us to conclude that our subjects' 'belief that they were the navigators of their own lives and their unwillingness to be completely disillusioned through dependency allowed them to change their lives without recourse to treatment and self-help' (Granfield and Cloud, 1999, 129).

From social capital to recovery capital

The more we unpacked our qualitative interviews, the more we came to appreciate the broader structural basis of our subjects' natural recovery experiences. The recognition that larger structural factors played a role in our subjects' natural recovery emerged because our sample was not randomly drawn from a larger population. Our sample contained individuals that can be best described as 'socially advantaged'. All our subjects completed high school and most possessed university degrees. Most were or had been employed in stable occupations. Most of the sample characterized themselves as middle class.

We determined that one way of capturing how structural factors could lead to differentials in emancipatory opportunities for overcoming addiction was through the concept of social capital. We reasoned that 'while the concept of social capital has been used to explain occupational and social mobility, the extent of civic culture as well as business transactions more generally, the concept has utility for understanding personal problems such as addictions and efforts to overcome these problems' (Granfield and Cloud, 1999, 138). Following the insights from Coleman (1988, S98) that 'social capital is productive, making possible the achievement of certain ends that would not be attainable in its absence', we sought to illustrate the broader structural context present within our participants' narratives. As William recalled:

> Those in natural recovery had social capital in their positions in society. They had pro-social values and they had expectations held of them by their family and community members. They had not taken on the addict identity. Many of these folks had lots of money and could spend thousands of dollars' worth of drugs in a week, but it wouldn't bother some of them because their assets were so deep. Drug use was very much a part of the lives of the natural remitters, but it was not the entirety of their lives. They had other stuff going on. And it was the presence of that other stuff that tipped the scales towards recovery. (White, 2016, 4)

Making the connection between natural recovery and social capital drew the attention of an international group of scholars working on the issue of self-remission from addiction. In March of 1999, The Kettil Bruun Society sponsored a conference on the 'Natural History of Addictions: Recovery from Alcohol, Tobacco, and Other Drug Problems without Treatment' in Les Diablerets, Switzerland, where our application of the concept of social capital was received favourably by scholars working in the area of self change, especially for its theoretical contributions to offering a deeper understanding of natural recovery.

Our interest in developing a theoretical understanding of natural recovery grew more intense as we continued to analyse our data. Because self-remitters could not point to treatment as the path to their success, we sought to identify the dimensions of natural recovery to articulate a general theory of recovery. The concept social capital seemed to offer explanatory power in understanding natural recovery, especially in Bourdieu and Wacquant's (1992, 119) formulation as 'the sum of the resources, actual or virtual, that accrue to an individual or a group by virtue of possessing a durable network of institutionalized relationships of mutual acquaintance and recognition'. The concept of social capital embodies both structure and agency. Social capital is a resource existing inside and outside all individuals that facilitates social action. Our extensive life history data pointed indisputably to the relevance of social capital in the lives of our subjects established through patterns of relationships formed through family, work, community groups, friendships, and social institutions. This led us to the conclusion that 'the social capital that had been established and maintained prior to as well as during their dependencies played a significant role in helping our respondents overcome their problems' (Granfield and Cloud, 1999, 154).

In our original formulation of the significance of social capital in the lives of our self-remitters, we identified three forms of social capital that helped facilitate their natural recovery. Many of our subjects experienced periods of stability during much of their lives. Most had relatively stable employment histories. Most of our subjects had a degree of financial security that minimized the need to engage in criminal activities to maintain their addiction. Our subjects also often pointed to the feelings of obligations they had to others as a motivation for overcoming their addiction. This sense of obligation can be, and was for our subjects, a very potent form of social capital. As Coleman (1988, S103) has argued, 'individuals in social structures with high levels of obligations outstanding at any time, whatever the source of those obligations, have greater social capital they can draw upon'. Our subjects were also able to maintain relationships with family members, friends, and other associates despite their substance misuse. In other words, most of our subjects had not entirely 'burned their bridges' with others. They continued to have supportive networks that aided in their recovery.

Had we concluded our analysis at this point, we would have broadened the literature on natural recovery by connecting it to the theoretical concept of social capital, but we would have missed the more complex multidimensionality in the recovery process. Instead, we continued to analyse and interrogate our data and each other. We were confident that social capital played a significant role in the lives of our subjects, but we also saw evidence of other factors including physical capital, human capital, and cultural capital. We came to conclude that social capital, while a critical dimension in recovery, was insufficient to explain the process of natural recovery. We realized that we needed a multidimensional theory that built upon the various behavioural capacities and opportunities created through social capital (relationships and networks), physical capital (tangible assets, housing, income), human capital (skills, knowledge, abilities), and cultural capital (norms, values, predispositions). Through the narratives of our subjects, we were hearing themes associated with quality of life, self-actualization, well-being, self-efficacy, and so on, but there was no singular concept in the addiction literature that captured this broad and multifaceted conceptualization of recovery. Ironically, the concept of recovery capital came to us in a prosaic manner. As William explains:

> The idea of recovery capital came, not in the context of a high-level professional conference, but during a conversation Bob and I were having during a Saturday barbecue in my back yard. That's when we shifted from the broad idea of social capital to a clearer concept of recovery capital. It was like a light bulb moment. (White, 2016, 5)

Developing the broader concept of recovery capital was a significant breakthrough that provided us with the conceptual framework to develop a multidimensional theory of addiction recovery. As we first outlined in our 1999 book:

> Recovery capital is used to refer to the sum total of one's resources that can be brought to bear in an effort to overcome alcohol and drug dependency. It is embodied in a number of tangible and intangible resources and relationships, including those that existed prior to a person's drug involvement, during the period of drug use, and conditions likely to prevail in the future. (Granfield and Cloud, 1999, 179)

Recovery capital embodies the internal and external attributes available to individuals that can promote the capacity to overcome life challenges including those associated with addiction. In our formulation, recovery capital is a resource that can be accumulated or depleted. In building one's recovery capital portfolio, investments made in social, human, physical, and cultural capital can help insulate individuals from crises or help restore them to a state of balance and well-being after experiencing life challenges that can result in self-destructive behaviours (Cloud and Granfield, 2008).

It is important, however, to view recovery capital not simply from the perspective of individual agency alone. The resources available to individuals through recovery capital are never equally distributed within society. Opportunities to build and activate recovery capital are shaped by the social structures within which an individual is embedded. For instance, the capacity to build and activate recovery capital for middle-class individuals is different from those living in poverty. Recovery capital can be enabling or constraining. This is the basis of positive and negative recovery capital (Cloud and Granfield, 2008). For example, a supportive network can empower an individual's recovery, but societal stigma, especially when associated with the criminal justice system, may limit the opportunities for employment and social integration (Connolly and Granfield, 2017). Individuals with higher socioeconomic backgrounds are often in a better position to manage the stigmatization associated with addiction than individuals from lower socioeconomic classes. Individuals from marginalized groups based on race and/or social class often have fewer resources to draw upon in pursuing recovery. Such individuals may possess limited access to recovery capital because of their structural positions within society (Connolly and Granfield, 2017).

Recovery capital can be best conceptualized as existing along a continuum of both positive recovery capital, those factors that promote and facilitate recovery, and negative recovery capital, those factors that diminish or interfere with the capacity for recovery. The private troubles that people encounter in their lives are always embedded within historical and biographical circumstances (Mills, 1967). While history and biography are never determinative of human agency, the embedded nature of it creates circumstances that can both enable and constrain individual actors (Giddens, 1984). The capacity to overcome problem behaviours like addiction are always based on the choices that individuals make, but the choices that people make are always embedded within circumstances that are often not of their own choosing. People are often born into poverty, have limited access to develop the human capital necessary for self-determination, have social networks that do not promote health, have unstable and dysfunctional families, or reside in communities that can be harmful to their well-being. The types of negative recovery capital can diminish the ability to develop and activate positive recovery capital. However, the presence of positive recovery capital that enables the capacity to overcome human travails as opposed to negative recovery capital that diminishes it is always experienced uniquely by individuals. One person's portfolio of positive or negative recovery capital is more or less greater than another person's and is always uniquely configured. Because of this, there is never a standard 'tipping point' where positive recovery capital becomes more facilitative of a recovery experience by overshadowing or reducing negative recovery capital. Since recovery capital exists along a continuum of positive and negative poles, efforts to build positive recovery capital and reduce, or at least neutralize, the effects of negative recovery capital can contribute to the reflexivity needed for behaviour change. In some circumstances, such as those within our study of natural recovery, because individuals may have an excess of positive recovery capital to begin with or the opportunity to draw upon it, they may be able to resolve their problems without or with minimal treatment. In other cases, individuals may need treatment or recovery communities to help cultivate their positive recovery capital (Connolly and Granfield, 2017).

In these latter cases, because of the dynamic quality of recovery capital, it may take a greater amount of time to build positive social capital due to the severity of use and/or degree of involvement with a drug using subculture. Ultimately, recovery is best facilitated when there is an excess of positive recovery capital relative to negative recovery capital.

Thus, from the previous discussion, the following set of propositions may be postulated:

1. Recovery involves a process of personal change and transformation.
2. As a process of change and transformation, recovery occurs within the context of social interaction and is not predetermined by genetics.
3. The social interaction related to change involves the accumulation of recovery capital.
4. A person's recovery capital is defined by the total sum of internal and external resources that promote their capacity for change.
5. The internal and external resources associated with recovery capital exist at the personal, social, and community levels across four distinct dimensions, consisting of social capital, human capital, physical capital, and cultural capital.
6. Recovery capital possesses a dynamic quality that has differential trajectories. It can be accumulated and depleted. It can be stored and it can be lost. It can be built (or rebuilt) at any stage in a person's life.
7. The development of positive recovery capital can be facilitated through participation in pro-social networks, communities, and institutions.
8. Like all forms of capital, recovery capital is not equally distributed throughout society. Systemic inequities in areas such as education, income, housing, and access to healthcare generate inequities in recovery capital.
9. Recovery is facilitated when there is an excess of positive recovery capital (those factors that promote and facilitate recovery) relative to negative social capital (those factors that diminish or interfere with the capacity for recovery).

Expansion of the recovery capital construct

While our work on recovery capital received some positive reaction from professionals and scholars in the field, especially those investigating the processes of natural recovery and self-change, many treatment professionals, as well as funding agencies were not initially receptive to the idea. Because our work on recovery capital did not emphasize treatment models nor was consistent with the treatment-centred funding streams at the state and federal levels, the concept of recovery capital did not receive broad support. Many working in the treatment field were not positively inclined towards our research due to their general disbelief that individuals could overcome addiction without treatment and even asserted that our subjects did not suffer from 'real' addiction if they were able to self-resolve. Additionally, our attempts to acquire federal funding to further study recovery capital proved unsuccessful.

As was pointed out earlier in this chapter, all scientific ideas exist within a broader social context. Scientific concepts and theories are accepted or rejected due to any number of conditions that are often external to their quality or empirical support they receive. Indeed, the alcoholism-as-disease concept became institutionalized largely without much empirical research. The disease concept of alcoholism and addiction, and its expansion, had much to do with the broader social context of the failure of prohibition, the emergence of influential advocacy groups, the rising concerns of youth protest and drug use during the 1960s, the establishment of federal policies and funding agencies such as NIDA and the NIAAA, as well as the proliferation of for-profit treatment in the 1970s and beyond.

The ever-widening expansion of recovery capital as a theory of recovery from addiction has been largely due to factors existing independently from the origins of the concept. The expansion and acceptance of recovery capital as a viable construct can be attributed to two significant factors. The initial formulation of recovery capital was as a theoretical construct developed to explain what we were observing in our natural recovery case studies. The concept became a way of describing a pattern of behaviour we observed in our data and offering insight into the limitations of the addiction-as-disease paradigm. As young assistant professors working in the academic 'field' that emphasized the production and dissemination of knowledge as the traditional pathways for achieving tenure, we were not part of the emerging recovery advocacy groups that were becoming popular during that time period. As the scholarship on institutionalism has demonstrated (DiMaggio and Powell, 1983; Powell and DiMaggio, 1991), the existence of advocacy groups in advancing the legitimacy of a theory or concept is crucially important to its circulation and viability.

The corresponding social movement of the 'Recovery-Oriented System of Care' (ROSC) played a significant role in the circulation and expansion of recovery capital theory. The basic tenets of ROSC include, among others, individual empowerment, community-based support, resiliency, multiple pathways to recovery, a long-term perspective, and the importance of the voices of individuals who have overcome addiction. Individuals within this burgeoning movement were critical to advancing the concept of recovery capital. In advocating for new approaches or new organizational forms, individuals acting as change agents can serve as 'institutional entrepreneurs' who often challenge existing institutional norms, introduce or promote new ideas, and influence the adoption of alternative practices. The circulation and advancement of recovery capital as a theory of addiction recovery has benefited significantly from the endorsement of leaders in advancing ROSC.

The contributions of William White stand out as a significant factor in the circulation, acceptance, and institutionalization of recovery capital theory. For several decades, he had been a prominent figure in the addiction recovery field and played a significant role in contributing to the development of the ROSC paradigm. In the late 1990s and early 2000s, a time that corresponds to our first publications on recovery capital, William White was working as a scholar/activist to advance models of ROSC 'with systems defined not as a treatment system but a larger mobilization of recovery support resources within local communities' (White, 2023). Working within this framework to help build a recovery management network emphasizing a comprehensive, community-based approach to support long-term recovery, he 'recognized recovery capital as a potentially transformative idea within the addiction treatment field and allied fields' (White, 2023). Due to his stature in the ROSC movement and in the addiction recovery field more generally, he provided valuable bridging social capital linking the concept of recovery capital to a larger network of researchers, practitioners, and policy makers. His numerous publications and monographs along with his extensive presentations at national conferences circulated and helped legitimize the concept of recovery capital. As he comments (2023), his status in the field helped spark:

> invitations to keynote national and state conferences of addiction professionals as well as my deep involvement with a new recovery advocacy movement that spawned hundreds of new grassroots recovery community organizations and new recovery support organizations. I think my long tenure in the field and my access to diverse professional academic/scientific, and people in recovery and their families helped spread the RC concept and support its importance. (White, 2023)

He also helped advance the science of recovery capital through his collaborations with other thought leaders interested in recovery processes, including Alexandre Laudet, David Best, and John Kelly (Laudet and White, 2008; Best and Laudet, 2010). These researchers along with several others have helped institutionalize recovery capital as a viable concept. This work eventually led to the development of assessment tools such as the Assessment of Recovery Capital (Groshkova et al, 2013), REC-CAP (Cano et al, 2017), the Brief Assessment of Recovery Capital (Vilsaint et al, 2017), and most recently, the Multidimensional Inventory of Recovery Capital (Bowen et al, 2023). Research on recovery capital has now been applied to diverse and vulnerable populations including African Americans (Connolly and Granfield, 2017), ethnic minorities (Pouille et al, 2021), the homeless (Neale and Stevenson, 2015), rural populations (Palombi et al, 2019), older adults (LaBarre et al, 2021), adolescents (Hennessy, 2019), and to examine gender differences (Gavriel-Fried et al, 2019). It has included studies in a diversity of settings such as drug treatment courts and criminal justice organizations (Kahn et al, 2019; Witbrodt et al, 2019; Hennessy et al, 2023), parenting (Hennessy et al, 2022), the workplace (Frone et al, 2022), mindfulness programmes (LaBelle et al, 2023), higher education (Hennessy et al, 2022), marital counselling (Lee and Ofori, 2022), post-incarceration (Bormann et al, 2023), and child welfare programmes. The concept has also been implemented in countries around the globe including the US, UK (Best et al, 2021), Canada, Iran (Moghanibashi-Mansourieh et al, 2022), Ireland (Foley et al, 2022), Norway, Sweden, and Australia. Additionally, the concept has been applied to a variety of problem behaviours beyond substance addiction, including gambling (Gavriel-Fried, 2018; Gavriel-Fried et al, 2020), mental health (Tew, 2013), eating disorders (Kline, 2023), suicide ideation (Haynes et al, 2021), sex addiction, and social media addiction.

A second source for the dissemination and legitimation of the recovery capital concept has been at the grassroots level. Institutional entrepreneurs within this sector often serve as advocates for the adoption of novel approaches, policies, laws, or practices within existing institutions. Such groups can introduce new practices, challenge existing norms, promote alternative structures and approaches, influence policy makers, help establish new networks, build capacity, and contribute to shaping and reshaping organizational fields. The development of environmental sustainability and corporate responsibility is a case in point. Social action groups such as Greenpeace, the World Wildlife Fund, and the Natural Resources Defense Council played crucial roles in raising awareness, mobilizing public support, emerging legislation, and changes in corporate practices. New organizational roles and practices within companies developed around this changing landscape, such as chief sustainability officers and the rise in corporate social responsibility. Investment funds now include opportunities for environmentally conscious individuals to invest with companies that prioritize ethical and environmentally sustainable practices.

With regards to recovery capital, grassroots organizations have had a substantial impact on its spread and legitimation. One grassroots organization that has helped raise awareness, mobilize public support, and spread recovery capital is the Last Door Recovery Society (LDRS) in New Westminster, British Columbia. This organization has had more than a 35-year history of providing addiction services that emphasizes a community-based model of recovery. Faced with 'evidence-based' policy paradigms promoting pathology, and funding limited acute-based services, LDRS established licensed, accredited services while building a grassroots recovery community in their city. Alongside other recovery advocates, LDRS sought out means to optimize recovery outcomes. LDRS broadened their collaborative, multidisciplinary approach to recovery by seeking health ministers' policy support for recovery-oriented systems of care and establishing a platform for broader public education highlighting recovery science.

The concept of recovery capital aligned with Last Door's recovery-oriented focus and was integrated into their philosophy and programming. The organization's mission of building recovery communities by promoting investments in recovery capital became the focus of its public education and awareness campaign. Begun in 2017, the annual Recovery Capital Conference of Canada organized by LDRS, with support from the British Columbia Mental Health and Addiction Ministry and many recovery advocacy groups, has brought leading international researchers, clinicians, and policy makers together to share evidence-based scientific and clinical knowledge on recovery and the processes of building recovery capital. Over 10,000 clinicians, health care providers, academics, and politicians have been educated in the principles of recovery capital over the past several years. The stated aims of the conference are to 'transform provincial policies, services, and systems toward a recovery-oriented paradigm responsive to the needs of people nationwide and within our own communities' (Recovery Capital Conference of Canada, 2023). The impact of this public education effort has not only helped LDRS solidify its reputation in the recovery world, but more importantly for the expansion of recovery capital as a theoretical concept, it helped legitimize the concept by embedding it within a professional context as well as in a policy domain. Professionalization can be a powerful force in building or transforming institutional fields and Last Door's professionalizing activities through its Recovery Capital Conference have contributed much to the circulation, legitimation, and expansion of this construct. The expansion of this professionalizing trend occurring within the recovery capital 'field' can be seen in the more recent establishment of the National Recovery Capital Conference of America, started in 2020, that is sponsored by the National Behavioral Health Association of Providers and the California Consortium of Addiction Programs and Professionals. This annual conference not only teaches participants the principles of recovery capital but also offers continuing education credits from various organizations.

The impact of these two institutional sectors, the academic sector and the applied sector, on the institutionalization of recovery capital theory cannot be overstated. The work within these two sectors has served as a catalyst for the expansion of recovery capital by building the scientific legitimacy of the concept as well as integrating it within various applied settings. As with all professionalizing projects, a theoretical foundation is an essential component to establishing professional jurisdiction (Abbott, 1988). Indeed, all professionalizing projects establish boundaries that include a knowledge base and levels of expertise. The growing recognition of recovery capital may represent a broader movement towards an interdisciplinary and holistic approach to addiction and recovery. Traditionally, the addiction field has been the domain of specific professions that place an emphasis on the biological and/or neurological aspects of addiction and recovery. The adoption of recovery capital as a concept reflects a more holistic and collaborative understanding of factors influencing recovery, potentially challenging the exclusive jurisdiction of specific professional constituencies. Recovery capital theory brings into the conversation fields that have, for the most part, been tangential to the reified 'truths' about addiction and recovery. Because recovery capital theory draws upon insights from various disciplines, including psychology, sociology, public health, and community development, as well as the experiences of individuals in recovery, the traditional boundaries within the field have become more porous allowing for the recognition of a more multifaceted approach to addiction and recovery. By doing so, it has broadened the narrow focus on treatment modalities towards a recognition of the social, cultural, and personal factors influencing recovery. This shift is challenging traditional notions of expertise within the addiction treatment field and is encouraging a more comprehensive, inclusive, accessible, and multilayered approach to understanding recovery.

Conclusion

In his 2000 book, *The Tipping Point*, Malcolm Gladwell recounts the story of Paul Revere and his famous midnight ride warning citizens of Boston and the surrounding area of the impending attack of British forces by land and by sea. Every child born in the US over the generations and many around the world have learned of Revere's ride as signalling the start of the American Revolution. However, what has been forgotten in this history is the fact that there was a second rider, William Dawes, who sped off on the same mission but in the opposite direction. Why every American citizen knows of Paul Revere but has little knowledge of William Dawes is precisely what Gladwell analyses in his book. For Gladwell, Paul Revere became a 'legend' not simply because of his ride, but because of the networks within which he was embedded. Unlike Dawes, Revere was connected to a multitude of social, business, and community groups. People knew Revere, they listened to him and shared the story of his ride with others. Dawes, on the other hand, was unknown by people and had none of the network connections that Revere possessed and subsequently his role in the beginning of the revolution went unnoticed by most.

The reception, circulation, and legitimation of the concept of recovery capital is not unlike Revere's famous ride story. It has grown exponentially from its humble beginnings as an inductively developed concept to explain the recovery experiences of 46 individuals in a major American city to a concept that has spawned a new scientific area of inquiry and now serves as foundation for a growing number of treatment and recovery programmes around the world. It has been recognized by policy makers at local and national levels and is being applied to an ever-growing number of life challenges that individuals experience. Currently, there are well over 100,000 unique references to recovery capital online. In the span of 25 years, the concept of recovery capital has become institutionalized and is considered by some as 'one of the most important concepts to understand for those who are concerned with substance abuse disorders and recovery' (Brown, 2021).

This chapter has charted the theoretical foundations, conceptual development, and institutional expansion of the concept of recovery capital. Generated from the study of a small sample of self-remitters in the late 1990s, the concept initially evolved from a focus on the importance of social capital in the recovery experiences of individuals with alcohol and drug addictions to a more multidimensional concept utilizing the insights from the concepts of human capital, physical capital, and cultural capital. As a general theory of recovery, recovery capital predicts that individuals overcome addiction when they can draw on and activate a sum of internal and external resources available to them that support the initiation and sustainment of recovery. The expansion of the concept in the scientific literature as well as in its practical applications across many domains has occurred largely due to the actions of individual and grassroots leaders within the recovery-oriented systems of the care movement who introduced the concept to a significantly broader social network of academics, community activists, policy makers, treatment professionals, and individuals in recovery. Like the case of Paul Revere, these individual and grassroot leaders have served as the institutional entrepreneurs helping to drive institutional change within the addiction field.

The future of recovery capital as a general theory of recovery and change will be shaped by researchers, community groups, treatment professionals, and policy makers who continue to explore its applications to multiple constituencies. One future possibility to be explored is the role that generative AI might play in the process of building recovery capital. AI is one of the fastest growing forms of technology in human history. This technology has changed and will continue to change multiple dimensions of people's lives, including our social, physical, psychological, health, recreational, educational, and occupational experiences. As with all technologies, there are always positive and negative attributes associated with these developments, but the progress of generative AI technology will be unstoppable. Could generative AI be used to help individuals build recovery capital? Research has already established that online communities can be an effective method of building recovery capital (Bliuc et al, 2017). It could be possible for AI applications to assess an individual's recovery capital, monitor a person's utilization of recovery capital, provide recovery capital analytics as early warnings of potential relapse, recommend peer matchings and suggested pathways into supportive community groups, or create messaging that communicates positive norms encouraging abstinence or moderation. Of course, AI will never be a replacement for the necessity for human contact and support, but as we have seen with the rise of telemedicine and telehealth, digital platforms have utility in health promotion and perhaps have applications to recovery capital.

A final potential consideration in the future of recovery capital concerns the role it might play in the construction of social policy at multiple levels. Treatment modalities associated with addictions have largely abstracted individuals from the broader circumstances related to their addictions (Granfield, 2004). From a recovery capital perspective, treatment does not 'cure' people's addictions, rather, when it is effective, treatment helps build the capacity of individuals to draw upon and/or develop internal and external resources to initiate, support, and maintain recovery. Treatment is a tool; recovery is a lived experience! In the large, complex societies and communities that permeate our lives, human travails are inevitable. Addictions and personal challenges of all kinds are normal outgrowths of a complex society. The grand challenge that we all face from rural communities to large global cities is how we create the capacities for people from diverse and unequal backgrounds to overcome the often-devastating life challenges they confront. At some point in all our lives, we are recovering from a personal challenge that could disrupt and perhaps destroy our lives and others' lives. If most people are faced with having to overcome some challenge, what social policies are in place to assist people to successfully resolve these problems? What would social policies or urban design look like if they were driven by tenets of recovery capital (Best and Colman, 2018)? Perhaps this is too grandiose of an expansion of the term but, as a thought experiment, it may include some of the following: access to affordable health care, access to supportive community groups, criminal justice reform to destigmatize people, opportunities for stable housing and living conditions when needed, employment and educational training, family and child supports, a culture that celebrates diversity and equity, and resources to support physical and mental health. The value of recovery capital as a general theory of recovery is that it recognizes the importance of people's own capacities in overcoming the problems they experience. How we create and facilitate the opportunities for cultivating people's capacity to overcome these problems is the greatest challenge we face in contemporary society.

References

Abbott, A. (1988) *The System of Professions: An Essay on the Division of Expert Labor*, Chicago: University of Chicago Press.

Ashford, R., Brown, A., Brown, T., Callis, J.H., Cleveland, H., Eisenhart, E., et al (2019) 'Defining and operationalizing the phenomena of recovery: A working definition from the recovery science research collaborative', *Addiction Research & Theory*, 27(3): 179–88.

Best, D. and Laudet, A.B. (2010) *The Potential of Recovery Capital*, London: Royal Society for the Arts.

Best, D. and Colman, C. (2018) 'Let's celebrate recovery: Inclusive cities working together to support social cohesion', *Addiction Research and Theory*, 27(1): 55–64.

Best, D. and Hennessy, E.A. (2022) 'The science of recovery capital: Where do we go from here?', *Addiction*, 117(4): 1139–45.

Best, D., Pickersgill, H.D., Higham, K., Hancock, R., and Critchlow, T. (2021) 'Building recovery capital through community engagement: A hub and spoke model for peer-based recovery support services in England', *Alcoholism Treatment Quarterly*, 39(1): 3–15.

Biernacki, P. (1986) *Pathways from Heroin Addiction: Recovery Without Treatment*, Philadelphia: Temple University Press.

Bliuc, A.M., Best, D., Iqbal, M., and Upton, K. (2017) 'Building addiction recovery capital through online participation in a recovery community', *Social Science & Medicine*, 193: 110–17.

Bormann, N.L., Weber, A.N., Miskle, B., Arndt, S., and Lynch, A.C. (2023) 'Sex differences in recovery capital gains post-incarceration', *Substance Use and Misuse*, 58(14): 1839–46.

Bourdieu, P. (1991) 'The peculiar history of scientific reason', *Sociological Forum*, 6(1): 3–26.

Bourdieu, P. and Wacquant, L. (1992) *An Invitation to Reflexive Sociology*, Chicago: The University of Chicago Press.

Bowen, E., Irish, A., Wilding, G., LaBarre, C., Capozziello, N., Nochajski, T., et al (2023) 'Development and psychometric properties of the Multidimensional Inventory of Recovery Capital (MIRC)', *Drug and Alcohol Dependence*, 247, 109875, DOI: 10.1016/j.drugalcdep.2023.109875.

Brown, A. (2021) 'Taking the measure of addiction recovery: A brief history of recovery capital', *Population Health Research Brief Series*, 149, Available from: https://surface.syr.edu/lerner/149

Cano, I., Best, D., Edwards, M., and Lehman, J. (2017) 'Recovery capital pathways: Modelling the components of recovery wellbeing', *Drug and Alcohol Dependence*, 181: 11–19, DOI: https://doi.org/10.1016/j.drugalcdep.2017.09.002

Cloud, W. and Granfield, R. (2008) 'Conceptualizing recovery capital: Expansion of a theoretical construct', *Substance Use and Misuse*, 43(12–13): 1971–86.

Coleman, J.S. (1988) 'Social capital in the creation of human capital', *American Journal of Sociology*, 94: S95–S121.

Connolly, K. and Granfield, R. (2017) 'Building recovery capital: The role of faith-based communities in the reintegration of formerly incarcerated drug offenders', *Journal of Drug Issues*, 47(3): 370–82.

Dawson, D., Grant, B.F., Chou, S.P., and Pickering, R.P. (1995) 'Subgroup variation in U.S. drinking patterns: Results of the 1992 national longitudinal alcohol epidemiologic study', *Journal of Substance Abuse*, 7(3): 331–44, DOI: 10.1016/0899-3289(95)90026-8.

DiMaggio, P.J. and Powell, W.W. (1983) 'The iron cage revisited: Institutional isomorphism and collective rationality in organizational fields', *American Sociological Review*, 48(2): 147–60.

Flint, T. and Ronel, N. (2023) 'From deprivation to capital – spirituality and spiritual yearning as recovery capital from PTSD', *Journal of Aggression, Maltreatment & Trauma*, 32(3): 325–45, DOI: https://doi.org/10.1080/10926771.2022.2146557

Foley, M., Reidy, M., and Wells, J.S.G. (2022) 'Recovery capital: Stakeholder's experiences and expectations for enabling sustainable recovery from substance use in the South East region of Ireland', *Journal of Substance Use*, 27(3): 283–8.

Frone, M., Chosewood, L.C., Osborne, J.C., and Howard, J.J. (2022) 'Workplace supported recovery from substance use disorders: Defining the construct, developing a model, and proposing an agenda for future research', *Occupational Health Science*, 6(4): 475–511.

Gavriel-Fried, B. (2018) 'The crucial role of recovery capital in individuals with a gambling disorder', *Journal of Behavioural Addictions*, 7(3): 792–9.

Gavriel-Fried, B., Moretta, T., and Potenza, M.N. (2019) 'Similar roles for recovery capital but not stress in women and men recovering from gambling disorder', *Journal of Behavioural Addictions*, 8(4): 770–9.

Gavriel-Fried, B., Moretta, T., and Potenza, M.N. (2020) 'Associations between recovery capital, spirituality, and *DSM–5* symptom improvement in gambling disorder', *Psychology of Addictive Behaviors*, 34(1): 209–17.

Giddens, A. (1984) *The Constitution of Society: Outline of the Structuration Theory*, The Constitution of Society: University of California Press.

Gladwell, M. (2000) *The Tipping Point: How Little Things Can Make a Big Difference*, New York: Little Brown.

Granfield, R. (2004) 'Addiction and modernity: A comment on a global theory of addiction', *NAD Publication*, 44: 29–34.

Granfield, R. and Cloud, W. (1999) *Coming Clean: Overcoming Addiction without Treatment*, New York: New York University Press.

Granfield, R. and Cloud, W. (2001) 'Social context and "natural recovery": The role of social capital in the resolution of drug-associated problems', *Substance Use and Misuse*, 36(11): 1543–70, DOI: 10.1081/ja-100106963.

Groshkova, T., Best, D., and White, W. (2013) 'The Assessment of Recovery Capital: Properties and psychometrics of a measure of addiction recovery strengths', *Drug and Alcohol Review*, 32(2): 187–94.

Haynes, C., Deane, F., and Kelly, P. (2021) 'Suicidal ideation predicted by changes experienced from pre-treatment to 3-month post-discharge from residential substance use disorder treatment', *Journal of Substance Abuse Treatment*, 131, 108542.

Hennessy, E.A., Cristello, J.V., and Kelly, J.F. (2019) 'RCAM: A proposed model of recovery capital for adolescents', *Addiction Research & Theory*, 27(5): 429–36, DOI: https://doi.org/10.1080/16066359.2018.1540694.

Hennessy E.A., Simpson, J.J., and Nash, A. (2022) 'Parenting to provide social recovery capital: A qualitative study', *Addiction Research & Theory*, 30(5): 368–74, DOI: 10.1080/16066359.2022.2055000.

Hennessy, E.A., Krasnoff, P., and Best, D. (2023) 'Implementing a recovery capital model into therapeutic courts: Case study and lessons learned', *International Journal of Offender Therapy and Comparative Criminology*, September 27, DOI: 10.1177/0306624X231198810.

Hennessy, E.A., Nichols, L.M., Brown, T., and Tanner-Smith, E. (2022) 'Advancing the science of evaluating Collegiate Recovery Program processes and outcomes: A recovery capital perspective', *Evaluation and Program Planning*, 91, DOI: 10.1016/j.evalprogplan.2022.102057.

LaBelle, O., Hastings, M., Vest, N., Meeks M., and Lucier, K. (2023) 'The role of mindfulness, meditation, and peer support in recovery capital among Recovery Dharma members', *Journal of Substance Use & Addiction Treatment*, 145: 208939, DOI: 10.1016/j.josat.2022.208939.

Laudet, A.B. and White, W. (2008) 'Recovery capital as prospective predictor of sustained recovery, life satisfaction, and stress among former polysubstance users', *Substance Use and Misuse*, 43(1): 27–54.

Lee, B.K. and Ofori Dei, S.M. (2022) 'Changes in work status, couple adjustment, and recovery capital: Secondary analysis of data from a congruence couple therapy randomized controlled trial', *Substance Abuse: Research and Treatment*, 16, DOI: 10.1177/11782218221088875.

Levine H.G. (1978) 'The discovery of addiction: Changing conceptions of habitual drunkenness in America', *Journal of Studies on Alcohol*, 39(1): 143–74.

Kahn, L., Vest, B.M., Kulak, J.A., Berdine, D.E., and Granfield, R. (2019) 'Barriers and facilitators to recovery capital among justice-involved community members', *Journal of Offender Rehabilitation*, 58(6): 544–65.

Kline, K. (2023) 'A conceptual framework for recovery from eating disorders: An adoptive approach to the recovery capital model', *Social Work in Mental Health*, 21(2): 162–79.

Kuhn, T. (1962/1970a) *The Structure of Scientific Revolutions* (2nd edn, with postscript), Chicago: University of Chicago Press.

LaBelle, O., Hastings, M., Vest, N., Meeks, M., and Lucier, K. (2023) 'The role of mindfulness, meditation, and peer support in recovery capital among Recovery Dharma members', *Journal of Substance Use and Addiction Treatment*, 145, DOI: 10.1016/j.josat.2022.208939.

LaBarre, C., Linn, B.K., Bradizza, C.M., Bowen, E.A., and Stasiewicz, P.R. (2021) 'Conceptualizing recovery capital for older adults with substance use disorders', *Journal of Social Work Practice in the Addictions*, 21(4): 1–11.

Lax, E. (2005) *The Mold in Dr. Florey's Coat: The Story of the Penicillin Miracle*, New York: Henry Holt & Company.

Lee, B. and Ofori Dei, S. (2022) 'Changes in work status, couple adjustment, and recovery capital: Secondary analysis of data from a congruence couple therapy randomized controlled trial', *Substance Abuse: Research and Treatment*, 16, DOI: 10.1177/11782218221088875.

Martin, L., Gutman, H., and Hutton, P. (eds) (1988) *Technologies of the Self: A Seminar with Michel Foucault*, Amherst: University of Massachusetts Press.

Mills, C.W. (1967) *The Sociological Imagination*, Oxford, UK: Oxford University Press.

Moghanibashi-Mansourieh, A., Alipour, F., Rafiey, H., and Arshi, M. (2022) 'The role of reflective consequences in developing recovery capital for the recovering substance abuser population of Tehran city', *Journal of Ethnicity in Substance Abuse*, 21(4): 1272–84.

Neale, J. and Stevenson, C. (2015) 'Social and recovery capital amongst homeless hostel residents who use drugs and alcohol', *International Journal of Drug Policy*, 26(5): 475–83.

Palombi, L., Hawthorne, A.N., Irish, A., Becher, E., and Bowen, E. (2019) '"One out of ten ain't going to make it": An analysis of recovery capital in the rural Upper Midwest', *Journal of Drug Issues*, 49(4): 680–702.

Peele, S. (1989) *Diseasing of America*, New York: Lexington Books.

Pouille, A., Bellaert, L., Vander Laenen, F., and Vanderplasschen, W. (2021) 'Recovery capital among migrants and ethnic minorities in recovery from problem substance use: An analysis of lived experiences', *International Journal of Environmental Research and Public Health*, 18(24): 3025.

Powell, W. and DiMaggio, P. (1991) *The New Institutionalism in Organizational Analysis*, Chicago: The University of Chicago Press.

Recovery Capital Conference of Canada (2023) [online], Available from: https://recoverycapitalconference.com

Reinarman, C. and Granfield, R. (2015) 'Addiction is not just a brain disease: Critical studies of addiction', in R. Granfield and C. Reinarman (eds) *Expanding Addiction: Critical Essays*, New York: Routledge Press, pp 1–21.

Room, R. (2003) 'The cultural framing of addiction', *Janus Head*, 6(2): 221–34.

Rose, N. (2003) 'The neurochemical self and its anomalies', in A. Doyle and D. Ericson (eds) *Risk and Morality*, Toronto: University of Toronto Press, pp 407–37.

Schneider, J.W. (1978) 'Deviant drinking as disease: Alcoholism as a social accomplishment', *Social Problems*, 25(4): 361–72.

Tew, J. (2013) 'Recovery capital: What enables a sustainable recovery from mental health difficulties?', *European Journal of Social Work*, 16(3): 360–74.

Valliant, G. (1983) *The Natural History of Alcoholism: Causes, Patterns, and Paths to Recovery*, Cambridge: Harvard University Press.

Vilsaint, C.L., Kelly, J.F., Bergman, B.G., Groshkova, T., Best, D., and White, W. (2017) 'Development and validation of a Brief Assessment of Recovery Capital (BARC-10) for alcohol and drug use disorder', *Drug and Alcohol Dependence*, 177: 71–6.

Waldorf, D., Reinarman, C., and Murphy, S. (1991) *Cocaine Changes: The Experience of Using and Quitting*, Philadelphia: Temple University Press.

White, W. (1998) *Slaying the Dragon: The History of Addiction Treatment and Recovery in America*, Bloomington, IL: Chestnut Health Systems/Lighthouse Institute.

White, W. (2016) 'Explorations in natural recovery and recovery capital': An interview with Dr William Cloud [online], Available from: www.chestnut.org/william-white-papers/

White, W. (2023) Personal communication, November 2.

Winick, C. (1962) 'Maturing out of narcotic addiction', *Bulletin on Narcotics*, 14: 1–7.

Witbrodt, J., Polcin, D., Korcha, R., and Li, L. (2019) 'Beneficial effects of motivational interviewing case management: A latent class analysis of recovery capital among sober living residents with criminal justice involvement', *Drug and Alcohol Dependence*, 200: 124–32.

3

Reflections on Initial Attempts at the Quantification of Recovery Capital

David Best, William White, and Lauren A. Hoffman

Overview

This chapter will follow one particular pathway for the development of the concept of recovery capital through the work of William White, initially in the form of a paper and an initial checklist that was intended to support the measurement of recovery capital in peer-based recovery support settings. This chapter will discuss the initial attempts at quantifying recovery capital, the origins of the Recovery Capital Scale (RCS), and how it was used and interpreted. Much of it is presented in the first person, initially with reflections from William White, and then from David Best, with the remaining sections contributed by all three authors. This developmental pathway will be reviewed to consider the approaches to measurement and the aspirations of this approach, how they reflect current thinking about recovery capital, and what the aims of measurement might be as we move forward.

William White's reflections on the history of recovery capital measurement

This section is a first-person account of William's experiences of the emergence of the concept of recovery capital and then its application and implementation.

> In 1998, I helped start the Behavioral Health Recovery Management (BHRM) project in Illinois – an effort to extend addiction treatment from models of acute care to

models of sustained recovery management nested in larger recovery-oriented systems of care (ROSC) – with systems defined not as the treatment system but a larger mobilization of recovery support resources within local communities (White, 2009). This project grew out of legislator and clinician concerns regarding large numbers of individuals recycling through repeated brief episodes of addiction treatment without achieving sustainable recovery and related achievements. The project explored the application of principles and practices from chronic disease management in primary medicine to the management of severe and complex substance use disorders. In conducting a recovery literature review during the initial stages of that project, I discovered Robert Granfield and William Cloud's early articles (1996, 2001) and their book *Coming Clean* (Granfield and Cloud, 1999) shortly after its publication. I immediately recognized recovery capital as a potentially transformative idea within the addiction treatment and allied fields and closely followed all subsequent published work related to recovery capital. Early papers disseminated through the BHRM project extolled the concept of recovery capital and its implications within the Recovery Management/ROSC process we were recommending.

When the BHRM funding was on the brink of ending due to sudden state budget cuts, it was replaced by a Substance Abuse and Mental Health Services Administration (SAMHSA) Addiction Technology Transfer Center (ATTC) multi-year contract to spread Recovery Management/ROSC concepts regionally and nationally. This involved countless presentations (75 to 100 per year in peak years), articles, and monographs promoting Recovery Management/ROSC that highlighted the import of recovery capital. The publications included a 2008 recovery capital primer co-authored with William Cloud (White and Cloud, 2008) that explored the clinical implications of the concept of recovery capital. The primer split recovery capital into four domains – personal, social, community, and cultural – and discussed how these domains interacted with varying levels of problem severity to identify individual needs. In the primer, we proposed that where individuals fall within the model can be used to determine the intensity and duration of planned service interventions (see Figure 3.1).

We suggested that careful measurement of matrix component interactions could be used to direct the appropriate level of care within addiction treatment and allied settings. Thus, 'a client with moderate problem severity but high recovery capital arriving at a treatment agency in response to a positive drug test might be quite appropriate for screening and brief intervention' (White and Cloud, 2008, 7). Similarly, 'a client with high problem severity/complexity and extremely low recovery capital requires services of high intensity, broad scope (for example, outreach, assertive case management, and sustained recovery coaching), and long duration' (White and Cloud, 2008, 7).

Figure 3.1: Recovery capital/Problem severity matrix

High Recovery Capital / High Problem Severity / Complexity	High Problem Severity / Complexity / Low Recovery Capital
Low Problem Severity / Complexity / High Recovery Capital	Low Recovery Capital / Low Problem Severity / Complexity

The fundamental logic of the recovery capital primer is summed up in White and Cloud's conclusion:

> We tend to evaluate our effectiveness based on what is subtracted from the lives of our clients (for example, AOD use, criminal activity, threats to public safety, financial problems, high health care consumption, and emotional distress). However, the short-term elimination or reduction of these ingredients may or may not have any linkage to the prospects of long-term recovery. A better predictor of long-term recovery may be what has been added to the lives of the individuals and families with whom we work, for example, radically altered perceptions of alcohol and other drugs, physical and emotional health, increased coping and communication skills, improved family relationships, new family rules and rituals, safe/stable housing and employment; clean and sober friends, membership in a community of recovering people, and life meaning and purpose. (White and Cloud, 2008, 8–9)

The BHRM and ATTC presentations, papers, and the Recovery Management/ROSC monograph series (2006–12) were warmly received, nationally and internationally, and stirred innumerable requests to me for information related to Recovery Management, ROSC, and recovery capital. ATTC Directors Lonnetta Albright and Dr Mike Flaherty promoted these publications throughout the regional ATTC Centers and advocated for recovery and Recovery Management/ROSC initiatives within SAMHSA and state addiction treatment authorities. The monographs went through multiple printings and were widely distributed at professional conferences. The national ATTC office also hosted Recovery Management/ROSC training seminars for trainers selected by states to later spread Recovery Management/ROSC methodologies and the import of recovery capital assessment. All of these activities increased interest in recovery capital-inspired language and changes in service practices, including early efforts to measure recovery capital and extend strictly clinical (intrapersonal) models of intervention to models focused on community social change.

In addition to the ATTC's influence, Dr Arthur Evans, then Director of the Philadelphia Department of Behavioral Health, invited me to consult on Recovery Management/ROSC implementation from 2005 to my retirement in 2013. I was similarly involved in multiple consultations with Dr Thomas Kirk, Commissioner of the State of Connecticut's mental health and addiction services authority. These consultations provided a laboratory to test novel ideas related to Recovery Management, ROSC, and recovery capital, which informed subsequent presentations and papers that emerged from this work. Drs Evans and Kirk later described these efforts in the book *Addiction Recovery Management* (Kelly and White, 2011). These professional involvements were accompanied by my deep involvement with a new recovery advocacy movement that spawned hundreds of new grassroots recovery community organizations and new recovery support organizations, for example, recovery community centers, recovery residences, recovery high schools, collegiate recovery programmes, recovery programmes within business and industry, recovery ministries, recovery cafes, recovery music festivals, recovery theatre and film projects, and recovery book clubs. Work with this growing network of recovery community organizations forged a second pathway of dissemination of concepts, language, and recovery support activities related to recovery capital development.

Key early collaborators in measurement of recovery capital: William White continues his reflections

Shortly after my discovery of Granfield and Cloud's seminal work, I began discussing this work with leaders in the field, including scientific investigators. Several of these people were very important in recovery capital concept dissemination in addition to those individuals noted earlier.

Dr Alexandre Laudet, a research scientist at National Development and Research Institutes, Inc (NDRI), was among the first collaborators to conduct research related to recovery capital. We published several early papers (2006, 2008, 2010) based on studies of recovery capital and quality of life in recovery. She was among the first researchers to focus her work exclusively on the recovery process rather than on addiction or its brief treatment. She authored many recovery capital and recovery related papers that helped spread recovery capital as a potentially transformative idea and was a tireless advocate for expanding recovery research.

The 2008 paper referred to earlier (Laudet and White, 2008) examined the concept of recovery capital in terms of its ability to predict recovery maintenance,[1] its impact on quality of life and stress, and the relationship between recovery capital and recovery stage, among a sample of individuals using heroin and crack who were interviewed twice in the space of one year in New York City. The authors' key finding was that greater levels of baseline recovery capital were predictive of better outcomes, contributing a significant percentage of variance across the outcome domains of sustained recovery, quality of life, satisfaction, and stress. Recovery capital remained significant when controlling for the baseline level of the domains under study (Laudet and White, 2008, 9). The authors concluded that the recovery capital framework offers a key theoretical foundation for the basis of subsequent recovery capital measurement. To continue William's reflections:

> Dr David Best from the UK, who was then chair of the Scottish Drugs Recovery Consortium and an academic based in Scotland, contacted me early in this work and invited me to collaborate with him on numerous studies related to recovery and the role of recovery capital in addiction treatment outcomes. In more recent years, his consultations with many organizations in the US and other countries spurred further dissemination and advancement of the concept of recovery capital and its service applications. David Best's reflections on the importance of recovery capital as a measurement approach are discussed in the next section.
>
> Dr John Kelly, an eminent researcher and academic at Harvard Medical School, was very interested in recovery-related research and founded the Recovery Research Institute at Massachusetts General Hospital and Harvard Medical School. He promoted and advanced research related to recovery prevalence, pathways and styles of recovery, recovery processes, and achievements in recovery. Both his published studies and his innumerable presentations at professional conferences helped spread the idea and application of recovery capital. He and several of his colleagues at the Recovery Research Institute have contributed to the advancement of recovery capital as a concept, as well as its measurement.
>
> As this early exploration and application of recovery capital unfolded, one limitation was our inability to respond to countless requests for a way to measure changes in recovery capital as part of the clinical or peer recovery support services assessment or service evaluation process. In 2009, out of futility, I drafted a Recovery Capital Scale (RCS; White, 2009) with some ideas of what a recovery capital measure might look like based on the three-domain model of recovery capital (that is, personal, social, and community capital) and posted it publicly on my website under the Recovery Toolkit heading (see Appendix 1).

The clinical import of the scale was based on the idea outlined previously that the interaction between levels of recovery capital and problem severity could be used to determine the intensity of treatment, ongoing supervision, and assertive linkage to recovery groups and services. Although the drafted scale had not yet been piloted and validated, it generated numerous requests for its use in clinical and recovery support settings. This later inspired collaborations and additional efforts to develop recovery capital measures and examine their psychometric properties with diverse populations (in the form of the Assessment of Recovery Capital [ARC; Groshkova, Best, and White, 2012 and subsequently the Brief Assessment of Recovery Capital [BARC-10; Vilsaint et al, 2017]). William's reflections continue:

> This early series of attempted recovery capital measures helped spread interest in recovery capital, particularly among frontline addiction counsellors, as these measures proved useful in the development of treatment and recovery plans. Also of note in this spread was the fact that these instruments were left in the public domain and could be accessed for free, with our permission always provided upon requests for their use. These early instruments (RCS, ARC, and BARC) were followed by other measurement efforts (the ARC, BARC, and Sterling publications to be discussed later) and the inclusion of recovery-capital scales within other larger assessment instruments, such as the Global Appraisal of Individual Needs (GAIN; Dennis et al, 2006).
>
> Other research professionals I communicated with who went on to be influenced in their writings include Dr Amy Krentzman, whose application of positive psychology to addiction recovery shows recovery capital influences, as well as Dr Robert Ashford and Dr Emily Hennessy. Also of note are the steady stream of emails from MA and PhD candidates requesting permission to cite recovery capital materials or use recovery capital instruments. These connections promise continued future publications on recovery capital.
>
> As far as professional dissemination of recovery capital, the Betty Ford Institute is also noteworthy. The institute hosted two recovery capital-related consensus conferences, the first on the definition of recovery and the second on the mobilization of community resources to support recovery. These were closed conferences with invited papers from addiction treatment leaders and people in recovery, with key papers later published in the *Journal of Substance Abuse Treatment*. Recovery capital language was very evident at these conferences, as was its influence on the published conclusions.
>
> David Best's work was very influential in the UK, Europe (Life in Recovery Surveys in multiple countries), and Canada. Several of the people I have mentioned also were invited to speak or consult internationally. These included presentations in Canada but also included meetings in Africa, Asia (Japan), Australia, India, Ireland, and other countries. In the case of Canada, I had numerous communications with various provinces about recovery capital/Recovery Management/ROSC, including communications with their major recovery advocacy organization, Faces and Voices of Recovery Canada. The interview I did with William Cloud also drew a large number of readers to my website.[2]

The next stage in this journey is described by David Best who was central to developing a number of measures of recovery capital, and who worked closely with William White in both the development and testing of the next wave of measures.

David Best's reflections on the development of measurement instruments

> My interest in recovery capital as a concept was driven by two concerns – as someone who had become increasingly interested in the concept and potential of recovery, I was frustrated by the criticisms levelled against recovery that it was both unscientific (relying as it did on vague and woolly concepts like spirituality and purpose in life) and so subjective that it was beyond measurement.
>
> However, in conversations with Dr Teodora Groshkova, I was also conscious that the existing array of outcome measures in addiction recovery (and I had been one of the authors of the Maudsley Addiction Profile [MAP], Marsden et al, 1998) were not suited to measuring recovery approaches.
>
> Teodora Groshkova had mainly worked in therapeutic communities in Bulgaria before moving to the National Addiction Centre in London, and we shared a concern that the traditional measures (like the Maudsley Addiction Profile and the Addiction Severity Index [ASI], McLellan et al, 1980) were completely unsuited to measuring the recovery journey. Because the aim of these measures was to assess the severity of addiction problems, they were based on the assumption that success could be defined as a reduction in the intensity or severity of a diverse range of symptoms. However, if your aim, as Laudet and White (2008) assert, is to build up one's quality of life and recovery capital, then such measures would not capture this, not because they were deficient in any way, but because that was not their objective. This also has significance for funding – if funding is based on outcomes, and the outcomes measured are around the reduction in symptoms or pathologies, acute services whose aim is pathology management and symptom reduction will fare much better. In such a world, services like recovery community organizations, aftercare programmes, and therapeutic communities will not achieve such good outcomes, because what they aspire to do (help people to build the lives they want through building sustainable strengths and overcoming residual barriers) is not captured by the measures, or indeed by the logic and implicit conceptualization of addiction and recovery that underpins this. Our aim was to measure the growth of strengths and resources, that would typically emerge in the post-acute period.
>
> There was also an increased awareness of some of the incredible advocacy and research going on in the US that encouraged me to make contact with both William White and then with Alexandre Laudet. The latter collaboration led to a position paper, published by the Royal Society for the Arts in England, entitled 'The potential of recovery capital' (Best and Laudet, 2010). This paper proclaimed the potential importance of strengths-based measurement but also the importance of the social and community components of the journey. We argued that:

Recovery unfolds in the lived, physical community as well as in the substance misusing communities and it has significant ramifications for those wider communities. The growth of recovery capital as a collective, community concept will involve mutual empowerment, support and recovery contagion in substance misusing groups, but it will manifest itself in improved functioning for the family and the wider community. (Best and Laudet, 2010, 6)

This suggests two critical developmental components for recovery capital measurement – the first, that it cannot focus exclusively on the individual, and the second, that it must be strengths-based. Behind this is the assumption that recovery transcends physical and psychological deficits and symptoms, and that the focus should as much be on what is 'out there' as what is happening 'in here', in terms of social support, belonging, and active citizenship. So, the underlying principles for a recovery capital model were that it should be inherently strengths-based, as well as social and community-focused.

Our first attempt at quantification of some of these concepts was the start of an incredibly fruitful collaboration between Best, White, and Groshkova that led to the publication of two measures – the Recovery Group Participation Scale in 2011 (Groshkova, Best, and White, 2011) and the Assessment of Recovery Capital in 2012 (Groshkova, Best, and White, 2012). However, before going on to describe these two scales in detail, and their origins, it is worth briefly reviewing what was emerging at that time in the UK, as the development of the scales were embedded in an emerging visible recovery movement that was striving for new ways of measuring the impact and effectiveness of various recovery support projects and services.

To a much smaller extent than across the Atlantic, in the early 2000s the UK was experiencing the first wave of visible recovery advocacy, recognized in grassroots activities and in public policy in both Scotland and England, and summarized in a special edition of the *Journal of Groups in Addiction and Recovery*[3] (Roth and Best, 2013. For the first time, there were public celebrations of recovery including annual recovery walks in Scotland and England, the opening of recovery cafes and community centres, and recovery research activity. There was also the emerging sense, through the Recovery Academy, of recovery as a social movement, with advocacy and activist components that were being coordinated across the country and backed by new recovery-oriented drug policies in both Scotland (Scottish Government, 2008) and England (HM Government, 2010).

It is against this background that we decided to collaborate on the development of new measures, which attempted to use a scientific framework for the mapping and measurement of recovery capital, actively engaging the recovery communities of the UK – in residential, quasi-residential, and community settings – in the development of the instruments. In particular, the Lothians and Edinburgh Abstinence Project (LEAP), established as a demonstration project under the Road to Recovery Scottish Government drug policy (Scottish Government, 2008), was a key partner in item development and testing of the two instruments: (1) the Recovery Group Participation Scale (RGPS) and

(2) the Assessment of Recovery Capital (ARC). There was a strong sense of dynamism and change at the time and the new measures were seen as something bespoke and suited to assessing the impact and effectiveness of this new wave of recovery support services. We worked closely with the clients of LEAP and with the staff (most of whom had their own lived experience) in the development of the measures.

The two instruments should really be considered together, as the RGPS is effectively a measure of one aspect of community recovery capital – the extent of engagement with a diverse range of recovery support services – while the ARC is a measure of two other domains of recovery capital – personal and social capital. There is an important distinction between the scales – the RGPS is largely behavioural (examples include 'I speak at recovery meetings' and 'I attend a recovery centre'); while the ARC is much more cognitive and affective (one example from the ARC's personal recovery capital scale is 'I am coping with the stresses in my life', while an example from the ARC's social recovery capital scale is 'I am proud of my home'), raising questions about what kinds of 'things' should be measured in assessing recovery capital.

Thus, there are two potential challenges for the measurement of recovery capital – what domains should be addressed (examined in Chapter 4 by Bunaciu and colleagues), but also what kinds of things should be counted (internal and personal experiences versus externally observable behaviours, or changes in knowledge, beliefs, awareness, and so on). This also provokes questions about the reliance on self-report and the criteria through which this can be validated. It is also important to note that the RGPS only measures one aspect of community recovery capital (links to the recovery community and not to professional services or to non-recovery local community assets and resources) and neither the ARC nor the RGPS attempts to address aspects related to cultural capital.

The ARC in particular, while widely used in research and, arguably, the most empirically scrutinized recovery capital measure (Bunaciu et al, 2023), is limited in that it fails one of the earliest requirements of the White and Cloud (2008) paper – that its results are used to direct recovery support options and activities. A similar accusation could be directed at the shortened version of the ARC (the BARC-10, Vilsaint et al, 2017) – that they are excellent research measures but that they offer little to the recovery community.

In the next section, we review the role of the largest recovery research centre, and in particular its director, Dr John Kelly, in the development of the concept of recovery capital and its subsequent translation to research and practice.

The role of John Kelly and the Recovery Research Institute

Kelly and Hoeppner (2015) proposed a biaxial model of recovery as a construct. This model built on the prior work of Edwards and Gross (1976) on the addiction syndrome, as well as the work of White and Cloud (2008) on recovery capital, and leveraged stress and coping theory to describe the reciprocal aspects of recovery capital and remission. Their model proposed that as remission becomes more stable and as recovery duration increases, recovery capital increases, and in a reciprocal manner, improvements in recovery capital also work to, in turn, support ongoing stable remission. This work contributed to initial attempts at defining recovery as a construct and promoted recovery capital as a key and dynamic aspect of recovery, both during early and sustained remission.

A systematic review conducted by Dr Emily Hennessy (2017; during her graduate work) revealed wide variability in the definition, conceptualization, and measurement of recovery capital within the scientific field, with inconsistencies in the use of recovery-capital domains and validated measures/scales. To continue advancing the science on recovery capital and its clinical utility, Hennessy concluded that there was a need for consistent use of recovery capital constructs, enhanced attention toward community-level factors within measures of recovery capital, and evaluation of recovery capital in the context of special populations (for example, adolescents and emerging adults). Building on these conclusions, Dr Hennessy and Dr Kelly proposed a novel model of recovery capital for adolescents (RCAM; Hennessy, Cristello, and Kelly, 2019) which leveraged original models of adult recovery capital to create developmentally-appropriate constructs that the field continues to adapt and test. Subsequently, Dr Hennessy joined the Recovery Research Institute where she and other faculty are examining the RCAM in their National Institutes of Health-funded research. More recently, Kelly and Hennessy advocated for additional research to enhance the clinical utility of recovery capital (Meisel et al, 2023), highlighting the need for a better understanding of social recovery capital, as well as novel ways to measure it and promote its growth during recovery. A detailed five-part research agenda was proposed to advance the field in a direction that enhances the clinical utility of social recovery capital research and leverages novel methods for increasing social recovery capital to facilitate positive recovery outcomes. This work exemplifies ongoing efforts to further characterize and measure specific elements of recovery capital across diverse populations, as well as the continued scientific support for the study of recovery capital as a key construct of addiction recovery.

Scientists at the Recovery Research Institute have also helped to advance the measurement of recovery capital, with the development of the Brief Assessment of Recovery Capital (BARC-10; Vilsaint et al, 2017), a shortened version of the ARC (Groshkova, Best, and White, 2012) that measures recovery capital as a single construct, with strong psychometric properties. However, this instrument may be better suited for the measurement of recovery capital in the context of research, as its clinical utility and its ability to guide early recovery pathways and individual needs may be limited, as discussed in greater detail later.

What lessons can we learn for the future growth of recovery capital models and measurement?

It was this early work, defining the concept of recovery capital and exploring its potential clinical and policy-related implications and applications, that laid the foundation for subsequent efforts toward the measurement of recovery capital. The need for a measure of recovery capital was driven by pressure from diverse constituencies: recovery advocates, clinicians in addiction treatment, peer recovery support leaders, allied health professionals, research scientists, and service funders, with each injecting different needs and concerns to be addressed within the measurement process.

These foundations have generated intensive activities in academic settings but also in practice. There has now been a proliferation of new scales and measures attempting to capture recovery capital (considered by Bunaciu and colleagues in Chapter 4) but one of the key changes has been the development of online delivery mechanisms that have achieved two critical outcomes – immediacy of scoring and therefore the potential for the provision of recovery capital score profiles to participants, and, second, fulfilling the requirements of the White and Cloud (2008) paper described earlier, directly linking scores to planned activities and actions. The development of recovery capital measures has benefited from the involvement of multiple disciplines, international collaborations, involvement across diverse cultural contexts, efforts to embrace multiple clinical subpopulations, and diverse pathways and styles of recovery.

The development of these tools has also helped in some ways with the conceptual development of recovery capital. Through measurement development, recovery capital was linked conceptually to allied ideas: recovery paradigm, recovery contagion (social transmission of recovery), recovery carriers/champions, recovery cascades (sudden surges in recovery prevalence), peer-based recovery support services, new types of recovery support institutions, and family and community recovery. This clustering of related concepts helped spread discussion of recovery capital and its application and contributed both to theory development and to subsequent empirical testing.

We remain at an early stage of framing, far less measuring, these core concepts of recovery contagion and cascade, yet the emerging evidence would suggest that exposure to recovery role models and their incorporation into social networks is strongly predictive of recovery growth (Litt et al, 2007;

Litt et al, 2009). However, we know far less about the underlying mechanisms of salutogenesis (transmission of recovery and related achievements within family, social networks, communities, and cultures), and it is to be hoped that recovery capital will provide a lens through which to test such questions. Thus, it may be the case that high levels of peer recovery capital (particularly social and community) increase the likelihood of 'recovery transmission' (for example, Petterson et al, 2019). Similar questions will arise about intergenerational transmission and whether high levels of recovery capital in parents is a protective/preventative factor or increases recovery transmission within families across generations. These questions should also drive us to change the focus of recovery measurement away from an exclusive focus on the individual in recovery to the social networks, community conditions, and collective forms of recovery capital that are associated with the effective transmission of recovery.

To this day, early measurement instruments also remain free and in the public domain, which has additionally encouraged their testing and utilization in diverse settings. However, one of the key components to expanding the application and utility of recovery capital measurement was moving it out of the clinical setting and starting to engage people at different stages of recovery, many of whom were unconnected to treatment – this was one of the big innovations with Granfield and Cloud's *Coming Clean* (as discussed in depth in Chapter 2 by Granfield and Cloud).

However, there is now an increasing risk of commercialization of recovery capital measures, linked to outcome monitoring and intervention systems that are for profit. This creates a risk of reducing collaboration and cooperation between research groups and of excluding peer researchers and peer recovery organizations who cannot afford the licensing fees or do not have the human resources to implement such systems.

Furthermore, we must acknowledge the intrinsic limitations of available measures, including the inherent biases of self-report questionnaires and their potentially limited ability to capture more dynamic concepts critical to recovery capital, such as recovery contagion. We continue to acknowledge the importance of context and social networks, yet the primary mechanism of assessment is a self-completion questionnaire (although Chapter 4 by Bunaciu and colleagues does attempt to suggest other types of measurement). Further, as Best, Collinson, and Patton acknowledge in Chapter 7, the measurement of community capital remains limited and there is considerable work to be done around including cultural and contextual factors in recovery capital assessment and subsequent interventions.

Ongoing efforts are needed to expand the practice of recovery capital measurement in clinical settings and recovery communities. Indeed, advances in recovery capital measurement are underway. Future steps include the integration of recovery capital assessment and related service planning into practice guidelines and regulatory standards governing the delivery of treatment and recovery support services. Moreover, four critical frontiers in the development and psychometric evaluation of recovery capital measures include:

1) The exploration of differences in recovery capital sources across cultural contexts and across the life cycle (for example, special concerns with recovery capital development among adolescents and transition-age youth, and recovery capital replenishment among older adults).
2) Recovery capital measurement among people with co-occurring medical/psychiatric conditions, people with disabilities, people experiencing unstable or unsafe shelter, and people within culturally marginalized communities (see Bowen and Hennessy, Chapter 6, for additional conceptual considerations).
3) Recovery capital assessments for families both in the sense of the family as a resource for recovery but also holistically to review the recovery resources available to support 'whole family' recovery.
4) Recovery capital assessments that consider peer recovery workers both in their own recovery but as a support to others and how this may have a multiplicative effect on their recovery capital growth through dynamic building of social recovery capital.

Indeed, given that the field has historically focused on personal assets within the context of recovery capital, significant progress also needs to be made to develop and test measures that assess family and community recovery capital, which are important to consider in the broader context of addiction recovery.

Conclusion

From those early origins, the model of recovery capital has developed considerably and with it a flourishing of measurement tools as outlined in Chapter 4 by Bunaciu and colleagues. Many of these have now been subjected to both scientific scrutiny to test psychometrics and subsequent peer review, such that the body of empirical work on recovery capital has expanded hugely in the last decade. However, we should not be too quick to congratulate ourselves on this achievement – there are significant gaps in the field, particularly around the measurement of community and cultural recovery capital and the adequacy of testing and application with various diverse populations, including women, ethnic minority groups, LGBTIQ+ populations, and those who reside in non-English speaking countries. The true establishment of recovery capital as a measure of strengths cannot be regarded as satisfactory until those gaps are addressed.

Notes

1. At this stage in the field, there was no single inventory available for the measurement of recovery capital – we measured recovery capital via five inventories that assessed social support, spirituality, religiousness, life meaning, and 12-step affiliation that corresponded to the four domains of recovery capital (personal, social, community, and cultural).
2. White, W. (2016) 'Explorations in natural recovery and recovery capital: An Interview with Dr William Cloud', [online], William White Papers | Chestnut Health Systems, Available from: https://www.chestnut.org/resources/94afc3b4-b689-4bc8-947a-17a2e3b83b52/2016-Dr.-William-Cloud-v2.pdf
3. The *Journal of Groups in Addiction and Recovery* is no longer active.

References

Best, D. and Laudet, A. (2010) *The Potential of Recovery Capital*, London: Royal Society for the Arts: London.

Bunaciu, A., Bliuc, A.-M., Best, D., Hennessy, E., Belanger, M., and Benwell, C. (2023) 'Measuring recovery capital for people recovering from alcohol and drug addiction: A systematic review', *Addiction Research & Theory*, 32(3): 225–36.

Dennis, M.L., Chan, Y., and Funk, R.R. (2006) 'Development and validation of the GAIN Short Screener (GSS) for internalizing, externalizing and substance use disorders and crime/violence problems among adolescents and adults', *American Journal of Addiction*, 15(s1): 80–91.

Edwards, G. and Gross, M.M. (1976) 'Alcohol dependence: Provisional description of a clinical syndrome', *British Medical Journal*, 1: 1058–61.

Granfield, R. and Cloud, W. (1996). 'The elephant that no one sees: Natural recovery among middle-class addicts', *Journal of Drug Issues*, 26(1): 45–61.

Granfield, R. and Cloud, W. (1999) *Coming Clean: Overcoming Addiction without Treatment*, New York: New York University Press.

Granfield, R. and Cloud, W. (2001) 'Social context and "natural recovery": The role of social capital in the resolution of drug-associated problems', *Substance Use & Misuse*, 36(11): 1543–70.

Groshkova, T., Best, D., and White, W. (2011) 'Recovery Group Participation Scale (RGPS): Factor structure in alcohol and heroin recovery populations', *Journal of Groups in Addiction and Recovery*, 6(1–2): 76–92.

Groshkova, T., Best, D., and White, W. (2012) 'The assessment of recovery capital: Properties and psychometrics of a measure of addiction recovery strengths', *Drug and Alcohol Review*, 32(2): 187–94.

Hennessy, E.A. (2017) 'Recovery capital: A systematic review of the literature', *Addiction Research & Theory*, 25(5): 349–60.

Hennessy, E.A., Cristello, J.V., and Kelly, J.F. (2019) 'RCAM: A proposed model of recovery capital for adolescents', *Addiction Research & Theory*, 27(5): 429–36.

HM Government (2010) *Drug Strategy 2010: Reducing Demand, Restricting Supply, Building Recovery: Supporting People to Live a drug-free life*, HM Government: London.

Kelly, J.F. and Hoeppner, B. (2015) 'A biaxial formulation of the recovery construct', *Addiction Research & Theory*, 23(1): 5–9.

Laudet, A. and White, W. (2008) 'Recovery capital as prospective predictor of sustained recovery, life satisfaction and stress among former poly-substance users', *Substance Use and Misuse*, 43(1): 27–54.

Laudet, A.B. and White, W. (2010) 'What are your priorities right now? Identifying service needs across recovery stages to inform service development', *Journal of Substance Abuse Treatment*, 38: 51–9.

Litt, M., Kadden, R., Kabela-Cormier, E., and Petry, N. (2007) 'Changing network support for drinking: Initial findings from the network support project', *Journal of Consulting & Clinical Psychology*, 75(4): 542–55.

Litt, M.D., Kadden, R.M., Kabela-Cormier, E., and Petry, N.M. (2009) 'Changing network support for drinking: Network support project two-year follow-up', *Journal of Consulting & Clinical Psychology*, 77(2): 229–42.

Marsden, J., Gossop, M., Stewart, D., Best, D., Farrell, M., Lehmann, P., et al (1998) 'The Maudsley Addiction Profile (MAP): A brief instrument for assessing treatment outcome', *Addiction*, 93(12): 1857–68.

McLellan, A.T., Luborsky, L., Woody, G.E., and O'Brien, C.P. (1980) 'An improved diagnostic evaluation instrument for substance abuse patients: The Addiction Severity Index', *Journal of Nervous and Mental Diseases*, 168(1): 26–33.

Meisel, S.N., Hennessy, E.A., Jurinsky, J., and Kelly, J.F. (2023) 'Improving social recovery capital research to enhance clinical utility: A proposed agenda', *Addiction Research & Theory*, 32(3): 153–9.

Pettersen, H., Landheim, A.S., Skeie, I., Biong, S. , Brodahl, M., Oute, J., and Davidson, L. (2019) 'How social relationships influence substance use disorder recovery: A collaborative narrative study', *Substance Abuse: Research and Treatment*, 13. DOI: 10.1177/1178221819833379.

Roth, J. and Best, D. (eds) (2013) *Addiction and Recovery in the UK*, Abingdon: Routledge.

Scottish Government (2008) *The Road to Recovery: A New Approach to Tackling Scotland's Drug Problem*, Edinburgh: Scottish Executive.

Vilsaint, C.L., Kelly, J.F., Bergman, B.G., Groshkova, T., Best, D., and White, W.L. (2017) 'Development and validation of a brief assessment of recovery capital (BARC-10) for alcohol and drug use disorder', *Drug & Alcohol Dependence*, 177(1): 71–6.

White, W. (2009) 'Recovery capital scale', *William White Papers* [online], Available from: https://www.chestnut.org/william-white-papers

White, W. and Cloud, W. (2008) 'Recovery capital: A primer for addictions professionals', *Counselor*, 9(5): 22–7.

White, W. (2016). Explorations in natural recovery and recovery capital: An Interview with Dr. William Cloud. Available at: 2016-Dr.-William-Cloud-v2.pdf

White, W.L., Laudet, A.B., and Becker, J.B. (2006) 'Life meaning and purpose in addiction recovery', *Addiction Professional*, 4(4): 18–23, Available from: https://www.chestnut.org/william-white-papers

Appendix 1: William White Recovery Capital Scale

___ I have the financial resources to provide for myself and my family.
___ I have personal transportation or access to public transportation.
___ I live in a home and neighbourhood that is safe and secure.
___ I live in an environment free from alcohol and other drugs.
___ I have an intimate partner supportive of my recovery process.
___ I have family members who are supportive of my recovery process.
___ I have friends who are supportive of my recovery process.
___ I have people close to me (intimate partner, family members, or friends) who are also in recovery.
___ I have a stable job that I enjoy and that provides for my basic necessities.
___ I have an education or work environment that is conducive to my long-term recovery.
___ I continue to participate in a continuing care programme of an addiction treatment programme (for example, groups, alumni association meetings, and so on).
___ I have a professional assistance programme that is monitoring and supporting my recovery process.
___ I have a primary care physician who attends to my health problems.
___ I am now in reasonably good health.
___ I have an active plan to manage any lingering or potential health problems.
___ I am on prescribed medication that minimizes my cravings for alcohol and other drugs.
___ I have insurance that will allow me to receive help for major health problems.
___ I have access to regular, nutritious meals.
___ I have clothes that are comfortable, clean, and conducive to my recovery activities.
___ I have access to recovery support groups in my local community.
___ I have established close affiliation with a local recovery support group.
___ I have a sponsor (or equivalent) who serves as a special mentor related to my recovery.
___ I have access to online recovery support groups.
___ I have completed or am complying with all legal requirements related to my past.
___ There are other people who rely on me to support their own recoveries.
___ My immediate physical environment contains literature, tokens, posters, or other symbols of my commitment to recovery.

___ I have recovery rituals that are now part of my daily life.
___ I had a profound experience that marked the beginning or deepening of my commitment to recovery.
___ I now have goals and great hopes for my future.
___ I have problem solving skills and resources that I lacked during my years of active addiction.
___ I feel like I have meaningful, positive participation in my family and community.
___ Today I have a clear sense of who I am.
___ I know that my life has a purpose.
___ Service to others is now an important part of my life.
___ My personal values and sense of right and wrong have become clearer and stronger in recent years.

Possible Score: 0–175

4

The Evolution of Approaches to Measure Recovery Capital

Adela Bunaciu, Matthew J. Belanger, Ana-Maria Bliuc, and Arun Sondhi

Introduction to the measurement of recovery capital

The field of recovery capital began to develop conceptually in the first decade of the 21st century, primarily in the United States and the United Kingdom (Best and Hennessy, 2022). The emergence of this new field meant a shift of focus in the addiction recovery literature towards a strengths-based and capital-building oriented approach (Best and Hennessy, 2022). One of the key drivers for the development of measures of recovery capital was the recognition that a strengths-based measurement approach was needed to challenge and complement the traditional deficit-based approach dominating the addiction literature (Burns, 2019). Consequently, measures that can assess recovery capital to advance the research in the field and to bring this concept to practical recovery support settings started to be developed (Sterling et al, 2008; White and Cloud, 2008; Groshkova et al, 2013; Burns, 2019). However, the processes of theoretical and measurement advancements are inherently intertwined. Although the conceptual groundwork influenced how recovery capital measures were developed, the reverse is also true, in the sense that theory development and refinement are also informed by the evolution of these measures (Best and Hennessy, 2022; Bunaciu et al, 2023).

The development of sound measurement tools for assessing recovery capital has played a central role in supporting approaches to substance use disorder treatment. However, measure development is not a simple process. Rigorous questionnaire development is a time-consuming iterative process involving input from many categories of stakeholders, such as researchers, practitioners, and individuals with lived experience (Boateng et al, 2018). How we measure recovery capital, typically in the form of questionnaires, is important because successful practical applications (for example, recovery support planning) and solutions based on research are only possible if the measurement can reliably and accurately capture recovery capital and how it may change over time.

In this chapter, we discuss the range of approaches used during the last two decades since the term 'recovery capital' was first introduced by Granfield and Cloud (1999). We first briefly review recovery capital measures in the form of questionnaires and their psychometric properties. We also include a discussion of alternative (not questionnaire-based) approaches to capturing recovery capital such as the social identity mapping tool (Cruwys et al, 2016; Beckwith et al, 2019). We will also address how the modality of recovery capital measurement has developed more recently and how the ability of electronic modalities can provide immediate practical use. We conclude the chapter by discussing the strengths and limitations of the current recovery capital measures, and with recommendations on aspects to consider when selecting a measurement approach for practical or research use.

Recovery capital questionnaires

This section will review in chronological order, according to their publication year, the 13 recovery capital questionnaires currently available in English (as shown in Table 4.1).

Table 4.1: Names of the reviewed recovery capital questionnaires

Questionnaire name	Authors	Year of publication
Sterling et al's Recovery Capital Scale	Sterling et al	2008
White's Recovery Capital Scale	White	2009
Assessment of Recovery Capital	Groshkova et al	2012
Recovery Capital Questionnaire	Burns and Marks	2013
The Brief Assessment of Recovery Capital	Vilsaint et al	2017
REC-CAP	Cano et al	2017
Recovery Capital Index	Whitesock et al	2018
Recovery Strengths Questionnaire	Rettie et al	2019
The Short Recovery Capital Scale	Hanauer et al	2019
The Strengths and Barriers Recovery Scale	Best et al	2020
The Social Recovery Capital questionnaire	Francis et al	2022
The Brief Adult Health Capital Scale	Hanauer and Svetina Valdivia	2022
The Multidimensional Inventory of Recovery Capital	Bowen et al	2023

Unnamed recovery capital scale (RCS) by Sterling and colleagues (Sterling et al's RCS)

The first questionnaire specifically tailored to capture overall recovery capital was developed in the US by Sterling and colleagues (2008). This measure combined pre-validated questionnaires that assessed psychosocial functioning, addiction severity, and spirituality, including the Drug Taking Confidence Questionnaire (DTCQ, Annis et al, 1997), the Addiction Severity Index (ASI, McLellan et al, 1980; McLellan et al, 1985), the Daily Spiritual Experiences – long form (DSE, Underwood and Teresi, 2002), the Fetzer Institute and National Institute on Aging Working Group's Brief Multidimensional Measure of Religiousness/Spirituality (BMMRS, Fetzer Institute/National Institute on Aging Working Group, 1999), the Spiritual Belief Scale (SBS, Schaler, 1996), and the Spiritual Experience Index (SEI, Genia, 1997).

Questions from these measures were subjected to exploratory factor analysis (EFA), resulting in 23 final questionnaire items. The authors did not report the types of response options for the scale. The 23 items fell into eight main subdomains, suggested by factor analysis: 1) proportion of life spent sober; 2) contentment with living and marital life; 3) recent sobriety; 4) level of formal education or training; 5) stable job or income; 6) sober living environment; 7) reliance on God and faith; and 8) sense of spirituality (Burns and Marks, 2013; Hennessy, 2017). The questionnaire lacked predictive validity, evidenced by weakly significant or non-significant associations between, for example, the overall RCS score and abstinence days, alcohol-related problems, and scores in the Addiction Recovery Index and the Drug Taking Confidence Questionnaire. It appears that the scale was primarily developed for research purposes, however, we did not find any research studies using the questionnaire. Currently, this questionnaire is not publicly available.

Recovery Capital Scale (White's RCS)

The second recovery capital questionnaire was developed and published in the US by William White in 2009. The scale is a self-assessment instrument designed to help individuals measure their level of recovery capital (White, 2009). The questionnaire consists of 35 items scored from 1 (strongly disagree) to 5 (strongly agree), resulting in a total score ranging between 35 and 175. The questionnaire includes three questions that allow the respondents to list five areas where they scored the lowest, four goals to improve recovery capital within the next year, and five activities to complete in the following week to aid the completion of the four goals. The recovery capital domains were not specified, but by inspecting the 35 items, the scale seems to incorporate physical, human, social, and cultural recovery capital components. The questionnaire is available online (see White, 2009). While the Assessment of Recovery Capital (ARC) is not a direct extension of White's RCS, its development was influenced by the questionnaire. White added a note for clinicians and researchers in 2018 to his original publication from 2009 stating that 'For those wishing to use this instrument as a clinical or recovery support tool or as a research instrument, these updated instruments and their psychometrics have been published' (White, 2009, 6), referring to the ARC and the Brief Assessment of Recovery Capital (BARC-10).

The psychometrics of this questionnaire have not been fully assessed. However, Polcin and colleagues (2021) found high correlations among the questionnaire items when examining it among sober living house residents, suggesting high internal consistency, indicating that White's RCS effectively measures the construct of recovery capital.

Assessment of Recovery Capital

The ARC (Groshkova et al, 2012) was developed in the UK to move from a 'diagnostic' instrument to an instrument that captures personal and social strengths and resources for helping individuals meet their needs and aspirations in their recovery journeys. The authors engaged in discussions with practitioners and individuals in various stages of recovery and reviewed the previous literature to identify key questionnaire items and critical domains of recovery capital. This resulted in ten domains and 50 questions (that is, five questions per domain). The final version of the ARC includes ten subdomains, each having five dichotomous (yes/no) questions, resulting in a total score ranging between 0 and 50, with a higher score indicating more recovery capital. The ten subdomains are: 1) Substance Use and Sobriety; 2) Global Health (psychological); 3) Global Health (physical); 4) Citizenship and Community Involvement; 5) Social Support; 6) Meaningful Activities; 7) Housing and Safety; 8) Risk Taking; 9) Coping and Life Functioning; and 10) Recovery Experience. The authors suggested that the ARC 'offers a model for mapping and measuring the positive changes in personal and social capital that can be applied in both clinical and research settings' (Groshkova et al, 2012, 192). Furthermore, several assessments either include or have been modelled on the ARC. The REC-CAP incorporates the ARC (Cano et al, 2017). The Brief Assessment of Recovery Capital is a shortened version of the ARC, created with busy clinical or research settings in mind (Vilsaint et al, 2017). Moreover, the Adult Health Capital Scale is a 35-item scale that was created modelling the ten-domain structure of the ARC, specifically tailoring the questionnaire for the context of health capital (Hanauer and Svetina Valdivia, 2022). So far, the ARC is one of the most used recovery capital questionnaires in research, with over 17 published studies having used it (Bunaciu et al, 2023). The ARC is available online (see Groshkova et al, 2012, Supplemental Materials). The ARC has also been translated into other languages, including Hindi (Basu et al, 2019), Spanish (Sión et al, 2022), and Finnish (Aalto and Jumpponen, 2021).

Several studies have evaluated the psychometric properties of the ARC in English and other languages. While the questionnaire has ten subdomains, studies assessing the factor structure of the questionnaire in English, Hindi, and Spanish have shown that the ten subdomains form a unified underlying construct, namely recovery capital (Groshkova et al, 2012; Arndt et al, 2017; Basu et al, 2019; Sión et al, 2022). Moreover, studies have predominantly shown that the ARC overall has a moderate to high internal consistency, meaning that the various items within the ARC are highly correlated with each other, suggesting that they reliably measure the construct of recovery capital (Mawson et al, 2015; Arndt et al, 2017; Cano et al, 2017; Basu et al, 2019; Bowen et al, 2022; Sión et al, 2022). The ARC has shown moderate to high test–retest reliability, with testing intervals ranging from four to seven days (Groshkova et al, 2012; Basu et al, 2019). The ARC has distinguished individuals who are in the early stages of recovery versus those in later stages (Groshkova et al, 2012; Sión et al, 2022), and those who are opioid-free versus in opioid substitution treatment (Basu et al, 2019). Studies have also shown that the ARC scores are correlated with the WHOQOL-BREF, which is a measure of quality of life (Groshkova et al, 2012; Basu et al, 2019; Sión et al, 2022). Conversely, the ARC was found to have no statistically significant positive relationship with the Addiction Severity Index (Basu et al, 2019). These findings are important since they suggest that the ARC aligns with a measure of a similar construct (concurrent validity), and it has no relationship with a measure that captures a fundamentally different construct (divergent validity).

Some research has identified issues with the ARC's psychometric performance. Bowen and colleagues (2020) reported that their psychometric analysis using a diverse low-income sample of individuals revealed that the 50 items did not consistently align with their intended domains. Moreover, Arndt and colleagues (2017) suggested that the high number of items might increase the chance of false positive findings. However, they acknowledged the necessity of the full item set for maximum predictive ability regarding recovery success. The evidence suggests that, overall, the ARC is a suitable questionnaire for practical and research settings, with further work required to clarify its composite domains.

Recovery Capital Questionnaire (RCQ)

The Recovery Capital Questionnaire (RCQ, Burns and Marks, 2013) was developed in Scotland (UK) to measure recovery capital, particularly to better understand its relationship with addiction problem severity (Burns and Marks, 2013; Burns, 2019; Burns and Yates, 2022). It originates from the author's work within a community-based addiction treatment centre and was driven by the aim of developing a tool for use in the treatment centre (Burns, 2019). Specifically, the questionnaire aimed 'to identify the assets people bring with them to addiction treatment which can be developed and mobilised in a way that helps achieve client outcomes' (Burns, 2019, 13).

While the RCQ shares similarities with the recovery capital questionnaires preceding it, it was designed to differ from them in several philosophical and methodological ways (Burns and Yates, 2022). One key difference between the RCQ and the ARC is that the latter assumes that an individual should be completely sober from alcohol and illicit drugs for a maximum recovery capital score. In contrast, Burns sought to develop a measure of recovery capital that was not abstinence-based. Furthermore, the RCS included items related to community recovery capital, which was not included in the ARC. The RCQ uses a Likert scale ranging from 1 (untrue of me) to 5 (true of me).

After reviewing the academic literature, Burns selected 82 questions based on the theoretical models by Cloud and Granfield (2008) and White and Cloud (2008). These questions were discussed with addiction treatment service staff and people in recovery, reducing the item pool to 67 items (Burns, 2019). This was followed by pilot testing on researchers in addiction studies and treatment service staff members, which further reduced the item pool to 36 items across four domains: 1) social recovery capital; 2) physical recovery capital; 3) human recovery capital; 4) and perceived community recovery capital. The questionnaire and more information regarding its use are available online (see Burns, 2019, 250).

Assessments were conducted using the 36-item RCQ with individuals in treatment across community and prison settings, including therapeutic communities (Burns and Marks, 2013; Burns, 2019; Burns and Yates, 2022). Burns & Yates (2022) found that the RCQ has good internal consistency, suggesting that the questionnaire reliably measures the construct of recovery capital. Moreover, the RCQ demonstrated consistently similar scores between two assessment times with a minimum of one week between the assessments, suggesting test–retest reliability. The authors also reported concurrent validity with WHOQOL-BREF (a measure of quality of life), indicating that the RCQ aligns with a measure of a similar construct. Strong content validity was also reported, suggesting that the RCQ can accurately represent the range of content that is relevant to the construct of recovery capital.

The Brief Assessment of Recovery Capital

The Brief Assessment of Recovery Capital (BARC-10, Vilsaint et al, 2017) is a shortened version of the 50-item ARC. Using item response theory to ensure the preservation of the ARC's content validity and psychometric properties, Vilsaint and colleagues (2017) reduced the 50 items of the ARC to establish a tool tailored for busy clinical and recovery support settings. The sample included individuals used in the original ARC study (Groshkova et al, 2012) and individuals recruited from therapeutic communities in Australia. The process of item reduction led to the retaining of one item for each of the ten subdomains, resulting in a total of ten items. These items were scored on a six-point Likert scale, with a score ranging from 1 to 6 and a potential total score ranging from 10 to 60. The subdomains of the BARC-10 are identical to the ARC. Over 15 research studies have used the BARC-10 (Bunaciu et al, 2023). The questionnaire is available online (see Vilsaint et al, 2017).

Like the ARC, Vilsaint and colleagues (2017) reported that the BARC-10 consisted of a single underlying component, that is, recovery capital. The BARC-10 was found to have high internal consistency, indicating that the questionnaire reliably measures the construct of recovery capital. Furthermore, the BARC-10 was shown to distinguish between individuals who have been in recovery for more than 12 months and those with less recovery time. While the authors stated that the scale 'could increase its adoption and implementation in busy clinical and recovery support service settings by increasing speed of administration and scoring' (Vilsaint et al, 2017, 72), shorter scales like the BARC-10 may be limited with respect to variability and potential ceiling effects, which makes it difficult to track changes over time. Despite these concerns, the BARC-10 appears to be a suitable measure of recovery capital.

REC-CAP

The REC-CAP (Best et al, 2017; Cano et al, 2017) was developed by a UK and US-based team to measure recovery strengths and barriers in recovery treatment and peer support settings. Moreover, the questionnaire supports recovery support workers in planning and measuring recovery progression fostering long-term community engagement. The REC-CAP is a compendium instrument that incorporates a range of pre-validated questionnaires, all of which are available from their associated publications. These include the ARC, quality of life, parts of the Treatment Outcome Profile (Marsden et al, 2008), the substance use grid from the Maudsley Addiction Profile (Marsden et al, 1998), the Recovery Group Participation scale (RGPS, Groshkova et al, 2012), the Social Support Scale (Haslam et al, 2005), and the Commitment to Sobriety Scale (Kelly and Greene, 2014).

The REC-CAP can be completed either on paper or online, and the standard completion schedule includes a baseline assessment, a second assessment after 45 days, and other assessments 90 days thereafter. An electronic version is accompanied by an online platform (licensed for a fee) which allows those using it to receive immediate scoring feedback, which is summarized in a traffic light system to ease interpretation and maximize its utility. This modality of presentation is a newer development for the field and may help recovery support services to more easily monitor the recovery progress of their participants and make adjustments to supports and linkages. While the REC-CAP is predominantly tailored for practical settings to use in recovery care planning, it has also been used for research purposes (Härd et al, 2022; Belanger et al, 2024; Best et al, 2023; Sondhi et al, 2024).

To date, there is no research which assesses the psychometric properties of the entire REC-CAP questionnaire (Best et al, 2017; Cano et al, 2017). However, the questionnaire was structured around pre-validated questionnaires, suggesting that its building blocks are well-established. Parts of the REC-CAP have undergone psychometric evaluation, including assessments of reliability and factorization (Cano et al, 2017), showing that two subcomponents, the ARC and quality of life measures, had a single-factor structure solution. Moreover, internal consistency was high to excellent for both subcomponents. An overarching assessment of the REC-CAP tool is absent, with further confirmatory analysis across different populations required to check the generalizability and validity of REC-CAP as a whole.

Recovery Capital Index (RCI)

The Recovery Capital Index (RCI, Whitesock et al, 2018) was developed in the US to measure recovery capital at any point of the recovery journey and across various settings, regardless of a person's treatment modality, recovery, or wellness pathway. The RCI's design is influenced by the principles of cognitive behavioural therapy and motivational interviewing, and the questionnaire's structure aligns with the recovery capital model outlined by Cloud and Granfield (2008). The questionnaire is a compendium instrument, including a range of pre-validated tools such as the Behavioural Risk Factor Surveillance System Questionnaire, World Health Organization Quality of Life, Spirituality, Religiousness, and Personal Beliefs Questionnaire, General Well-Being Schedule, and the PTSD Checklist – Civilian Versions. The RCI has 22 components through 68 metrics and three subdomains, which are: 1) personal recovery capital; 2) family and social recovery capital; and 3) cultural recovery capital.

The total score for the RCI is calculated by summing the raw scores in a non-weighted way, resulting in a score ranging between 0 and 100, with a higher score indicating greater recovery capital (Whitesock et al, 2018). Furthermore, the RCI is accompanied by an online platform (licensed for a fee) which provides an opportunity for recovery support services to monitor the recovery progress and recovery wellness of their supported individuals. The results of the RCI could support building strategies and interventions around areas of concern or success (Whitesock et al, 2018).

Whitesock and colleagues (2018) evaluated the psychometric properties of the RCI. Their study found that the RCI had high internal consistency, suggesting that the items of the RCI highly correlated with each other and therefore the questionnaire reliably measures the construct of recovery capital. Moreover, high intercorrelations among the nine subdomains of the RCI indicated that while the RCI appears to measure one underlying construct (that is, recovery capital), the domains measure slightly different aspects of it (Whitesock et al, 2018). The study also assessed inter-factor correlations of the personal, social, and cultural recovery capital domains, finding moderate positive correlations. This indicates that the three subdomains tap into different aspects of the RCI (Whitesock et al, 2018).

Recovery Strengths Questionnaire (RSQ)

The Recovery Strengths Questionnaire (RSQ, Rettie et al, 2019) was developed in the UK to measure recovery capital, particularly in recovery group settings. The development of the RSQ was based on a review of the academic literature, such as the theoretical model by White and Cloud (2008), and experience from working in clinical addiction recovery settings.

One of the key aspects of the scale is its focus on attitudinal strengths, such as questions related to having a positive attitude and high self-worth (Rettie et al, 2019). The RSQ adopts an 11-point Likert scale with scores ranging between 0 (not at all satisfied) and 10 (completely satisfied). The RSQ has 15 questions and five main domains of recovery capital, divided into two main factors: ' within-group recovery strengths' and 'externally generated recovery strengths'. The five domains of recovery capital include: 1) physical recovery capital; 2) activity recovery capital; 3) social recovery capital; 4) personal strengths; and 5) attitudinal strengths. The questionnaire is available online (see Rettie et al, 2019).

The RSQ has a two-component structure of recovery capital ('external strengths' and 'within-group strengths', Rettie et al, 2019). Moreover, the analysis showed high internal consistency, meaning that the RSQ measures the construct of recovery capital reliably. The RSQ scores also align with the scores of the ARC, suggesting concurrent validity. Predictive validity was demonstrated with the RSQ total score, successfully predicting the length of time in recovery groups. However, of the two subcomponents, only within-group strengths distinguished individuals in terms of the time in recovery groups and the length of time in recovery overall (Rettie et al, 2019).

The Short Recovery Capital Scale (SRCS-10)

The Short Recovery Capital Scale (SRCS-10, Hanauer et al, 2019) was developed in the US in addiction recovery treatment settings using White's 35-item scale. It was developed based on clinical feedback recommending a shorter version of White's 35-item scale. While the items of White's RCS differ from the ARC, there is enough overlap that the authors could match the items of the SRCS-10 to items from the BARC-10, and so suggested the questionnaire has content validity. The items used to develop the SRCS-10 were scored on a five-point Likert scale, ranging between 1 (strongly disagree) and 5 (strongly agree). The questionnaire items are available in Hanauer et al (2019).

The developers of the SRCS-10, Hanauer and colleagues (2019), assessed a range of psychometric properties of the questionnaire identifying a single underlying factor with good internal consistency, that is, recovery capital. Moreover, the questionnaire was consistent across various ethnicities, genders, and sexual orientations (Hanauer et al, 2019).

The Strengths and Barriers Recovery Scale (SABRS)

The Strengths and Barriers Recovery Scale (SABRS, Best et al, 2020) was developed by creating positive and negative recovery capital items from the Life in Recovery (LiR) surveys (Laudet, 2013; Best et al, 2015). The LiR surveys measured changes in crucial life domains from active addiction to recovery, consisting of family and relationships, finances, psychological and physical health, employment, education and training, and criminal legal system contact (Best et al, 2015). The SABRS was developed by removing items from the original item set used in the US version of the LiR that would not be relevant globally (for example, 'did not have health insurance' may not be applicable in countries where public healthcare systems are accessible for every citizen) and items that did not apply to all people in recovery (for example, 'professional license restored' may not be applicable for all types of workers). This process resulted in 32 items, divided into recovery strengths (15 items) and recovery barriers (17 items). The scale uses a dichotomous (yes/no) rating system. Several research articles using the SABRS have been published (Best et al, 2021; Abreu Minero et al, 2022; Roxburgh et al, 2023). The questionnaire is available online in Best et al (2020). The psychometric properties of the SABRS remain to be assessed.

Social Recovery Capital questionnaire (SRC-IPA)

The Social Recovery Capital questionnaire was developed in the US to measure social recovery capital (Francis et al, 2022). The SRC-IPA was created based on previous academic literature and the Important People and Activities Instrument (IPA, Clifford & Longabaugh, 1991; Longabaugh et al, 1998). Although the IPA was used as its base, the SRC-IPA has additional components that measure the stability and significance of a person's network and meaningful engagement in social activities (Francis et al, 2022). The SRC-IPA has ten items with varying scoring systems ranging from negative to positive. The questionnaire has three domains, supported by factor analysis: 1) network abstinence behaviours; 2) basic network structure; and 3) network importance. Notably, because the SRC-IPA is a modification of the IPA measure, it may also be used to analyse pre-existing data from multiple large-scale studies that have already used the IPA (Francis et al, 2022). It is available online and scoring guidance can be found in the Supplemental Materials of Francis and colleagues' publication (2022).

Francis and colleagues (2022) evaluated a range of the SRC-IPA's psychometric properties from a sample of individuals with alcohol use disorders. The authors reported acceptable internal consistency for the questionnaire overall. The items of the three subscales correlated with each other for the Network Abstinence Behaviours and Basic Network Structure subdomains at an acceptable level. However, this was not the case for the Network Importance subdomain, indicating that this subdomain does not have high internal consistency. These findings suggest that the measure can reliably measure the construct of overall social recovery capital, but may be a weaker measure of the subdomains. The SRC-IPA was found to align from weak to moderate levels with the Alcohol Expectancies Questionnaire (Brown et al, 1987), the Achenbach Self Report (Achenbach, Dumenci and Rescorla, 2003), and the Hassles and Uplifts scale (DeLongis et al, 1988). At the time of writing, there has been noted a need for replication in more diverse samples with a wider age range.

The Brief Adult Health Capital Scale (BAHCS-10)

The Brief Adult Health Capital Scale (BAHCS-10, Hanauer and Svetina Valdivia, 2022) was not designed as a direct measure of recovery capital; however, its components were modelled on the ARC. Specifically, the BAHCS-10 is a shorter version of the 35-item Adult Health Capital Scale (AHCS),[1] modelled using the 50 items of the ARC (Hanauer and Svetina Valdivia, 2022). The 35-item AHCS has ten subdomains, and the authors reported developing the BAHCS-10 by identifying one item per subdomain. This resulted in a total of ten items, rated on a five-point Likert scale, from 1 (strongly disagree) to 5 (strongly agree). The BAHCS-10 is aimed at self-completion or assisted completion and can be used to measure health capital progressions and aid treatment planning. The questionnaire items are available in Hanauer and Svetina Valdivia (2022).

Hanauer and colleagues (2022) found that the questionnaire measures a single factor (that is, health capital). Furthermore, it had a statistically significantly negative correlation with the Patient Health Questionnaire (PHQ-9). This finding supports the notion that since the PHQ-9 measures depressive symptoms, the BAHCS-10 has divergent validity. Furthermore, the BAHCS-10 measured health capital consistently across ethnicities with issues related to individuals of different genders and ages. Overall, the BAHCS-10 has met some key psychometric criteria indicating that it could be considered a robust questionnaire, however, using its current form (that is, as presented in the study by Hanauer and colleagues [2022]) comes with the issue related to measurement invariance among individuals of different genders and ages.

The Multidimensional Inventory of Recovery Capital (MIRC)

The Multidimensional Inventory of Recovery Capital (MIRC, Bowen et al, 2023) was developed in the US for adults (18+ years) at various stages of alcohol use disorder recovery and across community recovery settings based on the theoretical model of recovery capital by Cloud and Granfield (2008). The measure sought to address conceptual inconsistencies and methodological issues identified in the RCQ, ARC, and BARC-10: those previous measures do not systematically assess recovery obstacles, also referred to as 'negative recovery capital'. Further, the ARC and BARC-10 contain abstinence-based items, and the MIRC does not assume abstinence-based recovery (Bowen et al, 2023).

A new set of 90 initial items were developed based on a literature review and consultation with recovery research experts (Bowen et al, 2023). These were eventually reduced to a final set of 48 items through interviews with experts and individuals in recovery (Bowen et al, 2022), organized into five subdomains, including items measuring positive and negative recovery capital: 1) physical recovery capital; 2) human recovery capital; 3) social recovery capital; 4) cultural recovery capital; and 5) community recovery capital. The MIRC uses a four-point Likert scale, with scoring ranging from strongly disagree to strongly agree. The questionnaire is available in the supplemental materials in Bowen et al (2023).

A range of psychometric properties of the MIRC were evaluated by its developers, Bowen and colleagues (2022), who claimed strong face validity through a rigorous development process that incorporated iterative feedback from a diverse group of stakeholders, including persons in recovery, service providers, and research experts (Bowen et al, 2022). The MIRC's internal consistency was excellent for the whole questionnaire and ranged from moderate to strong for each of its four subscales. The MIRC demonstrated test–retest reliability, indicating that it consistently captures recovery capital. Correlations between the subscales were of moderate strength, and correlations between each subscale and the total MIRC score were stronger. These findings indicate that each subscale measured unique aspects of recovery capital. Moreover, the overall questionnaire aligned well with the WHOQOL-BREF. Its subdomains also aligned with parts of the WHOQOL-BREF (physical and human domains from the MIRC and domains one, two, and four from the WHOQOL-BREF). The social capital subdomain aligned with the Brief 2-Way Social Support Scale (Obst et al, 2019), and the cultural capital subdomain with the sense of community subscale of the Perceived Neighbourhood scale. These findings indicated that the MIRC as a whole and its subdomains have concurrent validity with measures of similar constructs.

Domains and subdomains of recovery capital measured by the recovery capital questionnaires

All recovery capital questionnaires align with the original definition of recovery capital by Robert Granfield and William Cloud.[2] However, authors have proposed slightly differing dimensional structures for the recovery capital construct, as reviewed by Bowen and Hennessy in Chapter 6 (for example, a three- versus four-dimensional structure). Some authors of the recovery capital questionnaires closely followed one or more of the proposed recovery capital conceptual models in designing their questionnaire (for example, Burns and Marks, 2013; Whitesock et al, 2018; Bowen et al, 2023), whereas others used recovery capital theory but did not structure their questionnaire based on a particular recovery capital model (for example, Sterling et al, 2008; Groshkova et al, 2013). Nevertheless, if a questionnaire item structure does not follow a particular recovery capital model, it does not mean its items could not align with a theoretical model.

We reviewed the recovery capital domains of each currently available recovery capital questionnaire[3] and Figure 4.1 shows that, overall, a wide range of names have been used in the questionnaires to reference different components of recovery capital. There is a clear overlap in the ARC-based questionnaires (that is, the ARC, the BARC-10, and REC-CAP) and those structured using the theoretical recovery capital models (that is, the MIRC, the RCI, the RCQ, and the RSQ). The SRC-IPA, Sterling's RCS, SABRS, and the RSQ and REC-CAP have unique questionnaire domains. This figure, alongside a similar analysis of these recovery capital questionnaires at the item-level (Bunaciu et al, 2023) may be used to help guide selection of the most suitable recovery capital questionnaire for practical or research purposes (more discussion regarding how to select the optimal measurement approach is provided later in this chapter).[4]

Figure 4.1: Recovery capital domains identified in the available questionnaires

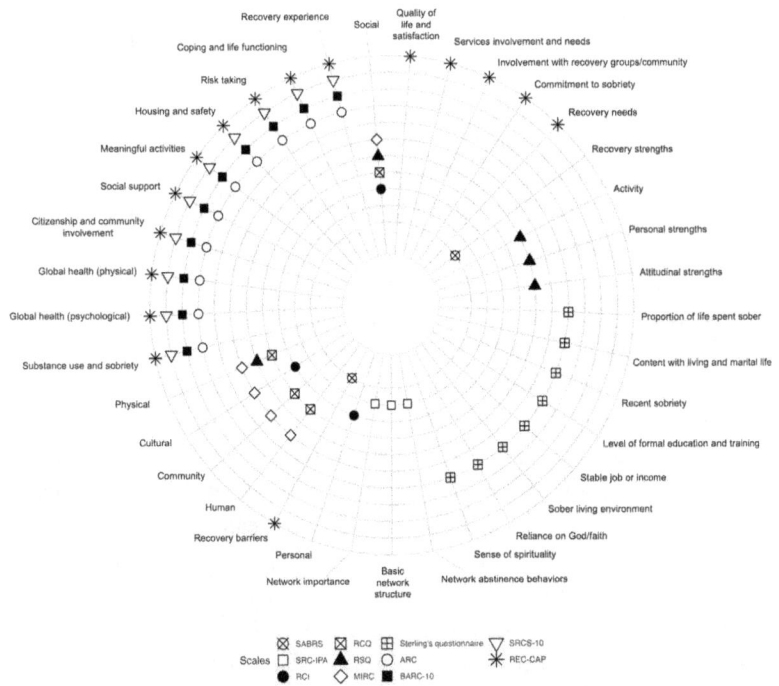

Alternative ways of mapping and measuring recovery capital

While questionnaires providing overall scores play an important role in the recovery capital measurement literature, there are contexts where using alternative approaches may be more suitable for the measurement of recovery capital. Recovery capital questionnaires measure recovery capital from multiple angles, as reviewed in this chapter, but these questionnaires might not capture every aspect of the construct. Furthermore, there are areas in which the administration of a questionnaire would not be convenient or even possible. Some examples of these areas include interactions on online settings, such as recovery forums or social media platforms like Facebook groups, Reddit, or X (previously Twitter). This section will review some of the approaches used to measure recovery capital which are not any of the previously reviewed recovery capital questionnaires.

When social recovery capital is of interest, the method of Social Identity Mapping in Addiction Recovery (SIM-AR, Beckwith et al, 2019; developed from Cruwys et al, 2016) provides an assessment of a recovering individual's social connections (Meisel et al, 2023). The process involves a series of structured questions about the social groups in which the individual participates, however, it does not result in an overall score like the recovery capital questionnaires. Specifically, the questions focus on understanding the group sizes and the importance of the group members to the individual in recovery, the relationships between the individual and the group members, and the substance use status of the identified social connections. The information gathered from these questions can be used to produce a visual map that positions the individual in recovery in their social network and provides quantifiable data to be used for analysis (Beckwith et al, 2019; Jurinsky et al, 2023). An advantage of this method is that it produces a highly individualized understanding of the individual's social recovery capital and potential recovery barriers in terms of the quantity and quality of social connections. Moreover, completing the SIM-AR may stimulate deeper reflection which may help individuals to have an in-depth understanding of their social recovery capital and barriers to recovery (Meisel et al, 2023).

Online settings provide ideal platforms for the development of recovery capital, but capturing it across different platforms can be a challenging task. In certain cases, individuals who are part of online platforms could be, for example, interviewed about their experiences with online platforms and how they influence the development of recovery capital. However, this is not always possible, and researchers may seek to collect data that is more objective in nature. One solution for measuring social recovery capital in online settings is to use linguistic data for the assessment of recovery capital. For large amounts of data that cannot be analysed manually, computerized linguistic analysis tools such as the Linguistic Inquiry and Word Count (LIWC, Pennebaker et al, 2015) can be used. LIWC is a text analysis tool that assesses the emotional, cognitive, and structural components of written speech. It provides information on social identity and is especially useful in online settings due to its suitability as a method for large datasets. Linguistic analyses can be used in conjunction with Social Network Analysis (SNA) to capture both psychological states underpinning the use of language in online communities of recovery and the levels of commitment and engagement within the community.

Bliuc and colleagues (2019) used this approach to capture social recovery capital in a naturalistic study of participants engaged in online recovery communities. Furthermore, the SNA provides detailed information on the strength of connections between individuals in the online community, and it maps changes in social connectedness over time (Bliuc et al, 2017; 2019; Best et al, 2018). Detailed, step-by-step guidance on conducting the SNA and LIWC analyses to capture social recovery capital in online settings is provided in Bliuc and colleagues (2019).

Collinson and Best developed the Asset Based Community Engagement Mapping (ABCE) in 2019, which is another potential method for measuring social and community recovery capital. It is addressed in more detail in

Chapter 7, but briefly, this approach involves mapping community resources and how individuals in recovery interact with them to identify engagement opportunities and challenges. The approach begins by mapping the current levels of community engagement and identifying the available resources. These assets are then examined regarding accessibility, affordability, connectedness, social networks, as well as for the identification of barriers (for example, cost, confidence, motivation). A recovery navigator then actively facilitates the connection between the individual and community assets. ABCE is an encompassing approach as it recognizes the personal, social, and community elements of recovery capital, and how each component interacts with the other.

Review of the strengths and limitations of the existing profile of recovery capital measures, how to choose a suitable measurement approach, and potential future directions for scale development

The various recovery capital measurement approaches discussed in this chapter have played a central role in transitioning recovery capital theory from academic settings to an increasingly integral component of practical recovery support settings. Addiction recovery support practitioners and researchers now have the option to select from over ten recovery capital questionnaires and employ other methods such as Social Identity Mapping or Social Network Analysis. Such a range of available measurement options may be regarded as essential, considering the diversity of different recovery settings and the complexity of recovery journeys (as discussed in this volume by Hennessy and colleagues). Thus, the choice of the optimal measure or instrument should be determined by a range of questions for both practitioners and researchers. That is, the most suitable approach to measurement will likely depend on several factors, including the specific population, the setting (face-to-face or online, research or practice), and the interest in the concept (whether overall recovery capital or specific aspects of it). While Figure 4.1 shows that construct names differ among the questionnaires, the item-level analysis in our systematic review (Bunaciu et al, 2023) showed that certain items are common in all or almost all questionnaires, such as housing, health, finances, and social support. These figures may be used for guidance in identifying questionnaires that fit the needs of a specific organization.

Despite shared elements across recovery capital questionnaires, they possess differences in design, methodology, and theory. Notably, one discrepancy lies in their stance on whether recovery requires abstinence from unwanted substance use. Similarly, recovery definitions vary in the literature, with more recent definitions avoiding abstinence and including considerations for controlled substance use and ongoing use of prescription medications

(Ashford et al, 2019). Although researchers generally agree on the core components of recovery capital theory, the specifics of recovery capital differ across populations and settings. As a result, the differences in the reviewed questionnaires may be viewed as a strength rather than a limitation, as they provide an increased opportunity to accurately measure a construct that is inherently multifaceted. Overall, the choice of which measure to use will be dependent on the theoretical perspective of the individual practitioner or researcher combined with practical considerations (length, appropriateness to the population, how often it is to be measured, sensitivity to change, cost). Notably, the two electronic recovery capital questionnaires that require a fee also come with specialized platforms that allow immediate scoring and feedback as well as a support system for practical settings (REC-CAP and RCI). Unlike research tools which may be difficult to score and to interpret, these approaches can become an important component of high-quality recovery support and monitoring provided by organizations.

Echoing the findings of a systematic review of recovery capital measurement approaches (Bunaciu et al, 2023), the recovery capital questionnaires reviewed in this chapter appear to be tailored predominantly for adult populations. While a large proportion of those in addiction recovery are considered adults due to the large span of ages that is considered adulthood, addiction impacts the youth and elderly as well. Theoretical and conceptual literature exists regarding recovery capital for youth (for example, Hennessy et al, 2019; Hennessy and Finch, 2019; Nash et al, 2019; Jurinsky et al, 2023) and the elderly (for example, LaBarre et al, 2021). However, recovery capital measures, particularly questionnaires, have not yet been published for these populations, although an adapted SIM-AR has been developed for use with youth (Blyth et al, 2023; Jurinsky et al, 2023). Similarly, literature has suggested that individuals simultaneously in recovery and in desistance from illegal activity form a unique subgroup of people in recovery (Best et al, 2017; Van Roeyen et al, 2017). Recovery capital literature is currently limited for this population, and further research is needed to understand better how to best measure recovery capital in this group (see Hamilton and Bartels, Chapter 11, in this volume). Literature on the recovery capital measurement approaches, particularly questionnaires, still need to be further expanded to focus research on a diverse range of individuals and settings, including a broader gendered approach (that is, other than a binary gendered approach), people from different cultures (Bunaciu et al, 2023), and with different primary substances (for example, primary alcohol versus primary opioid users).

Moreover, the psychometric properties of most recovery capital questionnaires have been examined, which is an integral part of developing and refining a high-quality questionnaire. However, ensuring that a questionnaire is psychometrically sound requires extensive research before reaching definitive conclusions. While the various instruments vary in their underlying domains, most appear to offer coherent measures of recovery capital with several key domains offering a consistent set of subscales. Our review here suggests that most scales have good internal reliability, but we argue that most lack external validation (measuring differences at different times, used on differing populations, and implemented by different parts of the workforce – for example, researchers, clinicians, paid workers, peer workers, or volunteers – each with their own power relationship with a person in recovery). Furthermore, most measures have been tested only once and in limited settings. We suggest that more data should be collected to increase confidence in the external validity of these measures. So far, only the ARC has been demonstrated to work well across different languages, and only some of the questionnaires may be appropriate or sufficiently sensitive to various cultural backgrounds.

Conclusion

Overall, while aspiring for a 'gold standard' measure may be an ideal pursuit, as previously suggested, the range of recovery capital measurement approaches may be considered a strength in the field. Furthermore, developing a single measure that would flawlessly capture the multifaceted nature of recovery capital for individuals from diverse backgrounds and settings would be optimal, however, this would likely be an unattainable goal. Nevertheless, the focus should be on creating the most effective realistically achievable measures, and the past decades have demonstrated a strong start in this.

Notes

1. While this scale was mentioned in Hanauer and Svetina Valdivia (2022), this scale was not reviewed in this chapter because we did not find a publication about the AHCS.
2. '… the sum of one's total resources that can be brought to bear in an effort to overcome alcohol and drug dependency' (1999, 179).
3. White's Recovery Capital Scale does not specify domains and therefore was not included here. The BAHCS-10 (Hanauer and Svetina, 2022) subdomains were not explicitly named but appear to be aligned with the ARC.
4. Detailed review of Figure 4.1, outlining the recovery capital questionnaires that measure each construct.
    1. Quality of life and satisfaction, measured by the REC-CAP.
    2. Services involvement and needs, measured by the REC-CAP.
    3. Involvement with recovery groups or community, measured by the REC-CAP.
    4. Commitment to sobriety, measured by the REC-CAP.
    5. Recovery needs, measured by the REC-CAP.
    6. Recovery strengths, measured by the SABRS.
    7. Activity, measured by the RSQ.
    8. Personal strengths, measured by the RSQ.
    9. Attitudinal strengths, measured by the RSQ.
    10. The proportion of life spent sober, measured by Sterling's questionnaire.
    11. Content with living and marital life, measured by Sterling's questionnaire.

12. Recent sobriety, measured by Sterling's questionnaire.
13. Level of formal education and training, measured by Sterling's questionnaire.
14. Stable job or income, measured by Sterling's questionnaire.
15. Sober living environment, measured by Sterling's questionnaire.
16. Reliance on God or faith, measured by Sterling's questionnaire.
17. Sense of spirituality, measured by Sterling's questionnaire.
18. Network abstinence behaviours, measured by the SRC-IPA.
19. Basic network structure, measured by the SRC-IPA.
20. Network importance, measured by the SRC-IPA.
21. Personal, measured by the RCI.
22. Recovery barriers, measured by the REC-CAP and SABRS.
23. Human, measured by the MIRC, and the RCQ.
24. Community, measured by the MIRC and the RCQ.
25. Cultural, measured by the MIRC and the RCI.
26. Physical, measured by the MIRC, the RSQ, and the RCQ.
27. Substance use and sobriety, measured by the REC-CAP, the SRCS-10, the BARC-10, and the ARC.
28. Psychological global health, measured by the REC-CAP, the SRCS-10, the BARC-10, and the ARC.
29. Physical global health, measured by the REC-CAP, the SRCS-10, the BARC-10, and the ARC.
30. Citizenship and community involvement, measured by the REC-CAP, the SRCS-10, the BARC-10, and the ARC.
31. Social support, measured by the REC-CAP, the SRCS-10, the BARC-10, and the ARC.
32. Meaningful activities, measured by the REC-CAP, the SRCS-10, the BARC-10, and the ARC.
33. Housing and safety, measured by the REC-CAP, the SRCS-10, the BARC-10, and the ARC.
34. Risk taking, measured by the REC-CAP, the SRCS-10, the BARC-10, and the ARC.
35. Coping and life functioning, measured by the REC-CAP, the SRCS-10, the BARC-10, and the ARC.
36. Recovery experience, measured by the REC-CAP, the SRCS-10, the BARC-10, and the ARC.
37. Social, measured by the MIRC, the RSQ, the RCQ, and the RCI.

References

Aalto, S. and Jumpponen, K. (2021) *Toipumispääomamittarin käyttökokemuksia hoitajan näkökulmasta päihdehoitotyössä*, dissertation, Laurea University of Applied Sciences, Available from [in Finnish]: https://www.theseus.fi/bitstream/handle/10024/497905/Opinn%C3%A4ytety%C3%B6.pdf?sequence=2

Abreu Minero, V., Best, D., Brown, L., Patton, D., and Vanderplasschen, W. (2022) 'Differences in addiction and recovery gains according to gender – gender barriers and specific differences in overall strengths growth', *Substance Abuse Treatment, Prevention, and Policy*, 17(1): 21.

Achenbach, T.M., Dumenci, L., and Rescorla, L.A. (2003) 'Ratings of relations between DSM-IV diagnostic categories and items of the Adult Self-Report (ASR) and Adult Behavior Checklist (ABCL)', *Research Center for Children, Youth and Families*, 1–11.

Annis, H.S. (1997) *The Drug Taking Confidence Questionnaire: User's Guide*, Toronto: Addiction Research Foundation.

Arndt, S., Sahker, E., and Hedden, S. (2017) 'Does the Assessment of Recovery Capital scale reflect a single or multiple domains?', *Substance Abuse and Rehabilitation*, 8: 39–43.

Ashford, R.D., Brown, A., Brown, T., Callis, J., Cleveland, H.H., Eisenhart, E., et al (2019) 'Defining and operationalizing the phenomena of recovery: A working definition from the recovery science research collaborative', *Addiction Research & Theory*, 27(3): 179–88.

Basu, A., Mattoo, S.K., Basu, D., Subodh, B.N., Sharma, S.K., and Roub, F.E. (2019) 'Psychometric properties of the Hindi-translated version of the 'Assessment of Recovery Capital' scale at a tertiary level de-addiction center in North India', *Indian Journal of Social Psychiatry*, 35(1): 40–6.

Beckwith, M., Best, D., Savic, M., Haslam, C., Bathish, R., Dingle, G., et al (2019) 'Social identity mapping in addiction recovery (SIM-AR): Extension and application of a visual method', *Addiction Research & Theory*, 27(6): 462–71.

Belanger, M.J., Sondhi, A., Mericle, A.A., Leidi, A., Klein, M., Collinson, B., et al (2024) 'Assessing a pilot scheme of intensive support and assertive linkage in levels of engagement, retention, and recovery capital for people in recovery housing using quasi-experimental methods', *Journal of Substance Use and Addiction Treatment*, 158, 209283.

Best, D. and Hennessy, E.A. (2022) 'The science of recovery capital: Where do we go from here?', *Addiction*, 117(4): 1139–45.

Best, D., Vanderplasschen, W., and Nisic, M. (2020) 'Measuring capital in active addiction and recovery: The development of the strengths and barriers recovery scale (SABRS)', *Substance Abuse Treatment, Prevention, and Policy*, 15(1): 1–8.

Best, D., Irving, J., Collinson, B., Andersson, C., and Edwards, M. (2017) 'Recovery networks and community connections: Identifying connection needs and community linkage opportunities in early recovery populations', *Alcoholism Treatment Quarterly*, 35(1): 2–15.

Best, D., Bliuc, A.M., Iqbal, M., Upton, K., and Hodgkins, S. (2018) 'Mapping social identity change in online networks of addiction recovery', *Addiction Research & Theory*, 26(3): 163–73.

Best, D., Albertson, K., Irving, J., Lightowlers, C., Mama-Rudd, A., and Chaggar, A. (2015) *The UK Life in Recovery Survey 2015: The First National UK Survey of Addiction Recovery Experiences*, Sheffield: Sheffield Hallam University.

Best, D., Sondhi, A., Brown, L., Nisic, M., Nagelhout, G.E., Martinelli, T., et al (2021) 'The Strengths and Barriers Recovery Scale (SABRS): Relationships matter in building strengths and overcoming barriers', *Frontiers in Psychology*, 12, 663447.

Best, D., Sondhi, A., Best, J., Lehman, J., Grimes, A., Conner, M., and DeTriquet, R. (2023) 'Using recovery capital to predict retention and change in recovery residences in Virginia, USA', *Alcoholism Treatment Quarterly*, 41(2): 250–62.

Bliuc, A.M., Iqbal, M., and Best, D. (2019) 'Integrating computerized linguistic and social network analyses to capture addiction recovery capital in an online community', *Journal of Visualized Experiments*, 147, e58851.

Bliuc, A.M., Best, D., Iqbal, M., and Upton, K. (2017) 'Building addiction recovery capital through online participation in a recovery community', *Social Science & Medicine*, 193: 110–17.

Boateng, G.O., Neilands, T.B., Frongillo, E.A., and Young, S.L. (2018) 'Best practices for developing and validating scales for health, social, and behavioral research: A primer', *Frontiers in Public Health*, 6, 366616.

Bowen, E.A., Scott, C.F., Irish, A., and Nochajski, T.H. (2020) 'Psychometric properties of the Assessment of Recovery Capital (ARC) instrument in a diverse low-income sample', *Substance Use & Misuse*, 55(1): 108–18.

Bowen, E., Irish, A., LaBarre, C., Capozziello, N., Nochajski, T., and Granfield, R. (2022) 'Qualitative insights in item development for a comprehensive and inclusive measure of recovery capital', *Addiction Research & Theory*, 30(6): 403–13.

Bowen, E., Irish, A., Wilding, G., LaBarre, C., Capozziello, N., Nochajski, T., et al (2023) 'Development and psychometric properties of the Multidimensional Inventory of Recovery Capital (MIRC)', *Drug and Alcohol Dependence*, 247: 109875.

Brown, S.A., Christiansen, B.A., and Goldman, M.S. (1987) 'The Alcohol Expectancy Questionnaire: An instrument for the assessment of adolescent and adult alcohol expectancies', *Journal of Studies on Alcohol*, 48(5): 483–91.

Bunaciu, A., Bliuc, A.M., Best, D., Hennessy, E.A., Belanger, M.J., and Benwell, C.S. (2023) 'Measuring recovery capital for people recovering from alcohol and drug addiction: A systematic review', *Addiction Research & Theory*, 32(3): 225–36.

Burns, J. (2019) *An Exploration of the Psychometric Properties of the Recovery Capital Questionnaire*, Doctoral thesis, University of Stirling, Available from: https://www.storre.stir.ac.uk/bitstream/1893/31142/1/Psychometric_properties_of_RCQ.pdf

Burns, J. and Marks, D. (2013) 'Can recovery capital predict addiction problem severity?', *Alcoholism Treatment Quarterly*, 31(3): 303–20.

Burns, J. and Yates, R. (2022) 'An examination of the reliability and validity of the recovery capital questionnaire (RCQ)', *Drug and Alcohol Dependence*, 232, 109329.

Cano, I., Best, D., Edwards, M., and Lehman, J. (2017) 'Recovery capital pathways: Modelling the components of recovery well-being', *Drug and Alcohol Dependence*, 181: 11–19.

Clifford, P.R. and Longabaugh, R. (1991) *Manual for the Administration of the Important People and Activities Instrument*, adapted for use by Project MATCH for NIAAA, 5R01AA06698-05.

Cloud, W. and Granfield, R. (2008) 'Conceptualizing recovery capital: Expansion of a theoretical construct', *Substance Use & Misuse*, 43(12–13): 1971–86.

Cruwys, T., Steffens, N.K., Haslam, S.A., Haslam, C., Jetten, J., and Dingle, G.A. (2016) 'Social Identity Mapping: A procedure for visual representation and assessment of subjective multiple group memberships', *British Journal of Social Psychology*, 55(4): 613–42.

DeLongis, A., Folkman, S., and Lazarus, R.S. (1988) 'The impact of daily stress on health and mood: Psychological and social resources as mediators', *Journal of Personality and Social Psychology*, 54(3): 486–95.

Fetzer Institute/National Institute on Aging Working Group (1999) *Multidimensional Measurement of Religiousness/Spirituality for Use in Health Research: A Report of the Fetzer Institute/National Institute on Aging Working Group*, Kalamazoo, MI: The John E. Fetzer Institute.

Francis, M.W., Bourdon, J.L., Chan, G., Dick, D.M., Edenberg, H.J., Kamarajan, C., et al (2022) 'Deriving a measure of social recovery capital from the Important People and Activities Instrument: Construction and psychometric properties', *Alcohol and Alcoholism*, 57(3): 322–9.

Genia, V. (1997) 'The spiritual experience index: Revision and reformulation', *Review of Religious Research*, 38(4): 344–61.

Granfield, R. and Cloud, W. (1999) *Coming Clean: Overcoming Addiction without Treatment*, New York: New York University Press.

Groshkova, T., Best, D., and White, W. (2012) 'Recovery Group Participation Scale (RGPS): Factor structure in alcohol and heroin recovery populations', in J. Roth and D. Best (eds) *Addiction and Recovery in the UK*, London: Routledge, pp 73–89.

Groshkova, T., Best, D., and White, W. (2013) 'The Assessment of Recovery Capital: Properties and psychometrics of a measure of addiction recovery strengths', *Drug and Alcohol Review*, 32(2): 187–94.

Hanauer, M. and Svetina Valdivia, D. (2022) 'Validation and utility study of the 10 item brief adult health capital scale (BACHS-10)', *Journal of Health Psychology*, 27(2): 332–40.

Hanauer, M., Sielbeck-Mathes, K., and Berny, L. (2019) 'Invariance of a recovery capital scale across gender, ethnicity, and sexual orientation in a substance use disorder treatment program', *The American Journal of Drug and Alcohol Abuse*, 45(3): 254–63.

Härd, S., Best, D., Sondhi, A., Lehman, J., and Riccardi, R. (2022) 'The growth of recovery capital in clients of recovery residences in Florida, USA: A quantitative pilot study of changes in REC-CAP profile scores', *Substance Abuse Treatment, Prevention, and Policy*, 17(1): 58.

Haslam, S.A., O'Brien, A., Jetten, J., Vormedal, K., and Penna, S. (2005) 'Taking the strain: Social identity, social support, and the experience of stress', *British Journal of Social Psychology*, 44(3): 355–70.

Hennessy, E.A. (2017) 'Recovery capital: A systematic review of the literature', *Addiction Research & Theory*, 25(5): 349–60.

Hennessy, E.A. and Finch, A.J. (2019) 'Adolescent recovery capital and recovery high school attendance: An exploratory data mining approach', *Psychology of Addictive Behaviors*, 33(8): 669–76.

Hennessy, E.A., Cristello, J.V., and Kelly, J.F. (2019) 'RCAM: A proposed model of recovery capital for adolescents', *Addiction Research & Theory*, 27(5): 429–36.

Jurinsky, J., Cowie, K., Blyth, S., and Hennessy, E.A. (2023) '"A lot better than it used to be": A qualitative study of adolescents' dynamic social recovery capital', *Addiction Research & Theory*, 31(2): 77–83.

Kelly, J.F. and Greene, M.C. (2014) 'Beyond motivation: Initial validation of the commitment to sobriety scale', *Journal of Substance Abuse Treatment*, 46(2): 257–63.

LaBarre, C., Linn, B.K., Bradizza, C.M., Bowen, E.A., and Stasiewicz, P.R. (2021) 'Conceptualizing recovery capital for older adults with substance use disorders', *Journal of Social Work Practice in the Addictions*, 21(4): 417–27.

Laudet, A. (2013) *Life in Recovery: Report on the Survey Findings*, Washington, DC: Faces and Voices of Recovery, Available from: https://facesandvoicesofrecovery.org/wp-content/uploads/2019/06/22Life-in-Recovery22-Report-on-the-Survey-Findings.pdf

Longabaugh, R., Wirtz, P.W., Zweben, A., and Stout, R.L. (1998) 'Network support for drinking, Alcoholics Anonymous and long-term matching effects', *Addiction*, 93(9): 1313–33.

Marsden, J., Farrell, M., Bradbury, C., Dale-Perera, A., Eastwood, B., Roxburgh, M., and Taylor, S. (2008) 'Development of the treatment outcomes profile', *Addiction*, 103(9): 1450–60.

Marsden, J., Gossop, M., Stewart, D., Best, D., Farrell, M., Lehmann, P., et al (1998) 'The Maudsley Addiction Profile (MAP): A brief instrument for assessing treatment outcome', *Addiction*, 93(12): 1857–67.

Mawson, E., Best, D., Beckwith, M., Dingle, G.A., and Lubman, D.I. (2015) 'Social identity, social networks and recovery capital in emerging adulthood: A pilot study', *Substance Abuse Treatment, Prevention, and Policy*, 10: 45.

McLellan, A., Luborsky, L., and O'Brien, C. (1980) 'Improved diagnostic instrument for substance abuse patients: The Addiction Severity Index', *Journal of Nervous and Mental Disease*, 168(1): 26–33.

McLellan, A.T., Luborsky, L., and Cacciola, J. (1985) 'New data from the addiction severity index', *Journal of Nervous and Mental Disease*, 173(7): 412–23.

Meisel, S.N., Hennessy, E.A., Jurinsky, J., and Kelly, J.F. (2023) 'Improving social recovery capital research to enhance clinical utility: A proposed agenda', *Addiction Research & Theory* 32(3): 153–9.

Nash, A.J., Hennessy, E.A., and Collier, C. (2019) 'Exploring recovery capital among adolescents in an alternative peer group', *Drug and Alcohol Dependence*, 199: 136–43.

Obst, P., Shakespeare-Finch, J., Krosch, D.J., and Rogers, E.J. (2019) 'Reliability and validity of the Brief 2-Way Social Support Scale: An investigation of social support in promoting older adult well-being', *SAGE Open Medicine*, 7, 2050312119836020.

Pennebaker, J.W., Boyd, R.L., Jordan, K., & Blackburn, K. (2015) *The Development and Psychometric Properties of LIWC2015*, Austin, TX: University of Texas at Austin.

Polcin, D.L., Mahoney, E., Witbrodt, J., and Mericle, A.A. (2021) 'Recovery home environment characteristics associated with recovery capital', *Journal of Drug Issues*, 51(2): 253–67.

Rettie, H.C., Hogan, L.M., and Cox, W.M. (2019) 'The Recovery Strengths Questionnaire for alcohol and drug use disorders', *Drug and Alcohol Review*, 38(2): 209–15.

Roxburgh, A.D., Best, D., Lubman, D.I., and Manning, V. (2023) 'Composition of social networks to build recovery capital differ across early and stable stages of recovery', *Addiction Research & Theory*, 32(3): 186–93.

Schaler, J.A. (1996) 'Spiritual thinking in addiction-treatment providers: The Spiritual Belief Scale (SBS)', *Alcoholism Treatment Quarterly*, 14(3): 7–33.

Sión, A., Jurado-Barba, R., Esteban-Rodríguez, L., Arias, F., and Rubio, G. (2022) 'Spanish validation of the assessment of Recovery Capital Scale in clinical population with alcohol use disorder', *The Spanish Journal of Psychology*, 25: e16, DOI: 10.1017/SJP.2022.12.

Sondhi, A., Bunaciu, A., Best, D., Hennessy, E.A., Best, J., Leidi, A., et al (2024) 'Modeling recovery housing retention and program outcomes by justice involvement among residents in Virginia, USA: An observational study', *International Journal of Offender Therapy and Comparative Criminology*, 68(15): 0306624X241254691.

Sterling, R., Slusher, C., and Weinstein, S. (2008) 'Measuring recovery capital and determining its relationship to outcome in an alcohol dependent sample', *The American Journal of Drug and Alcohol Abuse*, 34(5): 603–10.

Underwood, L.G. and Teresi, J.A. (2002) 'The daily spiritual experience scale: Development, theoretical description, reliability, exploratory factor analysis, and preliminary construct validity using health-related data', *Annals of Behavioral Medicine*, 24(1): 22–33.

Van Roeyen, S., Anderson, S., Vanderplasschen, W., Colman, C., and Vander Laenen, F. (2017) 'Desistance in drug-using offenders: A narrative review', *European Journal of Criminology*, 14(5): 606–25.

Vilsaint, C.L., Kelly, J.F., Bergman, B.G., Groshkova, T., Best, D., and White, W. (2017) 'Development and validation of a Brief Assessment of Recovery Capital (BARC-10) for alcohol and drug use disorder', *Drug and Alcohol Dependence*, 177: 71–6.

White, W. (2009) 'Recovery Capital Scale', Available from: https://www.chestnut.org/resources/4c4bb112-3d59-4984-98cb-3b637378965a/Recovery-Capital-Scale.pdf

White, W. and Cloud, W. (2008) 'Recovery capital: A primer for addictions professionals', *Counselor*, 9(5): 22–7.

Whitesock, D., Zhao, J., Goettsch, K., and Hanson, J. (2018) 'Validating a survey for addiction wellness: The recovery capital Index', *South Dakota Medicine: The Journal of the South Dakota State Medical Association*, 71(5): 202–12.

5

Recovery Capital as an Explanatory Model for Change and Growth

Emily A. Hennessy, Rebecca L. Smith, and Corrie L. Vilsaint

Introduction

This chapter will unpack the logic of recovery capital as a metric of change for use in both applied and research settings and will consider what the strengths and limitations of such an approach might be. Distinct from Chapter 4, which focuses on the more technical aspects of measurement (Bunaciu and colleagues), this chapter will draw on Hennessy (2017) and Best and Hennessy (2022), to consider some of the broader epistemological and empirical challenges around the development and use of recovery capital metrics for different settings and what lessons have been learned in this area to date. As an organizing framework, recovery capital has several key domains that fall into differing ecological levels (individual, interpersonal, community; Granfield and Cloud, 1999; Hennessy, 2017). Conceptually, these categories make intuitive sense. Yet, when we consider the broad scope of recovery capital – all the resources one can use for recovery – it would seem that measuring it to both understand one's current level of resources as well as to assess change across ecological domains and/or over time could get quite unwieldy. In addition to its utility as a broad theoretical organizing framework, there are many natural opportunities to use the assessment of recovery capital as both a research exercise and a practical one for identifying ways to support growth, assess change in recovery, predict outcomes, and address programme and system-level gaps in supporting recovery capital development (White and Cloud, 2008; Best and Hennessy, 2022). This is an important area to address both for the individual as well as for others, including organizations seeking to improve an individual's recovery capital to better support their recovery trajectory; yet, there are several challenges to selecting a recovery capital assessment or using the results of such an assessment in practice.

To address these issues, in the first section, we will cover the purpose and application of using recovery capital as a metric and describe differences for both (1) treatment planning and intervention and (2) research and programme evaluation. In the second section, we will expand the themes identified in section one and address important considerations for using recovery capital as a metric of change. In the third section, we will consider the challenges and lessons learned in the development of recovery capital metrics. In the fourth and final section, we will provide a summary for the future of developing recovery capital metrics for assessing growth and change in recovery.

Purpose and application of recovery capital metrics

There are different ways to measure and examine recovery capital (Bunaciu et al, 2023), and the current available recovery capital metrics were developed by and for different stakeholders. Thus, the decision of which metric to use will vary based on the key stakeholder asking the questions, and it can be difficult to choose which metric to use in practice given the many available options when the conceptual differences are not readily apparent. In the examples provided in Table 5.1, there are a variety of purposes for using a recovery capital measure and these purposes will change the types of questions each stakeholder may be interested in answering about recovery capital. For example, the reason an individual may be assessing their own recovery capital would likely be quite different than reasons of specialist treatment centres – the types of questions asked and the methods used would thus differ considerably.

Along these lines, we can consider two primary categories of reasons for using recovery capital metrics and how the different stakeholders may seek to use them. First, we will consider recovery capital assessment as a form of treatment planning and intervention. Then, we will consider recovery capital assessment in research and programme evaluation.

Recovery capital assessment in treatment planning and intervention

Measuring recovery capital as part of treatment planning and intervention was first formally suggested by White and Cloud when they posited that these findings could be part of how a clinician determined how to best support and assertively link an individual seeking treatment (White and Cloud, 2008 and discussed in Chapter 3 in this book). They suggested that by using both one's level of recovery capital and degree of problem severity, an individual could be 'triaged' to an appropriate level of care for their needs and thus maximize system resources. This could be done across the

Table 5.1: Purpose of recovery capital metric by key stakeholder

Stakeholder	Purpose of metric	Types of questions asked by stakeholder
Individual in recovery	Understand progress Celebrate progress Identify areas of challenges and potential roadblocks Determine where challenges may be due to factors outside the individual's control Identify strengths that can be used to support future progress	Am I improving? What is improving? What are the goals I should aim for? Where could I use some help? What are the resources and strengths I can rely on? What areas of capital do I need to continue to build?
Peer support worker	Understand and celebrate peer progress Identify areas of challenges and potential roadblocks that could be addressed by conversation and active linkages to supports Understand and develop their own skills in working on recovery capital	How is this person growing their recovery capital? Where are their barriers to growing recovery capital? How can I better support the individual? What resources do I have good access to in the community?
Specialist treatment	Identify when client is ready to leave programme Programme planning and development Demonstrate success of programme Outcome monitoring Performance management Identify needs for peer support and other forms of case management and coordination	Are we effective? For whom are our services working? What represents meaningful change? Are we identifying recovery support needs and continuity of care?
Recovery organization	Understand client trajectories Determine where challenges may be due to factors outside the organization's control Demonstrate success of programme to funders Identify gaps and areas for improvement Outcome monitoring Performance management – assess key areas of recovery capital that are strengths and weaknesses of the organization Effectiveness of community partnerships	Are we effective? For whom are our services working? What represents meaningful change? Where do we need to link clients to additional resources for improved/continued success? What recovery capital domains are our training and development needs
Researchers	Understand how recovery capital helps maintain recovery Understand which factors can lead to greater recovery capital Build recovery science	What are the strongest predictors of recovery? For whom, and under what circumstance are these predictors consistent?

recovery oriented system of care (or ROSC), for example, in screening and early intervention as well as later during someone's third or fourth treatment attempt when recovery capital might be quite low and problem severity high as a result of lack of responsive intervention and high consequences. In fact, the American Society of Addiction Medicine, which produces the most widely used set of clinical guidelines, has more recently formalized the use of recovery capital into patient placement criteria (American Society of Addiction Medicine, 2023). In this way, measuring recovery capital is both strengths-based and person-centred, allowing us to examine where an individual's strengths are and areas where that individual could use support in building recovery capital.

From a theoretical perspective, this approach to building recovery capital and seeing recovery progress mirrors what the G-CHIME framework suggests in its representation of a series of actions and experiences that one needs to engage in to initiate and sustain recovery (Ogilvie and Carson, 2022); essentially the vehicle of recovery (see Figure 5.1). The G stands for 'growth' or having a growth mindset where individuals adapt to their dynamic situation and learn flexible ways of thinking and behaving, something that has to happen while travelling the road of recovery. The C stands for 'connection' to others in positive and healthy ways, and could be considered the primary fuel of recovery: connection (often) initiates change in all other key areas. The H stands for the 'hope' that an individual has that they will be able to meet their recovery and other life goals. It can also provide an emotional boost to keep going in one's recovery journey when meeting stressors or unexpected challenges. The I stands for 'identity' and refers to the desire to conform and act in ways aligning with the norms, values, and behaviours of being in recovery (for example, sobriety); the acceptance of a recovery identity. The M stands for the 'meaning' in life that can help an individual see the value of living a life of recovery and can be a source of intrinsic motivation for sobriety. The E stands for the 'empowerment'

Figure 5.1: G-CHIME and the vehicle of recovery

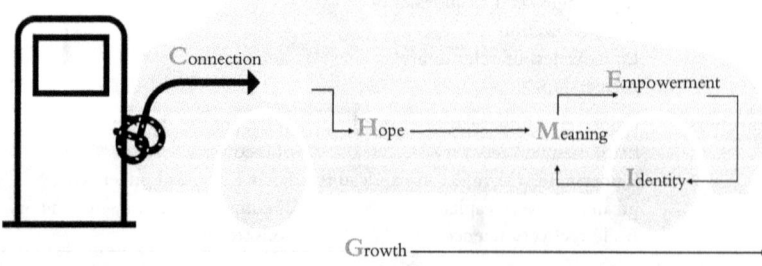

that an individual gains as they progress through recovery. Empowerment, 'individual determination over one's own life and democratic participation in the life of one's community'(Rappaport, 1987, 121), can only be developed by allowing the individual to begin to take ownership of their experience, actions, and outcomes (Rappaport, 1984, 1987; Wallerstein, 2006). In initiating recovery, an individual has taken back control of their life from substances. This has implications for how we define recovery capital and its progress, and who gets to define it.

Involving the individual in the process of assessing their own recovery capital, and barriers to building it, is where the strengths-based and person-centred approach inherent in understanding and developing recovery capital will shine, and where strength-building should be reflected across recovery organizations. This involvement – sharing the results of their recovery capital assessment with the individual, asking them to view the results and consider their next steps in partnership with a recovery navigator, such as a peer, mentor, clinician, or recovery coach – is one that will bring that individual in as a co-owner of their own outcomes and help to build the vital strength of self-efficacy and empowerment, especially if they are able to view changes over time as a result of their own actions. It should also help to build the relationship, or therapeutic alliance, between the individual and their navigator.

Illustrative case of recovery capital for treatment planning and intervention

Let us consider one example case to illustrate how, when assessed and used appropriately, recovery capital can be used as a way to plan and track individual growth and progress over time in collaboration with the individual in recovery.

Case study: Jane

In this case, Jane is appearing for her first day of drug treatment court programming with her probation officer. Jane had a long history of substance use and was engaged in behaviours while using substances that led to her arrest. Jane met the court's criteria for eligibility to be enrolled due to substance use leading to criminal activities which resulted in criminal legal system involvement. If she completes the drug court programme, she will have her charges dismissed. She is currently living with a sibling, was working part-time, but lost the job when she was arrested, and is trying to pay child support so she can see her young son. Jane's sibling is not very supportive of her recovery and is emotionally unhelpful, and Jane also has many friends who just want to see her enjoy life and continue to have fun ('party') with them. Jane is herself ambivalent about stopping substance use, but she recognizes it might be the only way to meet her other goals and get out of such severe consequences – she is terrified of the prospect of going to jail.

If we simply examine Jane's score on recovery capital metrics, as we might in a research context, we would probably see quite low levels of overall recovery capital and high problem severity and/or consequences, especially due to involvement with the criminal legal system. But we already have a sense of those elements given that she is presenting for a drug treatment court programme. An approach from a recovery capital perspective would examine in more nuance through discussion with Jane her sources of *both* recovery capital strengths and assets and barriers to building recovery capital. The conversation would centre around what areas of Jane's life have strengths and resources to build upon – her desire and motivation to have time with her child would be one source of human recovery capital – and where there might be barriers – her social support (or lack of it) might be considered low social recovery capital and a barrier to building social recovery capital. Discussing with Jane to identify in what ways she might find some additional relationships to support her recovery could be one way to initiate a process of change, knowing what her end goals for the programme are. But, with all we know about Jane's existing support system, it may be difficult for her to identify new, positive social groups and relationships and begin to create social network shifts on her own. This is where the role of a recovery navigator is essential, to work with Jane on both helping her to identify sources of new social supports (for example, mutual help groups in her community) and assertively link her with them.

Working with Jane over time we might see improvements in some of these areas, and roadblocks in others. Perhaps she identifies a goal of finding full-time work but does not have the skills needed to do her dream job. Throughout this process, identifying ways to make small and achievable goals as part of her recovery plan will be necessary to help move her forward. Additionally, identifying ways to build out her social network and community, and ways for them to continue to provide support and access to local resources, would help to fill in recovery capital gaps and increase her recovery capital. As she does this, we would likely see improvements in some areas of recovery capital – in personal or human recovery capital – as she gains confidence and more motivation. These wins may also lead to gains in other areas of recovery capital, such as financial recovery capital, as she is able to attain full-time employment and help to build a positive relationship with the recovery navigator. And, the process of assessing her recovery capital and reviewing it over time could be another way to help her gain human recovery capital through celebrating wins, developing insight, and learning how to develop coping skills with challenges, particularly if she is supported by a skilled peer navigator or coach. In this way, we can see how the different domains of recovery capital may develop and progress differently for each individual situation, how strength-building in one domain can have synergistic or ripple effects in other domains, and how critical the role is of co-ownership of the process as well as the role of the recovery navigator who can provide assertive linkage to broader contextual supports.

Challenges with using recovery capital as a metric for treatment planning and intervention

Yet, despite the potential of recovery capital as a metric for treatment planning and intervention, it is important to note that many of the recovery capital measurement tools developed after White and Cloud's (2008) suggestions are research-focused. That is, the majority of the existing measures allow us to understand an individual's recovery capital score on a scale, so we can compare individuals to each other and use this score to examine whether the score is predictive of substance use or some other meaningful outcome. Typically, however, this score does not help us – or the person seeking recovery – to understand what these numbers might mean to them on an everyday, practical basis. More recently, conceptual and technological advances have allowed organizations to implement a recovery capital assessment that also provides immediate and meaningful data to use in an applied setting, for example, to support recovery capital assessment which can feed directly into recovery goal setting: the Recovery Capital Index (RCI; Whitesock et al, 2018) and the REC-CAP (Cano et al, 2017) are two examples. It remains important for those considering recovery capital metrics to remember this point in comparing different recovery capital assessment options.

Recovery capital assessment in research and programme evaluation

Recovery capital is an increasingly used metric in addiction science research and programme evaluations (Hennessy, 2017; Bunaciu et al, 2023). Research that involves recovery capital typically aims to understand how recovery capital helps individuals maintain their recovery and which factors are associated with greater recovery capital. As a multidimensional metric used to effectively assess individuals' current functioning at a point in time, recovery capital can be used both as a predictor or as an outcome in research. Research that uses recovery capital as a predictor often involves using total scores calculated from quantitative measures of recovery capital to predict some other meaningful outcome(s), such as treatment completion, return to substance use, sustained remission, and quality of life, to understand how recovery capital relates to that outcome. In other words, using recovery capital as a predictor of key recovery-related outcomes serves as a proof-of-concept of sorts, whereby researchers can demonstrate the ways in which having recovery supports can influence growth and change across domains important to recovery.

On the other hand, programme evaluations and treatment effectiveness research may be more likely to examine recovery capital as an outcome to understand whether particular programmes (for example, mutual help groups, recovery community centres, recovery housing) effectively improve participants' recovery capital. Although implemented in different forms, the ideal and overarching goal of these types of programmes are to help individuals initiate and maintain their recovery through improving access to resources and reducing barriers. Recovery capital is therefore an ideal metric to assess whether programmes are effectively meeting these goals. This could be done by measuring all programme participants' recovery capital when they join or first interact with the programme, as well as at the end of their programme involvement or at regular follow-up intervals to assess the extent to which someone's recovery capital changed over time following engagement with the programme. In doing so, recovery capital can also be viewed as a process, allowing the organization to examine both individual and programme-level strengths and barriers, including how individuals change across time and programming, and when changes are made to organizational structures and procedures.

By assessing individual programme participants' recovery capital and aggregating that data to draw themes and trends, programmes can collect information about how well certain aspects of their programmes are working (or overall) and if there are system-level barriers to improving recovery capital. In doing so, programmes can then use that feedback to adapt and improve the programme. For example, we can consider a recovery helpline programme, where individuals at any stage of recovery and/or their loved ones can call a helpline to be connected with call-takers who assist in navigating services ('service navigators'). To ensure they are capturing programme outcomes, all individuals in recovery who call in are asked to complete a measure of recovery capital at the point of first contact. Individuals also provide their contact information, so the programme can follow up with them at one and three months post-contact. After collecting baseline and follow-up data on a number of programme participants, the programme analyses the data and sees that most participants show an increase in understanding of the available recovery services in their area and which services require insurance and what type (an important first step). However, the majority of participants have not yet established connections to care, and of those who were able to make an initial appointment, service usage rates as a follow-up step were low.

From these trends, the programme directors can determine that they are helping increase participants' awareness of available services, but they also identify that they are not helping participants address common barriers. As part of the iterative evaluation process, this programme could decide to expand their programming by expanding the role of service navigators to provide a warm hand-off and create those care linkages while callers are on the phone. The programme could continue to collect baseline and follow-up data on how this change impacts individuals' recovery capital. They may find this change yielded a significant improvement, whereby participants are more likely to be connected to care and necessary services; however, they learn that service usage rates are still low. The programme could continue with this iterative process of identifying strengths and challenges and adapting the programme as necessary, as a form of both performance and outcomes management, as well as service development. As a result of this process, the programme may realize they are not helping participants address key barriers to service usage, such as transportation challenges, lack of childcare, and difficulty managing multiple appointments.

The programme then determines that service navigators are helpful, but certain participants may benefit from case managers who can help them problem-solve ways to address their unique constellation of barriers. To hire case managers, however, the programme would need additional funding, and collaboration with partner agencies to help address the identified barriers, like transportation services. The programme director can then apply for additional funding and/or approach partner agencies, using the data collected from the programme evaluation to make the case that their programme is effective at improving participants' recovery capital, but additional funding and collaboration could result in an even larger improvement (for a detailed example of this occurring in recovery residences, see Chapter 10 by Yearwood and colleagues). In sum, programme evaluations can be used to develop and test evidence-based strategies for improving recovery capital, which extant research has shown is associated with key recovery-related outcomes (Laudet and White, 2008; Kelly and Hoeppner, 2015; Best et al, 2017).

Challenges with using recovery capital as a metric for research and programme evaluation

Despite parallel lines of research suggesting that recovery capital may be an intervening variable, recovery capital is rarely examined as a mediator in research studies. This may be due to several factors, including ongoing debate about whether recovery capital constitutes a measure of progress or an outcome (see the 'Recovery capital as progress or outcome' section later in this chapter) and the challenges with collecting longitudinal data that follows individuals from a treatment episode into the community and over the long term. Additionally, unlike other concepts in addiction and recovery, which may have a standardized measure and scoring system, recovery capital metrics do not, aside from several basic assumptions: they assume that higher recovery capital is better than lower and that over time, an individual should be building and growing their recovery capital to see increased scores. There is not yet a standardized way of interpreting these recovery capital scores. That is, aside from assessing whether an individual's score has improved, there is no particular standard of recovery capital as an outcome to which all individuals should be working. From a person-centred approach, success will vary by the values of individual people and cultures and as a result of intersectional identities.

Some individuals (or organizations) might conceptualize recovery capital as the intended outcome, which is achieved through the completion of a given programme or intervention. From a programming perspective, there may be less motivation to consider it beyond that scope to understand how recovery capital is predictive of other outcomes. Furthermore, other outcomes, like sustained remission, may necessitate a longer participant follow-up, which can be complex, costly, and labour-intensive. Despite these challenges, it remains important to empirically measure recovery capital so that we can better appreciate the ways that recovery programmes and interventions help people grow and accumulate resources, and then how that recovery capital relates and translates to other key recovery-related outcomes over time.

Important considerations for any stakeholder when using recovery capital metrics

As noted earlier, different stakeholders will need to use different recovery capital metrics depending on their intended purpose and application. However, there are additional important considerations that stakeholders should keep in mind, regardless of their purpose and application.

Recovery capital approaches may not capture barriers, especially structural barriers

A recovery capital framework considers an individual's strengths and resources within their particular context. Yet, barriers and risks can impede an individual's accrual of recovery capital, which is sometimes also referred to as forms of negative recovery capital or recovery-related discrimination (Vilsaint et al, 2020; for further discussion of 'negative recovery capital', see Bowen and Hennessy, Chapter 6); these areas are, however, not naturally considered as part of recovery capital assessments. This raises the question of whether recovery capital should be measured in tandem with barriers and risks to get a fuller picture of individuals in recovery. A strengths-based approach does not mean ignoring risks and barriers. Rather, strengths should be celebrated and identified as areas to build or continue reinforcing and used as foundational building blocks to help address where risks and barriers are present. Indeed, some more recent tools have started to do this (for example, SABRS and REC-CAP, covered in Chapter 4).

In addition, a recovery capital framework often focuses on factors most easily identified and measured at the individual and social level – for example, one's own motivation and commitment and perceived emotional and instrumental supports for recovery. Yet, there are many barriers that may get in the way of building recovery capital or moderate the effects of recovery capital on recovery. Recovery trajectories are the result of synergistic effects between a variety of influences. Structural barriers, which stem from laws, policies, and institutional practices, and are mutually reinforced across systems (healthcare, social welfare, criminal legal, employment), are formidable determinants of recovery. Structural barriers are largely recognized as the drivers of health inequities despite the bulk of health science focusing on individual behaviour change (Alegría et al, 2019), which has resulted in inconsistent improvement over time.

The course of substance use disorder treatment and recovery is marked by glaring health disparities. Black and Hispanic people are half as likely to remit compared to their White counterparts (Bommersbach et al, 2022) and fatal opioid drug poisonings among Black Americans surpassed that of White Americans for the first time in recent US history (Friedman and Hansen, 2022). These racial health disparities are largely explained by disproportionate exposure to structural barriers in the criminal legal system, where 77 per cent of people incarcerated in federal prisons for drug offenses are Black or Latino, yet these groups comprise only 30 per cent of the US population (Carson, 2014). Additionally, unequal receipt of harm reduction services and access, use, and continuity of treatment services (Gibbons et al, 2023) also explain racial health disparities. The National Recovery Study found that individuals who are exposed to recovery-related discrimination, in terms of individual sleights (micro level) or violation of personal rights (macro), have less recovery capital, lower quality of life, and more psychological distress (Vilsaint et al, 2020). Consistent with theory and research on how health disparities are created, it was the macro (not micro) discriminations that Black Americans were disproportionately exposed to in terms of losing their job, being denied housing, not getting a new job, or not getting a promotion because someone knew about their resolved history with problematic substance use (Vilsaint et al, 2021). Notably, barriers in the employment system are where racial health inequities in recovery continue to play out (Eddie et al, 2020) and Black people are no more likely to be employed than someone with multiple arrests. This suggests that recovery-ready workplaces may be an important mechanism for building recovery capital and creating racial health equity in recovery.

In sum, although recovery capital metrics do not often include risks and barriers, and have failed to capture structural-level factors impacting recovery, this is an area requiring major attention when attempting to use recovery capital to understand one's recovery trajectory.

Recovery capital metrics are more than the sum total of their parts

Recovery capital metrics should be considered as more than the sum total of their parts, as it is possible that individuals may show growth in some domains but not others. That is, in assessments that allow for an overall average recovery capital 'score' with all items equally weighted, an individual could have an unchanged overall score due to increases in one recovery capital domain but declines in another; simple interpretation and use of the overall score, then, may not be helpful on its own for ongoing recovery care planning. Alternatively, they could have sources of social support from family but social barriers from friends, differences that, from a scoring perspective, could 'cancel' each other out (for example, see Meisel and colleagues for a review of the issue related to the social recovery capital domain [Meisel et al, 2023]). And, as discussed previously, it may not be feasible for individuals to overcome certain barriers (for example, stigma, marginalization, structural barriers). Although many treatment programmes and recovery-oriented support services aim to increase recovery capital across all domains, prior research has shown that people post-treatment may exhibit heterogeneous patterns of functioning (Witkiewitz et al, 2019, 2020). Given that pathways to recovery often emphasize surrounding oneself with others in recovery, and that individuals often exhibit high stress levels and low functioning during the early stages of self-reported recovery (Dennis et al, 2007; Kelly et al, 2018), it might be expected that people who are earlier in their recovery would have higher social than personal capital. This highlights the multidimensional and multidirectional aspects of recovery capital, all of which should be considered by researchers, treatment and service providers, policy makers, and others within the recovery-oriented system of care (see Figure 5.2).

To that end, stakeholders who use recovery capital metrics should consider total recovery capital and specific recovery capital domains in tandem. For those that use quantitative metrics, this might suggest the need to use domain sub-scores, rather than total recovery capital scores, when conducting research or programme evaluations. For treatment and service providers, examining functioning within each of the domains might help with the identification of barriers and aid in the customization of treatment plans. For individuals in recovery themselves, thinking about strengths and needs across each of these domains may be helpful in illuminating areas of achieved and potential growth in their recovery journeys.

Looking within each domain may also provide a sense of 'small wins' that can facilitate a sense of hope and accomplishment for individuals in recovery. Extant research suggests a momentum-building phenomenon in which

Figure 5.2: Visualization of the potential within-person heterogeneity in recovery capital

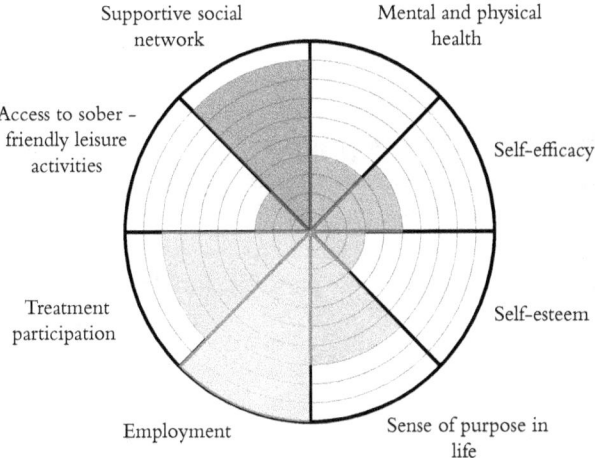

increases in recovery capital in one domain contribute to increases in other domains (Hennessy, 2017), so focusing on growth within specific domains that might be easier to achieve and/or have fewer barriers to overcome might be more fruitful than trying to increase capital across all domains simultaneously. For individuals and those supporting them, this is where having a recovery capital assessment that allows for immediate feedback and supports recovery care planning is crucial.

Recovery capital is dynamic

Another important consideration is that recovery capital is dynamic, such that we would expect it to look very different over time and at different stages of recovery. According to a study by Kelly and colleagues (2018), individuals who resolved a problem with alcohol or other drugs accrued recovery capital at a rapid pace in the first five years since problem resolution, and while this growth continues into long-term, stable recovery, the pace of recovery capital change was more gradual. This rapid growth during the early stages of recovery may be due in part to the synergistic effect of recovery capital accrual, whereby gains in one domain contribute to gains in other domains.

Moreover, recovery capital accrual tends to interact with other dynamic socioecological factors, including barriers (negative recovery capital), which vary over time. For example, someone might have a strong support system, healthy coping skills, and financial stability, contributing to high levels of recovery capital. One day, that person might be laid off from their job (a major life challenge) and have to work multiple part-time jobs to make ends meet, which could take away from time spent with prosocial peers and engaging in healthy, stress-relieving activities. In this way, their recovery capital might dramatically change in response to their current context, potentially placing them at risk of returning to substance use. Thus, understanding that recovery capital is dynamic and responsive to socioecological factors is paramount. To that end, recovery capital should be regularly assessed alongside other metrics that can better capture individuals' socioecological context and barriers. By understanding the ways that recovery capital varies longitudinally, stakeholders can better identify normative trajectories of growth, understand the individualized process of recovery capital accrual in its current context, and create more person-centred treatment, interventions, and programming that is tailored to individuals' ever-changing needs throughout their recovery journeys.

Challenges and lessons learned in the development of recovery capital metrics

In the development and application of recovery capital metrics, scholars have faced several conceptual challenges. The three we will focus on include the following: (1) the shifting definition of recovery over time, including the question of whether it should be considered a process or an outcome; (2) equity issues around who gets to define what constitutes capital and how meaningful change should be considered and captured; (3) the issue of whether there is a prototypical course of recovery capital change and development.

Shifting definition of recovery

One major challenge to the development of recovery capital metrics is that, over time, the way recovery is defined has been changed and refined. Recovery is the basis for recovery capital – without a standardized definition of recovery, it will be difficult for the field to accurately and systematically conceptualize what resources that support recovery would be and how to measure them (Best and Hennessy, 2021). A variety of leading addiction treatment and recovery organizations have proposed their own definitions of recovery. For example, the Betty Ford Institute defined recovery as 'a voluntarily maintained lifestyle characterized by sobriety, personal health and citizenship' (The Betty Ford Institute Consensus Panel, 2007), the Substance Abuse and Mental Health Services Administration defined recovery as 'a process of change through which individuals improve their health and wellness, live a self-directed life, and strive to reach their full potential' (SAMHSA, 2012), the Recovery Research Institute defined it as 'a dynamic process characterized by increasingly stable remission resulting in and supported by increased recovery capital and enhanced quality of life' (Kelly and Hoeppner, 2015), and the Recovery Science Research Collaborative defined it as 'an individualized, intentional, dynamic, and relational process involving sustained efforts to improve wellness' (Ashford et al, 2019). More recently, the US National Institute on Alcohol and Alcohol Use (Hagman et al, 2022) provided recovery definitions that allow researchers to measure it as both a process and an outcome, albeit with different criteria: 'A *process* through which an individual pursues both remission from AUD and cessation from heavy drinking. Recovery can also be considered an *outcome* such that an individual may be considered 'recovered' if both remission from AUD and cessation from heavy drinking are achieved and maintained over time' (pp 809–10). The definition also expanded to include suggestions of indicators that recovery is happening: 'recovery is often marked by the fulfilment of basic needs, enhancements in social support and spirituality, and improvements in physical and mental health, quality of life, and other dimensions of well-being.' This definition suggested that some attention to reducing alcohol use is part of recovery but recovery itself is considered something broader than that (Hagman et al, 2022).

These definitions have been driven by key stakeholders and encompass recovery as both a process and an outcome, and something that represents change beyond substance use. The definitions do not emphasize one type of outcome over another, suggesting that any (or all) of their key elements could indicate recovery (see Table 5.2). As may be clear from reviewing the definitions across each organization, there is substantial overlap and differing interpretations of how recovery can be measured. Even some of the distinct factors – for example, citizenship – could be operationalized in different ways in different contexts. Additionally, aside from the definition provided by the National Institute on Alcohol and Alcohol Use, other recovery definitions do not delineate whether or in what ways recovery would differ by the primary substance of use. For example, they do not address the current debate in abstinence-focused recovery spaces around how individuals using medication to support their recovery (for example, using prescribed methadone to support opioid use disorder recovery), might demonstrate successful recovery. This suggests that any improvements in the factors/areas mentioned, regardless of the substance and ways of resolving the problem, might be viewed as successful recovery. Thus, although the recovery capital model is well-positioned to consider this broad array of outcomes, it also presents a challenge for systematically assessing recovery capital growth and change, and how change can be flagged as meaningful growth or if it has stalled.

Recovery capital as progress or outcome

Similar to the old adage that progress is often two steps forward and one step back, recovery capital is not always linear. We expect to see variation

Table 5.2: Recovery definitions and implications for recovery capital as a model of growth and change

Group	Definition key words	Implications
Betty Ford	Voluntarily maintained lifestyle Sobriety Personal health Citizenship	• Maintenance suggests that time needs to elapse with continuous positive recovery outcomes • Choice/building personal power (empowerment) is important to recovery • Measures need to capture substance use so 'sobriety' can be determined • Personal health could include physical and mental health • Citizenship could be assessed in many ways. There is a need to operationalize 'citizen' of what kind of 'community' in these assessments.
SAMHSA	Process of change Improve their health and wellness Live a self-directed life Strive to reach their full potential	• Process and change could represent indefinite end points • Changes to health and wellness; indicators of wellness need to be operationalized • Empowerment • Education/training/work/employment
Recovery Research Institute	Dynamic process Increasingly stable remission Resulting in/supported by increased recovery capital and enhanced quality of life	• A process that cannot be static • 'Stable' suggests some degree of maintenance over time of outcomes • Recovery capital shows improvement (does not specify which areas of recovery capital)
RSRC	Individualized, intentional, dynamic, and relational process Sustained efforts to improve wellness	• An indefinite end point involving change across individual and interindividual levels • Focus/work on personal wellness; indicators of wellness need to be operationalized • Engaging and sustaining efforts seems to imply some aspect of engaging motivation
NIAAA	Process (but can be an outcome if remission/cessation is achieved and maintained) Remission from AUD Cessation from heavy drinking Fulfilment of basic needs Enhancements in social support and spirituality Improvements in physical and mental health, quality of life, and other dimensions of well-being	• Change – potential to have end point with AUD status • Day-to-day needs are met • Improvements in many domains (unclear weight/importance of these): social support, spirituality, physical and mental health, quality of life, other types of well-being (needs to be operationalized) • Perhaps also that 'remission' and 'cessation' imply changes in patterns of use and consequences

in one's recovery capital growth and progression, which may be the result of individual factors (for example, gender, age), interpersonal factors (for example, family system dynamics, social connectedness), or community factors (for example, stigma, self-help groups). When assessed over time using established metrics, treatment and service providers can then respond to this natural variation by adapting services to better meet the unique needs of individuals.

Recovery capital and recovery are linearly and reciprocally related, such that greater recovery capital is associated with a longer time in recovery and vice versa (Kelly and Hoeppner, 2015). Given the bidirectional relationship, recovery capital can be conceptualized as both a measure of progress and an outcome. For example, treatment or programme providers might use recovery capital as a benchmark by which they assess whether individuals receiving services are progressing in their recovery. On the other hand, the ultimate goal of treatment or recovery programmes may be to help individuals increase their recovery capital. While we acknowledge that recovery capital may be framed as either (or both), depending on the stakeholder and their purpose for measuring capital, we make the argument here that recovery capital is best understood and conceptualized as a metric of progress and growth, which has far-reaching implications for an individual's abstinence, remission from problems, and psychosocial functioning in recovery.

Thus, framing recovery capital as a measure of progress assumes its accrual is an ongoing, interactive, and experiential process that can continue indefinitely. This is borne out in the lived experience of individuals in long-term recovery and peer workers who can continue to grow and cocreate capital when engaging with and giving back to their recovery communities. Conversely, framing recovery capital as an outcome perpetuates the idea that recovery capital is time-limited and bounded by upper parameters, like a goal that can be accomplished and moved on from. The way that we conceptualize recovery capital is important because it shapes the way we define recovery, the ways in which stakeholders engage with individuals in recovery, and how individuals in recovery make meaning out of their experiences. Understanding recovery capital as a measure of growth and progress gives the empowering message that life in recovery can and will continue to get better over time.

Who defines 'capital' and meaningful change

In addition to the shifting definition of recovery, when we consider what capital is – the sum of all resources an individual has to use towards their recovery journey – we also have to consider who gets to decide what constitutes recovery capital and what meaningful change in this construct looks like. As empowerment is a key aspect of recovery, according to consensus across several recovery definitions and theoretical frameworks (for example, G-CHIME [Ogilvie and Carson, 2022]), this decision must be driven by key stakeholders, including those in recovery themselves. The challenge is that the choice of defining and measuring recovery, and therefore recovery capital, happens by the group or organization measuring it, and from what they perceive is important for an individual to change. These beliefs can be driven by the desire to see an individual improve but may also involve a variety of norms and assumptions from one's own place in life or driven by those funding the organization's efforts. Even the relative weight to place on certain domains, factors within those domains, and certain outcomes over others, may shift depending on the particular individual and their context (Jahan et al, 2023).

A prototypical course of recovery capital change

Although recovery capital is individualized and dynamic, one area of interest for researchers and scholars alike is whether there is a prototypical course by which an individual's recovery capital changes and develops. For instance, social and community capital may be a mechanism by which people in recovery can accrue personal capital (Collinson and Best, 2019). In other words, forms of personal capital such as self-efficacy and mental and physical well-being may be accrued primarily through engaging in prosocial activities and building up one's social network (Longabaugh et al, 2010; Best et al, 2012; Mawson et al, 2015; Collinson and Best, 2019). Social support can buffer against negative effects of stressors (Cohen and Wills, 1985; Ditzen and Heinrichs, 2014), which is critical during early recovery. Moreover, social support can facilitate social learning whereby individuals in recovery can begin to adopt a recovery identity (Dingle et al, 2015; Collinson and Hall, 2021). In contrast, those with recovery-hostile peer networks may be precluded from or face severe barriers to accruing personal capital. Thus, as we saw with Jane, our case example, we might expect that focusing on building social and community capital might be a catalyst for individual change and development, particularly the accrual of personal capital. In first focusing on these resources that build social and community capital, key stakeholders can set people on the path to success and building their personal capital.

Summary of future areas use of recovery capital for assessing growth and change

In summary, recovery capital is being widely used as a construct to understand and support growth and change in one's recovery journey, to understand how a programme or organization is supporting individuals in the recovery process, and to identify successful pathways to recovery. There remains the question of whether there is a prototypical pathway of recovery capital growth and a need to establish a standardized approach to using recovery capital measures to assess change over time, within and across recovery domains, and within structural barriers and oppression. This must happen despite a somewhat shifting understanding of recovery over time, which naturally influences how recovery capital should be assessed and used. Further research is needed to better understand recovery capital across all ecological levels and how each of these levels may interact and influence each other. For example, existing recovery capital metrics (and theories more broadly) have not been expanded to examine how families, communities, or even recovery programmes accrue resources to help them. Families must learn to navigate treatment systems and adapt to new family dynamics alongside the person in recovery, all of which can be stressful and time-consuming. Thus, families that have more sources of support upon which they can lean may fare better. Similarly, communities must react and adapt to its members in recovery. Communities and programmes with more capital may be more agile and able to adjust to the needs of its members, like providing recovery-friendly spaces and implementing recovery-oriented policies. Moreover, we would expect that individuals, families, and communities may coproduce recovery capital through ongoing and regular engagement (Edwards et al, 2018), a measurement challenge that has yet to be addressed.

Recovery is an individualized and personal process, occurring within and interacting with the context of complex social systems. Thus, the tension lies in creating a standardized approach that does not negate the individual's own role and understanding of recovery and takes into account health disparities at the broader system level.

References

Alegría, M., Araneta, M.R., and Rivers, B. (2019) 'The National Advisory Council on Minority Health and Health Disparities reflection', *American Journal of Public Health*, 109(S14–S15), DOI: https://doi.org/10.2105/AJPH.2019.304961.

American Society of Addiction Medicine (2023) 'ASAM Supplemental Resources', in *ASAM Criteria 4th Edition*, Center City, MN: Hazelden.

Ashford, R.D., Brown, A., Brown, T., Callis, J., Cleveland, H.H., Eisenhart, E., et al (2019) 'Defining and operationalizing the phenomena of recovery: A working definition from the recovery science research collaborative', *Addiction Research & Theory*, 27(3): 179–88.

Best, D. and Hennessy, E.A. (2022) 'The science of recovery capital: Where do we go from here?', *Addiction* 117(4): 1139–45.

Best, D., Irving, J., Collinson, B., Andersson, C., and Edwards, M. (2017) 'Recovery networks and community connections: Identifying connection needs and community linkage opportunities in early recovery populations', *Alcoholism Treatment Quarterly*, 35(1): 2–15.

Best, D., Honor, S., Karpusheff, J., Loudon, L., Hall, R., Groshkova, T., and White, W. (2012) 'Well-being and recovery functioning among substance users engaged in posttreatment recovery support groups', *Alcoholism Treatment Quarterly*, 30(4): 397–406.

Bommersbach, T.J., Jegede, O., Stefanovics, E.A., Rhee, T.G., and Rosenheck, R.A. (2022) 'Diagnostic remission of substance use disorders: Racial differences and correlates of remission in a nationally representative sample', *Journal of Substance Abuse Treatment*, 136: 108659.

Bunaciu, A., Bliuc, A.M., Best, D., Hennessy, E.A., Belanger, M.J., and Benwell, C.S. (2023) 'Measuring recovery capital for people recovering from alcohol and drug addiction: A systematic review', *Addiction Research & Theory*, 32(3): 225–36.

Cano, I., Best, D., Edwards, M., and Lehman, J. (2017) 'Recovery capital pathways: Modelling the components of recovery wellbeing', *Drug and Alcohol Dependence*, 181: 11–19.

Carson, E.A. (2014). 'Prisoners in 2013', NCJ 247282, U.S. Department of Justice.

Cohen, S. and Wills, T.A. (1985) 'Stress, social support, and the buffering hypothesis', *Psychological Bulletin*, 98(2): 310–57.

Collinson, B. and Best, D. (2019) 'Promoting recovery from substance misuse through engagement with community assets: Asset based community engagement', *Substance Abuse: Research and Treatment*, 13, DOI: 10.1177/1178221819876575.

Collinson, B. and Hall, L. (2021) 'The role of social mechanisms of change in women's addiction recovery trajectories', *Drugs: Education, Prevention and Policy*, 28(5): 426–36.

Dennis, M.L., Foss, M.A., and Scott, C.K. (2007) 'An eight-year perspective on the relationship between the duration of abstinence and other aspects of recovery', *Evaluation Review*, 31(6): 585–612.

Dingle, G.A., Cruwys, T., and Frings, D. (2015), 'Social Identities as Pathways into and out of Addiction', *Frontiers in Psychology*, 6, DOI: https://doi.org/10.3389/fpsyg.2015.01795.

Ditzen, B. and Heinrichs, M. (2014) 'Psychobiology of social support: The social dimension of stress buffering', *Restorative Neurology and Neuroscience*, 32(1): 149–62.

Eddie, D., Vilsaint, C.L., Hoffman, L.A., Bergman, B.G., Kelly, J.F., and Hoeppner, B.B. (2020) 'From working on recovery to working in recovery: Employment status among a nationally representative U.S. sample of individuals who have resolved a significant alcohol or other drug problem', *Journal of Substance Use and Addiction Treatment*, 113, 108000, DOI: https://doi.org/10.1016/j.jsat.2020.108000.

Edwards, M., Soutar, J., and Best, D. (2018) 'Co-producing and reconnecting: A pilot study of recovery community engagement', *Drugs and Alcohol Today*, 18(1): 39–50.

Friedman, J.R. and Hansen, H. (2022) 'Evaluation of increases in drug overdose mortality rates in the US by race and ethnicity before and during the COVID-19 pandemic', *JAMA Psychiatry*, 79(4): 379–81.

Gibbons, J.B., Harris, S.J., Solomon, K.T., Sugarman, O., Hardy, C., and Saloner, B. (2023) 'Increasing overdose deaths among Black Americans: A review of the literature', *Lancet Psychiatry*, 10(9): 719–26.

Granfield, R. and Cloud, W. (1999) *Coming Clean: Overcoming Addiction without Treatment*, New York: New York University Press.

Hagman, B.T., Falk, D., Litten, R., and Koob, G.F. (2022) 'Defining recovery from alcohol use disorder: Development of an NIAAA research definition', *The American Journal of Psychiatry*, 179(11): 807–13.

Hennessy, E.A. (2017) 'Recovery capital: A systematic review of the literature', *Addiction Research & Theory*, 25(5): 349–60.

Jahan, N., Gade, N., Zhen-Duan, J., Fukuda, M., Estrada, R., and Alegría, M. (2023) 'Investigating the role of interpersonal relationships on low-income SUD patients' recovery: A qualitative analysis of various stakeholders in New York state', *Addiction Research & Theory*, 32(4): 291–8.

Kelly, J.F. and Hoeppner, B. (2015) 'A biaxial formulation of the recovery construct', *Addiction Research & Theory*, 23(1): 5–9.

Kelly, J.F., Greene, M.C., and Bergman, B.G. (2018) 'Beyond abstinence: Changes in indices of quality of life with time in recovery in a nationally representative sample of US adults', *Alcohol, Clinical & Experimental Research*, 42(4): 770–80.

Laudet, A. and White, W. (2008) 'Recovery capital as prospective predictor of sustained recovery, life satisfaction, and stress among former poly-substance users', *Substance Use & Misuse* 43(10): 27–54.

Longabaugh, R., Wirtz, P.W., Zywiak, W.H., and O'Malley, S.S. (2010) 'Network Support as a Prognostic Indicator of Drinking Outcomes: The COMBINE Study', *Journal of Studies on Alcohol and Drugs*, 71(6): 837–46.

Mawson, E., Best, D., Beckwith, M., Dingle, G.A., and Lubman, D.I. (2015) 'Social identity, social networks and recovery capital in emerging adulthood: A pilot study', *Substance Abuse Treatment, Prevention, and Policy*, 10, 45, DOI: https://doi.org/10.1186/s13011-015-0041-2.

Meisel, S.N., Hennessy, E.A., Jurinsky, J., and Kelly, J.F. (2023) 'Improving social recovery capital research to enhance clinical utility: A proposed agenda', *Addiction Research & Theory*, 32(3): 153–9.

Ogilvie, L. and Carson, J. (2022) 'Positive addiction recovery therapy: A pilot study', *Advances in Dual Diagnosis*, 15(4): 196–207.

Rappaport, J. (1984) 'Studies in empowerment', *Prevention in Human Services*, 3(2–3): 1–7.

Rappaport, J. (1987) 'Terms of empowerment/exemplars of prevention: Toward a theory for community psychology', *American Journal of Community Psychology*, 15(2): 121–48.

Substance Abuse and Mental Health Services Administration (SAMHSA) (2012) *SAMHSA Working Definition of Recovery: 10 Guiding Principles of Recovery*, Rockville, MD: Department of Health and Human Services.

The Betty Ford Institute Consensus Panel (2007) 'What is recovery? A working definition from the Betty Ford Institute', *Journal of Substance Use and Addiction Treatment*, 33(3): 221–8.

Vilsaint, C.L., Hoffman, L.A., and Kelly, J.F. (2020) 'Perceived discrimination in addiction recovery: Assessing the prevalence, nature, and correlates using a novel measure in a US National sample', *Drug and Alcohol Dependence*, 206: 107667.

Vilsaint, C.L., Homan, L.A., and Kelly, J.F. (2021) 'Racial-ethnic disparities in recovery-related discrimination: A population based study of adults in recovery from alcohol use', *Alcoholism: Clinical and Experimental Research*, 1(4): 1–12.

Wallerstein, N. (2006) *What is the Evidence on Effectiveness of Empowerment to Improve Health? (Health Evidence Network)*, Copenhagen: WHO Regional Office for Europe.

White, W. and Cloud, W. (2008) 'Recovery capital: A primer for addictions professionals', *Counselor*, 9(5): 22–7.

Whitesock, D., Zhao, J., Goettsch, K., and Hanson, J. (2018) 'Validating a survey for addiction wellness: The recovery capital index', *Journal of the South Dakota State Medical Association*, 71(5): 202–12.

Witkiewitz, K., Pearson, M.R., Wilson, A.D., Stein, E.R., Votaw, V.R., Hallgren, K.A., et al (2020) 'Can alcohol use disorder recovery include some heavy drinking? A replication and extension up to 9 years following treatment', *Alcohol: Clinical & Experimental Research*, 44(9): 1862–74.

Witkiewitz, K., Wilson, A.D., Pearson, M.R., Montes, K.S., Kirouac, M., Roos, C.R., et al (2019) 'Profiles of recovery from alcohol use disorder at three years following treatment: Can the definition of recovery be extended to include high functioning heavy drinkers?', *Addiction*, 114(1): 69–80.

6

Conceptualizing Recovery Capital: Domains and Critical Perspectives

Elizabeth Bowen and Emily A. Hennessy

Introduction

Like many scientific concepts, as the concept of recovery capital has gained popularity in both research and practice over the years, it has also generated critical questions. While there is growing recognition of the salience and value of recovery capital as a general concept to guide recovery research and practice, questions remain regarding the unique domains of recovery capital, its utility with specific populations, and the valence of the concept as solely positive and strengths-based, versus reflecting both assets and barriers to recovery (Best and Hennessy, 2022; Patton et al, 2022). In this chapter, we review the major conceptualizations of recovery capital, including how its various domains have been described and operationalized. We then address critical inquiries about the relative importance of different domains of recovery capital, the issue of negative recovery capital, and considerations regarding population-specific recovery capital and the importance of applying an intersectional lens. In addressing these issues, we point to important directions for future research and practice to advance understanding of recovery capital and ultimately improve recovery outcomes for the many diverse groups of people impacted by substance use disorders.

Major conceptualizations of recovery capital

Recovery capital has been conceptualized as a strengths-based construct that has several interrelated and ecologically nested domains. The domains are nested in a manner consistent with Bronfenbrenner's Ecological Systems

Theory (Bronfenbrenner, 1977), which considers individuals within their immediate and more distal environments. Since Cloud and Granfield's (Cloud and Granfield, 2008; Granfield and Cloud, 1999, 2001) original research introducing the concept of recovery capital, researchers have conceptualized the recovery capital model as having three (for example, White and Cloud, 2008; Best and Laudet, 2010) to five domains (for example, Neale et al, 2014) that span individual, interpersonal, and community levels.

As illustrated in Figure 6.1, these domains have been recognized as: physical/ financial, human, personal (combination of human recovery capital and financial recovery capital), health, growth, social (also termed family/social), cultural, and community recovery capital (Hennessy, 2017). Physical/financial capital includes tangible resources such as financial stability, housing, transportation, and access to evidence-based treatment and continuing care supports. Human capital includes primarily intangible and internal resources such as motivation, self-efficacy, physical health, and cognitive skills, while health capital emphasizes physical health as a distinct domain (Neale et al, 2014). Growth capital is the momentum built in a recovery process that contributes to further building of recovery capital (Hewitt, 2007). Although conceptualized as its own domain, its properties are largely related to human recovery capital. Social capital includes sober and supportive peers, friends, and family as well as social processes related to those interactions (for example, social influence and social identity: Best et al, 2016; Kay and Monaghan, 2019). Cultural recovery capital includes the norms, values, and predispositions of others in proximity to the individual, while community capital references accessible resources in the community. Although cultural recovery capital has often been encompassed within the broader domain of community capital as intangible factors such as community attitudes toward people with substance use disorders and recovery and attitudes around substance use more generally (Cloud and Granfield, 2008; White and Cloud, 2008), the way it is enacted and studied is often within interpersonal relationships, at the level of social recovery capital.

Some scholars have included the idea of negative recovery capital in their conceptualizations of the construct. Negative recovery capital reflects any factor that undermines one's efforts to actively pursue recovery within any of the recovery capital domains, including a lack of resources in these areas (Cloud and Granfield, 2008). Negative recovery capital has been operationalized in different ways. Some scholars have considered it a distinct broad construct, representing direct barriers or risks to the recovery process (Hennessy et al, 2018), while others have conceptualized negative recovery capital along a continuum with positive recovery capital (Cloud and Granfield, 2008); see Figure 6.2. In this second definition, negative recovery capital could appear as barriers within each specific recovery capital

Figure 6.1: Recovery capital domains across ecological levels. Domains in the middle square boxes (personal, social, and community) indicate domains comprising the three-domain recovery capital model. The three domains in the ovals (human, financial/physical, and cultural) indicate domains that have been conceptualized on their own, but also included as components of other domains. The two remaining domains in ovals (growth and health) indicate domains generated through qualitative research that have not been incorporated into new recovery capital models.

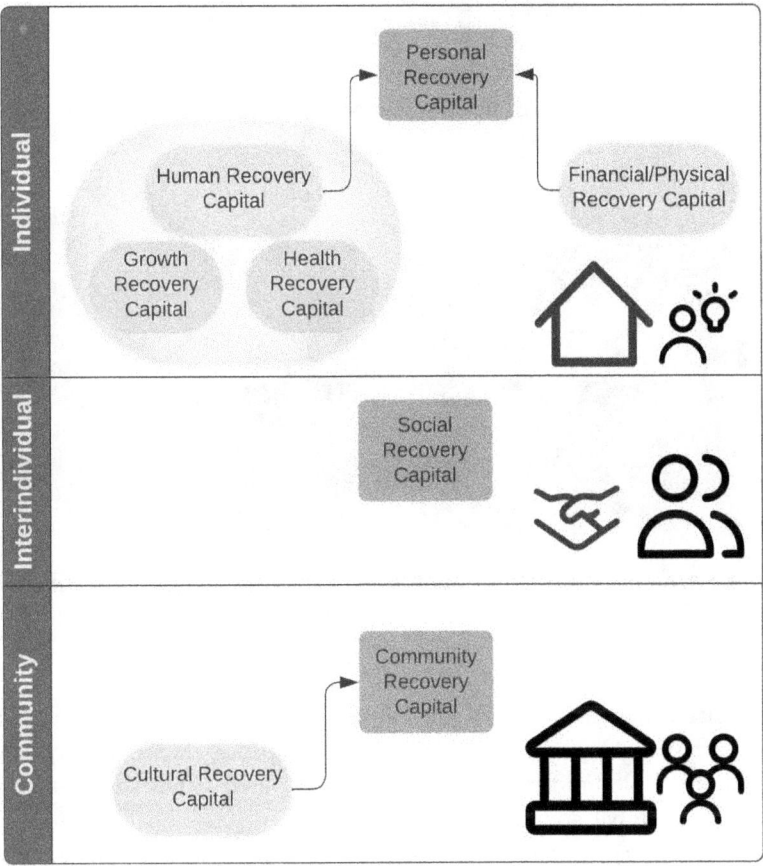

domain. We discuss debates and questions regarding negative recovery capital in a later section.

Although various configurations of the different recovery capital domains are possible, three major recovery capital models have been used consistently in research and practice to date. Granfield and Cloud's initial recovery capital model had three domains: social, human, and physical recovery capital (Granfield and Cloud, 2001, 1999). They later expanded the model to include cultural recovery capital (Cloud and Granfield, 2008). This model also

Figure 6.2: Different ways to conceptualize positive and negative dimensions of recovery capital

The Continuum of Recovery Capital: Negative to Positive Recovery Capital. Example from social recovery capital.

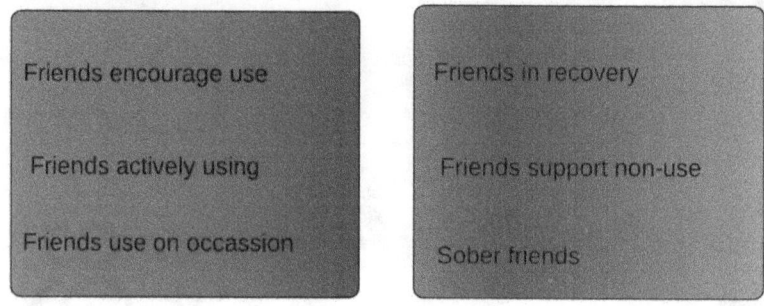

Barriers to Recovery Capital (Left) and Recovery Capital (Right).
Example from social recovery capital.

conceptualized recovery capital along a continuum rather than on a summative scale, with both positive and negative recovery capital included. Finally, White and Cloud (2008) and Best and Laudet (2010) used a three-domain model specifying personal, social, and community recovery capital. The category of personal recovery capital includes both physical/financial and human capital, while social capital is essentially the same as in previous models. The domain of community recovery capital references culturally appropriate, community-based recovery supports, aligned with Cloud and Granfield's (2008) cultural capital component. Notably, the conceptualization of community and cultural capital has evolved from static notions of cultural or community-level factors that facilitate or create barriers to recovery, to a more dynamic sense of the community as a modifiable target for intervention that can support recovery through inclusion and social cohesion (Best and Colman, 2019).

The use of multiple conceptual models of recovery capital has at times generated confusion for researchers and practitioners in the recovery field.

On the one hand, the first four-domain model with social, physical, human, and cultural recovery capital (Granfield and Cloud, 1999; Cloud and Granfield, 2008) and the later three-domain model with personal, social, and community recovery capital (White and Cloud, 2008; Best and Laudet, 2010) essentially have the same domains and cover the same conceptual ground. On the other hand, each model offers some distinct advantages.

The three-domain model reorganizes domains and their indicators more distinctly into ecological levels (individual, interpersonal, and community). In this model, the attention to the community overall that embeds cultural elements is an important one, because it is not just cultural aspects that influence recovery capital but also the broader community structures. This brings attention to the recovery infrastructure and emphasizes the responsibility of institutions, policy makers, and funders to create more robust public health systems to support recovery and overall health and thriving (Best and Colman, 2019). The four-domain model also offers unique value in terms of separating physical/financial and human capital, disentangling tangible personal resources (for example, housing, income, transportation) from less tangible ones (for example, education, attitudes, and spirituality). For individuals in challenging financial situations or highly dependent on others for tangible support (for example, youth), it provides an emphasis on what strengths they can bring to the situation irrespective of their material resources. In sum, while researchers have varied in their conceptualizations of recovery capital, including the number of domains and the labels used for them, the core notion of recovery capital as encapsulating a person's recovery resources at individual, interpersonal, and environmental levels remain consistent.

Critical perspectives on conceptualizing recovery capital

Although both conceptual and empirical work on recovery capital has advanced considerably over the past few decades, several critical questions remain regarding the conceptualization of recovery capital. In this section, we discuss questions regarding the relative importance of differing domains of recovery capital and questions about the conceptualization of negative capital. We then delve into the topic of population-specific recovery capital, highlighting important issues for ongoing research and theory-building on recovery capital with populations including adolescents and young adults, women, people of colour, lower-income people, criminal legal system-involved individuals, and individuals who have differing primary substance of use profiles. We conclude with a discussion about the value of using an intersectional lens to understand recovery capital and its meanings and functions in various population groups.

The relative importance of different domains

Very little research has empirically examined the salience and utility of different domains of recovery capital. Therefore, it is largely unknown if recovery capital functions primarily as a unidimensional construct, or if and how various domains have differential effects on recovery. Some qualitative studies have honed in on particular domains of recovery capital, such as social capital (Cheney et al, 2016; Zschau et al, 2016), community capital (Connolly and Granfield, 2017), and physical capital (Irish et al, 2020). While providing valuable insights into the nuances of recovery capital within these domains, such studies do not probe the question of if and how recovery capital domains interact and influence recovery for differing populations over time.

Research on these questions has been limited by constraints and challenges in recovery capital measurement, discussed in greater depth in other chapters of this book (for example, see Chapter 4, Bunaciu and colleagues). A recent systematic review located ten survey measures of recovery capital covering a total of 41 unique subconstructs, assessed through single items or multi-item subscales (Bunaciu et al, 2023). Although most of these measures are considered reliable and valid as complete instruments, their accuracy in assessing specific recovery capital domains is less clear and there needs to be further attention to their predictive validity in understanding recovery outcomes. For example, the Assessment of Recovery Capital (ARC; Groshkova et al, 2012) is proposed to measure two recovery capital domains, personal and social recovery capital, and contains ten subscales to assess recovery capital subdomains (for example, Coping and Life Functioning; Global Physical Health). Yet, psychometric analyses have indicated that the ARC appears to reflect a single factor rather than distinct domains (Arndt et al, 2017; Bowen et al, 2020).

Newer measures, such as the Multidimensional Inventory of Recovery Capital (MIRC; Bowen et al, 2023), have been developed with the aim of measuring total recovery capital as well as differentiating between recovery capital domains, such as social, physical, human, and cultural capital. Longitudinal studies using such instruments could clarify if social, physical, human, and cultural capital change at the same rates over time and how they are related to different kinds of recovery outcomes. For example, it is possible that certain domains could be more closely associated with sustained sobriety and well-being indicators in recovery than others. A close examination of overall recovery capital and its domains over time could also illuminate individual growth and areas where change is happening, even if the overall score is not changing much. Furthermore, measures that are developed primarily for assessing recovery capital in practice, such as the REC-CAP instrument, could establish if and how different domains are linked to meaningful outcomes and goals for people in recovery on an individual basis (Cano et al, 2017). For example, a service provider using the REC-CAP could help a person in recovery see trends in different categories or domains of their recovery capital over time and explore together how these changes relate to the person achieving their personal recovery goals.

The question of negative recovery capital

Another key question regards if recovery capital should be wholly understood as a strengths-based concept, or if it should reflect both positive and negative influences on recovery. Patton and colleagues (2022) expanded Cloud and Granfield's (2008) notion of negative recovery capital to integrate the concept of 'pains of desistance', articulating common challenges of the recovery process, such as addressing unresolved trauma and learning how to navigate relationships in sobriety. In contrast, other researchers have conceptualized recovery capital as entirely positive, or considered barriers to recovery as a separate domain in measurement and conceptualization, rather than along a continuum of recovery capital (see Figure 6.2; Best and Hennessy, 2022; Bunaciu et al, 2023).

One criticism of the concept of negative recovery capital is that it is etymologically confusing, since 'capital' is a positive term referring to wealth or resources (Hennessy, 2017; Best and Hennessy, 2022). Another concern is that in many conceptualizations of recovery capital, it is unclear if negative capital refers simply to a lack of positive capital in a given area (for example, not having adequate income) or to factors that actively deter recovery, such as having friends or family members who use substances in problematic ways (also see Table 11.1 in Chapter 11 for additional examples of negative *justice* capital). Further, recovery advocates champion the focus on recovery capital as a positive construct within the field of addiction, given the history of focusing on problems, harms, and risks related to an individual's addiction recovery experience, which can lead to increased stigma.

On the other hand, solely focusing on the resources that support recovery without simultaneous attention to barriers and challenges – regardless of the terminology that is used – risks minimizing the complexities of the recovery process (Patton et al, 2022). Further, attention to recovery barriers can direct service providers to focus resources and interventions accordingly. For example, probing health challenges as a form of negative human capital could prompt a service provider to link a client to healthcare resources, as well as discuss how health issues might be contributing to the client feeling discouraged and less optimistic about their recovery (Kahn et al, 2019).

Going forward, both research and practice would benefit from clarity regarding positive and negative aspects of recovery capital. There may be contexts in which framing recovery capital only in terms of strengths and assets makes sense, but this assumption should be explicit and a rationale should be provided. Similarly, researchers and service providers interested in measuring recovery capital should choose a measure that aligns with their conceptualization of recovery capital and indicate whether negative capital is included. For example, the ARC (Groshkova et al, 2012) and its briefer version, the BARC-10 (Vilsaint et al, 2017) contain only positively framed items, whereas other measures such as the MIRC (Bowen et al, 2022, 2023) and REC-CAP (Cano et al, 2017) include items assessing positive as well as negative capital or recovery barriers. The resulting challenge for research is to develop an understanding of positive and negative conceptualizations of recovery capital in a complementary way to provide predictive value for recovery and other meaningful outcomes, through rigorous, longitudinal studies of individuals from diverse backgrounds at various stages in their recovery process.

Population-specific recovery capital

Another critical area of inquiry in the conceptualization of recovery capital is to explore if recovery capital has differing features or functions for specific population groups. The qualitative research from which Cloud and Granfield (2001; 2008) developed the theory of recovery capital consisted entirely of adults aged 20 and over and was predominantly White, male, middle class, and struggling with alcohol. This generates questions about what recovery capital looks like and how it functions among more diverse populations, including those impacted by marginalization and systemic disadvantage (Nash et al, 2019; Wagner and Baldwin, 2020; Pouille et al, 2021). In particular, the domain of cultural capital – including values, norms, and traditions related to substance use and recovery – is likely to manifest in distinct ways for different groups.

Later, we review emerging research and key questions about recovery capital for some specific (and not mutually exclusive) population groups, including adolescents and young adults, women, LGBQ people, people of colour, lower-income people, criminal legal system-involved populations, and those with specific primary substance of use profiles. This is not an exhaustive account of population groups for which recovery capital should be conceptually examined, but rather is intended to illustrate the range of factors – including age, gender, sexual orientation, race, ethnicity, income, system involvement, and types of substances used – that are salient to consider in conceptualizing recovery capital. We then discuss the implications of adopting an intersectional lens regarding these and other factors.

Adolescents and young adults

The process of recovery is markedly different between adolescents and adults. Adolescents – young people aged 11 to 19 (Sacks, 2003) – and their emerging adult counterparts (up to around age 25) are in a unique developmental phase marked by many biological, physical, and neurological changes. Adolescents are still developing the skills of self-regulation and future thinking, which can support slowing or stopping substance use. For individuals who initiate substance use during adolescence, there may be delays in developing these skills. Adolescents are also seeking independence and desire to make their own choices and decisions. Many adolescents and young adults have additional mental health difficulties and/or trauma (Tanner-Smith et al, 2018; Substance Abuse and Mental Health Services Administration, 2022), experiences which are strongly linked to one's ability to engage in recovery. Finally, this age group typically presents with different substance use patterns than adults, including a faster transition to substance use disorders for some substances (for example, cannabis and prescription drugs [Volkow et al, 2021]), being more likely to use multiple substances, and being more resistant to complete abstinence.

Given these developmental and substance use disorder-related differences, adolescents' and young adults' sources of recovery capital are also likely to differ from adults' sources of recovery capital. As a result, Hennessy and colleagues made developmental adaptations to the original recovery capital model and proposed the Recovery Capital for Adolescents Model (RCAM) to use when examining youth recovery processes (Hennessy et al, 2018; Nash et al, 2019; Jurinsky et al, 2022). The RCAM has the same domains as the common recovery capital models developed for adults, but the domain indicators differ due to these key developmental considerations.

In the RCAM, human recovery capital for adolescents involves their motivations, skills, and abilities that directly influence to what degree they can and will engage in a recovery process. Internal resources such as intrinsic motivation may take the longest to develop as the adolescent's initiation of treatment, for example, is often enforced by parents or other adult figures (Gonzales et al, 2012; Hennessy et al, 2022; Jurinsky et al, 2022). As they have sought independence, having an adult step in to curb that independence, however well intentioned, can feel disempowering and in direct contradiction to their growing developmental need to act as a free agent. In terms of financial recovery capital, unlike adults who can freely support themselves through employment, adolescents are typically supported by an adult. As a result, unless they are emancipated, adolescent financial recovery capital is directly tied to their caregiver(s) and may be harder or slower to change.

Moving to the broader environmental context, social recovery capital is represented through relationships with family, friends, peers, and other adults, as these can each uniquely support a recovery journey through different pathways (for example, sober and recovery-supportive friends and family) or act as barriers to recovery (for example, substance-using friends and family, relationship conflict). One's peers and friends start to become especially important during adolescence as adolescents seek to individuate themselves from their families and experiment with creating their own social identity (Boyadjian et al, 2023). And, once these groups are formed, adolescents have less mobility than adults to shift their day-to-day environments on their own (for example, by moving neighbourhood or changing schools). As a result, it can be challenging to avoid peers and friends that are risks to their recovery. Research has also demonstrated the unique contribution of parents to an adolescent's recovery journey (Hennessy et al, 2022; Jurinsky et al, 2022); for adults, one's parents typically have reduced, if any, influence on their behaviour. It is important to recognize that parents can provide mixed levels of recovery capital; although parental monitoring that occurs within the context of a healthy relationship with their child is a protective factor (Rusby et al, 2018), relationship conflict and parental substance use can be barriers to recovery (Nichols et al, 2021).

At the broader community level, a growing body of research has demonstrated the value of having adolescent-specific services to support their recovery experience in the community, including education-based programmes such as recovery high schools and collegiate recovery communities, or peer support services such as alternative peer groups and recovery clubhouses (Finch et al, 2018; Tanner-Smith et al, 2018; Nash et al, 2019; Hennessy et al, 2021; Smith et al, 2023). These supports attend to this developmental stage by providing an adolescent with an adult-monitored and structured space where they can begin to develop new sober relationships and peer groups while engaging in fun, substance-free activities, fostering social and human recovery capital development. Through this socialization, recovery is modelled by peers and adults and they can begin to engage (or re-engage) in skill building to meet the key developmental goals of adolescence (Nash et al, 2019). Leaders of these programmes recognize the need to highlight how recovery can be fun and appealing to youth, to draw them in and begin to create new connections with the recovery community (for example, cultural capital), despite the fact that many youth do not initially choose to attend these programmes but do so as a result of parent or other adult involvement (Nash et al, 2019a; 2019b). This is a shift in thinking from adult models that assume that recovery is beneficial by the fact that adults are often seeking to gain (recover) what has been lost. In sum, adolescents and young adults clearly have important and different influences on their substance use and recovery than adults. These factors should be taken into account in conducting research on recovery capital with young people, and in turn, better understanding of recovery capital in youth can inform the design of youth-oriented recovery services that use a strengths-based and developmentally informed approach.

Women

A small body of research has explored recovery capital using a gendered lens, with most of these studies focusing on the experiences of cisgender women in recovery (Evans et al, 2014; Gueta and Addad, 2015; Blount et al, 2021) and differences between cisgender women and men (Neale et al, 2014; Gilbert et al, 2021; Gavriel-Fried et al, 2022). Some of this research highlights salient aspects of recovery capital for pregnant and/or parenting women. For example, in Blount and colleagues' (2021) qualitative study of African American women's recovery capital, participants frequently spoke of the desire to rebuild stable and caring relationships as a motivating factor in their recovery – a powerful source of human capital. However, participants also discussed challenges in securing physical capital resources, such as housing and childcare, to support their children and families.

Studies comparing and contrasting women and men's recovery capital accumulation and recovery experiences have noted some interesting differences. In Neale and colleagues' (2014) study of women and men recovering from heroin addiction, women reported higher levels of physical and sexual abuse – traumatic experiences that can be considered a form of negative human capital. However, women reported higher levels of social support from family members and others, which in some instances facilitated their access to housing and other material resources. More recently, Gilbert and colleagues (2021) found that recovery capital had a protective effect on preventing relapse from alcohol use disorder during the COVID-19 pandemic, though some risk factors for returning to substance use varied by gender. For instance, educational attainment was a protective factor for men, but not for women in the sample.

Given that women face a number of adverse recovery outcomes, including lower rates of treatment utilization (Gilbert et al, 2019), further gendered examinations of recovery capital are needed. Future studies could explore barriers to building recovery capital that women commonly experience and that may underlie gender-based disparities in recovery outcomes, as well as gender-specific recovery strengths. Other aspects of the intersection of recovery capital and gender are vastly under-explored and warrant further attention. Very little research has looked at recovery capital beyond binary notions of gender, examining recovery capital for transgender, nonbinary, and gender-fluid individuals who experience additional unique challenges to their well-being and recovery (Lyons et al, 2015; Wolfe et al, 2021). Research on the influence of fatherhood and parenting for men in recovery is also under-researched, in comparison to studies focusing on recovery capital for women with children.

LGBQ populations

People identifying as lesbian, gay, bisexual, or queer – sometimes referred to as sexual minorities – experience elevated problems related to substance use. For example, one study found that people identifying as lesbian, gay, or bisexual, as well as those who reported being unsure of their sexual identity, were more likely to experience severe alcohol, tobacco, and drug use disorders, compared to heterosexual-identifying individuals (Boyd et al, 2019). The increased risk of substance-related problems for LGBQ populations is linked to individual and structural discrimination and stigma (Slater et al, 2017).

Although little research has focused on the recovery experiences of LGBQ people, one study using data from the National Recovery Study found that people identifying as lesbian, gay, bisexual, or 'something else' had poorer outcomes than heterosexual-identifying individuals on many recovery indicators, including lower levels of recovery capital (Haik et al, 2022). Given these disparities, there is a need for treatment and recovery services that are explicitly affirming of diverse sexualities. A recent qualitative study of people identifying as sexual and/or gender minorities (for example, LGBTQ+) found that most participants reported experiencing discrimination, stigma, and/or bullying in substance use services (Paschen-Wolff et al, 2024). Participants offered several recommendations for providing affirming services, including developing LGBTQ+-specific programming, developing non-discrimination policies and staff trainings, and hiring staff whose identities reflect this community (Paschen-Wolff et al, 2024). Although recovery capital extends beyond treatment and service use, increasing access to LGBQ-affirming services is an important step toward reducing recovery disparities for sexual minorities. Further research should explore how sexuality-affirming practices in treatment, recovery, and other community-based services can help this population to build recovery capital, as well as continue to examine – and ultimately dismantle – the structures, policies, and attitudes that contribute to the oppression and discrimination that LGBQ people routinely face.

People of colour

In general, research to date on substance use and people of colour in the US and elsewhere has focused primarily on epidemiology and consequences of substance-related problems, rather than examining recovery in depth for these populations (Wagner and Baldwin, 2020). Thus, more research is needed on all aspects of the intersection of race/ethnicity and recovery, including looking at characteristics of recovery capital for different populations of colour and exploring how racism at individual and systemic levels impacts recovery capital accumulation. Critically, Subica and Link (2022) postulate that cultural trauma – including historical and recent acts of genocide, hate crimes, and legalized discrimination – functions as a fundamental cause of health disparities. From this perspective, it is important to examine how cultural trauma may underlie the development of substance use problems for people of colour, as well as contribute to recovery capital-related challenges, such as lack of access to high-quality, culturally resonant treatment services.

Recent research on recovery capital for people of colour has noted some interesting nuances. For example, one study of residents of Oxford House recovery homes in the US found that Black residents had greater acquisition of recovery capital and better recovery outcomes, compared to residents of other races (Jason et al, 2022). However, another study noted worse retention for Black residents of recovery homes located in the US state of Virginia, suggesting a need to continue exploring recovery capital accumulation and barriers for this population (Best et al, 2023), taking into account potential regional and geographic differences in racism and discrimination.

Although it is critical to address how racism and discrimination affect recovery capital, research should also examine the nuances of culture identity and cultural strengths as forms of recovery capital. Culture can intersect with recovery in complex ways. Some studies have reported people of colour feeling a sense of disconnection from their culture or feeling stigmatized within their community because of their substance use (Douglass et al, 2023; Pouille et al, 2021). Thus, reconnecting with cultural communities, identities, and traditions can be a potent form of recovery capital (Pouille et al, 2021). Matamonasa-Bennett (2017) referred to this process as 'retraditionalization' in her study with Native American men in recovery from alcohol problems, illustrating how participants reclaimed and reconstructed their Native American values and identities in ways that were vital to their recovery. Another example of this is Cheney et al's (2016) study, which highlighted the importance of connecting with family networks and faith communities for Black Americans in the rural Arkansas Mississippi Delta region recovering from problems with cocaine use. Studying culturally specific recovery capital can inform the development of services that maximize these recovery strengths, build a culturally competent workforce, and provide people with opportunities to participate in activities, ceremonies, and traditions that affirm both their cultural identity and their recovery pathway (Pouille et al, 2021).

Lower-income people

A limited body of research addresses the intersection of recovery capital and income, highlighting considerations for lower-income people in recovery. Studies have established that factors such as employment (Sahker et al, 2019) and having adequate income or other resources (for example, Supplemental

Nutrition Assistance Program benefits) to meet basic needs (Kahn et al, 2019) are salient forms of recovery capital for lower-income people. Other research with people experiencing homelessness explores the centrality of safe and stable housing – a form of physical recovery capital – in providing a foundation for recovery (Neale and Stevenson, 2015; Collins et al, 2016). Further research is needed to clarify associations between different forms of recovery capital for lower-income people. For example, is having fewer resources in terms of physical capital – such as housing, transportation, and income – associated with limited social support for recovery, or do people with fewer economic resources develop strong social relationships, despite or perhaps because of their economic constraints?

There may also be meaningful differences in community-level recovery capital for lower-income people. Bowen and colleagues (2022) found that lower-income participants perceived neighbourhood triggers to use substances, such as walking by liquor stores or being offered drugs on the street, as a powerful form of negative community capital – a concern that was not raised by middle-income participants in the study. Other research points to particular challenges in building recovery capital in under-resourced communities, such as the lack of employment opportunities for people in recovery in both urban and rural areas (Connolly and Granfield, 2017; Irish et al, 2020). In sum, there is a need for further research to examine how socioeconomic resources affect access to all forms of recovery capital, how the availability of these resources varies by geographic context, and to document recovery strengths and challenges for people with limited economic means and in areas with fewer community resources.

Criminal legal system-involved populations

In many countries, including the United States, there is considerable overlap between people with substance use problems and people involved in the criminal legal system (National Institute on Drug Abuse, 2020). People with substance use problems may enter into cycles of frequent arrests and incarceration for issues such as possession of controlled substances or driving under the influence. In the United States, Black, Latino, and Native American persons and lower-income people are disproportionately targeted by law enforcement and the legal system for substance-related violations (Camplain et al, 2020).

As advocates pursue systemic reform to address these injustices (for example, via drug treatment or recovery courts and drug policy changes), there is an imperative to examine how the criminal legal system at present impacts recovery capital. Having a record of arrests or incarceration presents a barrier to acquiring recovery capital, particularly in terms of access to housing, employment, and higher education and training opportunities

(Kelly et al, 2018; Kahn et al, 2019). People returning to the community from incarceration also experience high rates of physical and mental health problems and trauma (McCauley et al, 2023), presenting further impediments to human recovery capital development. Although organizations focused on serving clientele in the transition from incarceration can help people generate recovery capital, including rebuilding their support networks (Connolly and Granfield, 2017), some research suggests that over-reliance on professional support – rather than 'natural' support from friends and family – can render legal system-involved people vulnerable in recovery (Zschau et al, 2016). While criminal legal system involvement is generally an obstacle to building recovery capital, the nuances of how system-involved people acquire positive capital and reduce sources of negative capital, and which types of capital are most critical in this context, are key areas for further study.

Substance-specific recovery capital

Another area of difference with implications for recovery capital regards the primary substance(s) a person has a history of using. Research on recovery trajectories focusing on specific substances suggests that different substances are likely to produce distinct recovery challenges (Neale et al, 2014; Brookfield et al, 2019; Subhani et al, 2022). As a result, it seems likely that recovery capital may develop differently for individuals across the spectrum of types of substance use disorders.

There are several illustrations of this in existing research. Individuals who use methamphetamine frequently encounter a lack of local treatment and recovery resources (compared to other types of common substance-specific treatments and recovery supports) and may struggle to fulfil their social, family, and work functions that the stimulant previously helped them keep up with (Brookfield et al, 2019). Another example is that individuals with opioid use disorder who use medications to manage their recovery may face stigma from treatment providers or others for the use of medication and have trouble finding recovery-supportive groups in their community (Paquette et al, 2018; Andraka-Christou et al, 2022). In addition, people recovering from alcohol-related problems often report challenges related to the easy availability of alcohol and the social desirability and culture of drinking in many contexts (Collins et al, 2016; Subhani et al, 2022).

Neale's qualitative work with individuals with a history of heroin use found that physical health and individuals' ability and desire to take care of their bodies was so salient in individuals' recovery narratives that this area should be its own recovery capital domain separate from human recovery capital (Neale et al, 2014). This is a finding that has not been replicated or examined in other recovery capital studies, but most recovery capital research has not focused on individuals with specific substance use disorders. Future qualitative work could recruit participants with different primary substances of use and examine their recovery and recovery capital experiences to understand if there are key differences deriving from their specific substance(s) of use. These examinations could identify new domains of recovery capital, new indicators of recovery capital, or novel ways of understanding how recovery capital develops by the primary substance of use.

Intersectionality

People cannot be defined by a single characteristic. The concept of intersectionality, originating in Black feminist scholarship, conveys the reality that people's identities reflect a range of social categories – including but not limited to race, ethnicity, age, gender, sexual orientation, socioeconomic status, and disability – and that these categories infer different degrees of privilege and oppression (Bowleg, 2012). Thus, in conceptualizing population-specific recovery capital, one should not assume that all members of a particular group (for example, criminal legal system-involved populations) will have the same experiences, or that membership in that group is the most salient factor to understanding individuals' recovery experiences and needs.

As researchers continue to examine population-specific recovery capital, it is critical to apply an intersectional lens by collaborating in research with individuals and communities with lived experience of recovery, recruiting diverse samples within specific population groups, and conducting analyses in a manner that accounts for how this diversity might affect recovery and recovery capital. One illustration of this would be to carry out a qualitative study to explore how youth of colour perceive their recovery capital and encounter barriers related to racial and age-related discrimination and stigma, as well as culturally specific strengths. Although it can be challenging to operationalize intersectionality in research designs (Bowleg, 2012), acknowledging and accounting for it is critical to advancing recovery capital research and disrupting research paradigms that centre privileged perspectives (for example, White, male, adult, heterosexual, middle/upper class, able-bodied) as the basis of knowledge. Research that is coproduced with people with lived experience of recovery through participatory research designs may be especially powerful in illuminated nuanced conceptions of recovery capital from an intersectional lens.

Conclusion

In the decades since Granfield and Cloud (1999) introduced the concept of recovery capital, researchers have refined the concept and its application in a variety of populations to understand their recovery experiences. This scholarship has arguably generated more questions than solid answers. In particular, we encourage researchers to consider the following key questions in their ongoing work to further the conceptualization of recovery capital: (1) Are the different domains of recovery capital differentially associated with recovery outcomes such as abstinence, moderated use, improved quality of life, and/or remission of substance use disorder symptoms, or does recovery capital primarily function as a unidimensional construct? (2) How can conceptualizations of positive and negative recovery capital be refined to reflect barriers and challenges commonly encountered in recovery, while still maintaining a strengths-based foundation? and (3) How can an intersectional lens in recovery capital research yield new insights about recovery experiences and the nature and functions of recovery capital for populations that are diverse with regard to factors including age, gender, sexuality, race, culture, income, criminal legal system involvement, and substance use history? There is a particular need for research that goes beyond documenting the elevated risks that many marginalized populations face in terms of substance-related problems and examines both the unique challenges and the distinctive assets that these groups may encounter and draw from in recovery.

The evolution of the concept of recovery capital reflects shifting understandings of recovery itself as an individualized and holistic process of change (Ashford et al, 2019). The definition and domains of recovery, as well as recovery capital, are likely to continue to change and evolve. In the decades to come, we encourage researchers in the recovery field to apply an intersectional lens that centres lived experience in advancing the understanding of recovery capital and its practical applicability for enhancing recovery strengths and reducing barriers at individual and collective levels.

References

Andraka-Christou, B., Totaram, R., and Randall-Kosich, O. (2022) 'Stigmatization of medications for opioid use disorder in 12-step support groups and participant responses', *Substance Use & Addiction Journal*, 43(1): 415–24.

Arndt, S., Sahker, E., and Hedden, S. (2017) 'Does the assessment of recovery capital scale reflect a single or multiple domains?', *Substance Abuse and Rehabilitation*, 8: 39–43.

Ashford, R.D., Brown, A., Brown, T., Callis, J., Cleveland, H.H., Eisenhart, E., et al (2019). 'Defining and operationalizing the phenomena of recovery: A working definition from the recovery science research collaborative', *Addiction Research & Theory*, 27(3): 179–88.

Best, D. and Laudet, A. (2010) *The Potential of Recovery Capital*, London: The Royal Society for the Arts.

Best, D. and Colman, C. (2019) 'Let's celebrate recovery. Inclusive cities working together to support social cohesion', *Addiction Research & Theory*, 27(1): 55–64.

Best, D. and Hennessy, E. (2022) 'The science of recovery capital: Where do we go from here?', *Addiction*, 117(4): 1139–45.

Best, D., Beckwith, M., Haslam, C., Alexander Haslam, S., Jetten, J., Mawson, E. and Lubman, D.I. (2016) 'Overcoming alcohol and other drug addiction as a process of social identity transition: The social identity model of recovery (SIMOR)', *Addiction Research & Theory*, 24(2): 111–23.

Best, D., Sondhi, A., Best, J., Lehman, J., Grimes, A., Conner, M., and DeTriquet, R. (2023) 'Using recovery capital to predict retention and change in recovery residences in Virginia, USA', *Alcoholism Treatment Quarterly*, 41(2): 250–62.

Blount, T.N., LaGuardia, A.C., and Fitzpatrick, D.C. (2021) 'African American women's substance use recovery experiences: A phenomenological inquiry', *Counseling and Values*, 66(1): 92–110.

Bowen, E.A., Scott, C.F., Irish, A., and Nochajski, T.H. (2020) 'Psychometric properties of the Assessment of Recovery Capital (ARC) instrument in a diverse low-income sample', *Substance Use & Misuse*, 55(1): 108–18.

Bowen, E., Irish, A., LaBarre, C., Capozziello, N., Nochajski, T., and Granfield, R. (2022) 'Qualitative insights in item development for a comprehensive and inclusive measure of recovery capital', *Addiction Research & Theory*, 30(5): 403–13.

Bowen, E., Irish, A., Wilding, G., LaBarre, C., Capozziello, N., Nochajski, T., et al (2023) 'Development and psychometric properties of the Multidimensional Inventory of Recovery Capital (MIRC)', *Drug and Alcohol Dependence*, 247: 109875.

Bowleg, L. (2012) 'The problem with the phrase women and minorities: Intersectionality – an important theoretical framework for public health', *American Journal of Public Health*, 102(7): 1267–73.

Boyadjian, T., Sabelli, R.A., Wong, I.L., and Skeer, M.R. (2023) 'Perceptions on transition to college among high school students in recovery', *Contemporary School Psychology*, 27: 662–70.

Boyd, C.J., Veliz, P.T., Stephenson, R., Hughes, T.L., and McCabe, S.E. (2019) 'Severity of alcohol, tobacco, and drug use disorders among sexual minority individuals and their "not sure" counterparts', *LGBT Health*, 6(1): 15–22.

Bronfenbrenner, U. (1977) 'Toward an experimental ecology of human development', *American Psychologist*, 32(7): 513–31.

Brookfield, S., Fitzgerald, L., Selvey, L., and Maher, L. (2019) 'Turning points, identity, and social capital: A meta-ethnography of methamphetamine recovery', *International Journal of Drug Policy*, 67: 79–90.

Bunaciu, A., Bliuc, A.M., Best, D., Hennessy, E.A., Belanger, M.J., and Benwell, C.S. (2023) 'Measuring recovery capital for people recovering from alcohol and drug addiction: A systematic review', *Addiction Research & Theory*, 32(3): 225–36.

Camplain, R., Camplain, C., Trotter, R.T., Pro, G., Sabo, S., Eaves, E., and Baldwin, J.A. (2020) 'Racial/ethnic differences in drug-and alcohol-related arrest outcomes in a southwest county from 2009 to 2018', *American Journal of Public Health*, 110: 85–92.

Cano, I., Best, D., Edwards, M., and Lehman, J. (2017) 'Recovery capital pathways: Modelling the components of recovery wellbeing', *Drug and Alcohol Dependence*, 181: 11–19.

Cheney, A.M., Booth, B.M., Borders, T.F., and Curran, G.M. (2016) 'The role of social capital in African Americans' attempts to reduce and quit cocaine use', *Substance Use & Misuse*, 51(6): 777–87.

Cloud, W. and Granfield, R. (2008) 'Conceptualizing recovery capital: Expansion of a theoretical construct', *Substance Use & Misuse*, 43(12–13): 1971–86.

Collins, S.E., Jones, C.B., Hoffmann, G., Nelson, L.A., Hawes, S.M., Grazioli, V.S., and Clifasefi, S.L. (2016) 'In their own words: Content analysis of pathways to recovery among individuals with the lived experience of homelessness and alcohol use disorders', *International Journal of Drug Policy*, 27: 89–96.

Connolly, K. and Granfield, R. (2017) 'Building recovery capital: The role of faith-based communities in the reintegration of formerly incarcerated drug offenders', *Journal of Drug Issues*, 47: 370–82.

Douglass, C.H., Win, T.M., Goutzamanis, S., Lim, M.S., Block, K., Onsando, G., et al (2023) 'Stigma associated with alcohol and other drug use among people from migrant and ethnic minority groups: Results from a systematic review of qualitative studies', *Journal of Immigrant and Minority Health*, 25(6): 1402–25.

Evans, E., Li, L., Buoncristiani, S., and Hser, Y.-I. (2014) 'Perceived neighborhood safety, recovery capital, and successful outcomes among mothers 10 years after substance abuse treatment', *Substance Use & Misuse*, 49(11): 1491–1503.

Finch, A.J., Tanner-Smith, E., Hennessy, E., and Moberg, D.P. (2018) 'Recovery high schools: Effect of schools supporting recovery from substance use disorders', *The American Journal of Drug and Alcohol Abuse*, 44(2): 175–84.

Gavriel-Fried, B., Vana, N., Lev-El, N., and Weinberg-Kurnik, G. (2022) 'Recovery capital in action: How is gender understood and employed by men and women recovering from gambling disorder?', *Social Science & Medicine*, 313: 115401.

Gilbert, P.A., Pro, G., Zemore, S.E., Mulia, N., and Brown, G. (2019) 'Gender differences in use of alcohol treatment services and reasons for nonuse in a national sample', *Alcoholism: Clinical and Experimental Research*, 43(4): 722–31.

Gilbert, P.A., Soweid, L., Kersten, S.K., Brown, G., Zemore, S.E., Mulia, N., and Skinstad, A.H. (2021) 'Maintaining recovery from alcohol use disorder during the COVID-19 pandemic: The importance of recovery capital', *Drug and Alcohol Dependence*, 229(A): 109142.

Gonzales, R., Anglin, M.D., Beattie, R., Ong, C.A., and Glik, D.C. (2012) 'Perceptions of chronicity and recovery among youth in treatment for substance use problems', *Journal of Adolescent Health*, 51(2): 144–9.

Granfield, R. and Cloud, W. (1999) *Coming Clean: Overcoming Addiction without Treatment*, New York: New York University Press.

Granfield, R. and Cloud, W. (2001) 'Social context and 'natural recovery': The role of social capital in the resolution of drug-associated problems', *Substance Use & Misuse*, 36(11): 1543–70.

Groshkova, T., Best, D., and White, W. (2012) 'The assessment of recovery capital: Properties and psychometrics of a measure of addiction recovery strengths', *Drug and Alcohol Review*, 32(2): 187–94.

Gueta, K. and Addad, M. (2015) 'A house of cards: The long-term recovery experience of former drug-dependent Israeli women', *Women's Studies International Forum*, 48: 18–28.

Haik, A.K., Greene, M.C., Bergman, B.G., Abry, A.W., and Kelly, J.F. (2022) 'Recovery among sexual minorities in the United States population: Prevalence, characteristics, quality of life and functioning compared with heterosexual majority', *Drug and Alcohol Dependence*, 232, 109290.

Hennessy, E.A. (2017) 'Recovery capital: A systematic review of the literature', *Addiction Research & Theory*, 25(5): 349–60.

Hennessy, E.A., Cristello, J.V., and Kelly, J.F. (2018) 'RCAM: A proposed model of recovery capital for adolescents', *Addiction Research & Theory*, 27(5): 429–36.

Hennessy, E.A., Jurinsky, J., Simpson, H., and Nash, A. (2022) 'Parenting to provide social recovery capital: A qualitative study', *Addiction Research & Theory*, 30(5): 368–74.

Hennessy, E.A., Tanner-Smith, E., Nichols, L.M., Brown, T.B., and McCulloch, B.J. (2021) 'A multi-site study of emerging adults in collegiate recovery programs at public institutions', *Social Science & Medicine*, 278: 113955.

Hewitt, A.J. (2007) *After the Fire: Post Traumatic Growth in Recovery from Addictions*, Bath, UK: University of Bath.

Irish, A., Bowen, E.A., Hawthorne, A.N., and Palombi, L. (2020) '"Me, the street, and a backpack": Employment, income, and physical capital in rural recovery', *Journal of Social Work Practice in the Addictions*, 20(3): 194–207.

Jason, L.A., Guerrero, M., Bobak, T., Light, J.M., and Stoolmiller, M. (2022) 'Reducing health disparities among black individuals in the post-treatment environment', *Journal of Ethnicity in Substance Abuse*, 21(4): 1452–67.

Jurinsky, J., Cowie, K., Blyth, S., and Hennessy, E.A. (2022) '"A lot better than it used to be": A qualitative study of adolescents' dynamic social recovery capital', *Addiction Research & Theory*, 31(2): 77–83.

Kahn, L.S., Vest, B.M., Kulak, J.A., Berdine, D.E., and Granfield, R. (2019) 'Barriers and facilitators to recovery capital among justice-involved community members', *Journal of Offender Rehabilitation*, 58(6): 544–65.

Kay, C. and Monaghan, M. (2019) 'Rethinking recovery and desistance processes: Developing a social identity model of transition', *Addiction Research & Theory*, 27(1): 47–54.

Kelly, J.F., Greene, M.C., and Bergman, B.G. (2018) 'Beyond abstinence: Changes in indices of quality of life with time in recovery in a nationally representative sample of US Adults', *Alcoholism: Clinical and Experimental Research*, 42(4): 770–80.

Lyons, T., Shannon, K., Pierre, L., Small, W., Krüsi, A., and Kerr, T. (2015) 'A qualitative study of transgender individuals' experiences in residential addiction treatment settings: stigma and inclusivity', *Substance Abuse Treatment, Prevention, and Policy*, 10: 17.

Matamonasa-Bennett, A. (2017) '"The poison that ruined the nation": Native American men – alcohol, identity, and traditional healing', *American Journal of Men's Health*, 11(4): 1142–54.

McCauley, E.J., LeMasters, K., Behne, M.F., and Brinkley-Rubinstein, L. (2023) 'A call to action to public health institutions and teaching to incorporate mass incarceration as a sociostructural determinant of health', *Public Health Reports*, 138(5): 711–14.

Nash, A., Collier, C., Engebretson, J., and Cron, S. (2019a) 'Testing the feasibility of measuring recovery in adolescent participants of an alternative peer group: Lessons learned and next steps', *Journal of Adolescent Research*, 34(6): 655–82.

Nash, A.J., Hennessy, E.A., and Collier, C. (2019b) 'Exploring recovery capital among adolescents in an alternative peer group', *Drug and Alcohol Dependence*, 199: 136–43.

National Institute on Drug Abuse (2020) 'Criminal Justice DrugFacts', Available from: https://nida.nih.gov/publications/drugfacts/criminal-justice

Neale, J. and Stevenson, C. (2015) 'Social and recovery capital amongst homeless hostel residents who use drugs and alcohol', *International Journal of Drug Policy*, 26(5): 475–83.

Neale, J., Nettleton, S., and Pickering, L. (2014) 'Gender sameness and difference in recovery from heroin dependence: A qualitative exploration', *International Journal of Drug Policy*, 25(1): 3–12.

Nichols, L.M., Pedroza, J.A., Fleming, C.M., O'Brien, K.M., and Tanner-Smith, E.E. (2021) 'Social-ecological predictors of opioid use among adolescents with histories of substance use disorders', *Frontiers in Psychology*, 12, DOI: 10.3389/fpsyg.2021.686414.

Paquette, C.E., Syvertsen, J.L., and Pollini, R.A. (2018) 'Stigma at every turn: Health services experiences among people who inject drugs', *International Journal of Drug Policy*, 57: 104–10.

Paschen-Wolff, M.M., DeSousa, A., Paine, E.A., Hughes, T.L., and Campbell, A.N. (2024) 'Experiences of and recommendations for LGBTQ+-affirming substance use services: An exploratory qualitative descriptive study with LGBTQ+ people who use opioids and other drugs', *Substance Abuse Treatment, Prevention, and Policy*, 19(1): 2.

Patton, D., Best, D., and Brown, L. (2022) 'Overcoming the pains of recovery: The management of negative recovery capital during addiction recovery pathways', *Addiction Research & Theory*, 30(5): 340–50.

Pouille, A., Bellaert, L., Vander Laenen, F., and Vanderplasschen, W. (2021) 'Recovery capital among migrants and ethnic minorities in recovery from problem substance use: An analysis of lived experiences', *International Journal of Environmental Research and Public Health*, 18(24): 13025.

Rusby, J.C., Light, J.M., Crowley, R., and Westling, E. (2018) 'Influence of parent–youth relationship, parental monitoring, and parent substance use on adolescent substance use onset', *Journal of Family Psychology*, 32(3): 310–20.

Sacks, D. (2003) 'Age limits and adolescents', *Paediatrics & Child Health*, 8(9): 577.

Sahker, E., Ali, S.R., and Arndt, S. (2019) 'Employment recovery capital in the treatment of substance use disorders: Six-month follow-up observations', *Drug and Alcohol Dependence*, 205: 107624.

Slater, M.E., Godette, D., Huang, B., Ruan, W.J., and Kerridge, B.T. (2017) 'Sexual orientation-based discrimination, excessive alcohol use, and substance use disorders among sexual minority adults', *LGBT Health*, 4(5): 337–44.

Smith, C., Hennessy, E., Davidson, K., and Rodriguez, W. (2023) 'Recovery support clubhouses and alternative peer groups to support youth recovery: Comparing models, existing research, and future directions', Presented at the Association of Recovery in Higher Education Annual Meeting, Columbus, Ohio.

Subhani, M., Talat, U., Knight, H., Morling, J. R., Jones, K. A., Aithal, G. P., et al (2022) 'Characteristics of alcohol recovery narratives: Systematic review and narrative synthesis', *PLOS One*, 17(5): e0268034.

Subica, A.M. and Link, B.G. (2022) 'Cultural trauma as a fundamental cause of health disparities', *Social Science & Medicine*, 292, 114574.

Substance Abuse and Mental Health Services Administration (2022) *Key Substance Use and Mental Health Indicators in the United States: Results from the 2021 National Survey on Drug Use and Health*, No. HHS Publication No. PEP22-07-01-005, NSDUH Series H-57, Rockville, MD: Center for Behavioral Health Statistics and Quality, Substance Abuse and Mental Health Services Administration.

Tanner-Smith, E.E., Finch, A.J., Hennessy, E.A., and Moberg, D.P. (2018) 'Who attends recovery high schools after substance use treatment? A descriptive analysis of school aged youth', *Journal of Substance Use & Addiction Treatment*, 89: 20–7.

Vilsaint, C.L., Kelly, J.F., Bergman, B.G., Groshkova, T., Best, D., and White, W. (2017) 'Development and validation of a Brief Assessment of Recovery Capital (BARC-10) for alcohol and drug use disorder', *Drug and Alcohol Dependence*, 177: 71–6.

Volkow, N.D., Han, B., Einstein, E.B., and Compton, W.M. (2021) 'Prevalence of substance use disorders by time since first substance use among young people in the US', *JAMA Pediatrics*, 175(6): 640–3.

Wagner, E.F. and Baldwin, J.A. (2020) 'Recovery in special emphasis populations', *Alcohol Research Current Reviews*, 40(3): 5.

White, W. and Cloud, W. (2008) 'Recovery capital: A primer for addictions professionals', *Counselor*, 9: 22–7.

Wolfe, H.L., Biello, K.B., Reisner, S.L., Mimiaga, M.J., Cahill, S.R., and Hughto, J.M.W. (2021) 'Transgender-related discrimination and substance use, substance use disorder diagnosis and treatment history among transgender adults', *Drug and Alcohol Dependence*, 223: 108711.

Zschau, T., Collins, C., Lee, H., and Hatch, D.L. (2016) 'The hidden challenge: Limited recovery capital of drug court participants' support networks', *Journal of Applied Social Science*, 10(1): 22–43.

7

Community Recovery Capital and How it Contributes to Building Recovery Capital at an Individual Level

David Best, Beth Collinson, and David Patton

Introduction

As understandings and definitions of addiction recovery have evolved over the years, themes of improved health and well-being, strengthened social outcomes (Betty Ford Institute Consensus Panel, 2007; Timpson et al, 2016; Martinelli et al, 2020), and work and citizenship (Best et al, 2015) have become increasingly important. The Substance Abuse and Mental Health Services Administration (SAMHSA, 2012) defined recovery as 'a process of change through which individuals improve their health and wellness, live a self-directed life, and strive to reach their full potential'. A recent definition of recovery synthesizing the ten most common definitions of recovery framed the concept as 'an individualized, intentional, dynamic, and relational process involving sustained efforts to improve wellness' (Ashford et al, 2019). Yet, despite the necessity of an individualized recovery process, the factors identified as contributing to recovery do not sit within a vacuum. In fact, most of them are either situated within, or must be supported by, the community, and the networks, groups, and institutions that make up that community; therefore, this is an important area of emerging theory and measurement in considering recovery capital.

More than a decade ago, William White stated that the 'invitation for social inclusion' often lies within the community (2009, 155), yet we have continued to focus insufficient attention in this direction. The concept (and subsequent operationalization) of recovery capital affords us that opportunity.

Community capital is a key pillar of recovery capital, yet there is far less published on this in comparison to its counterparts – personal and social capital. When research does focus on community capital, it has tended to focus on the specific role of circumscribed recovery groups and communities, as these are easiest to measure from an empirical perspective. The emergence of recovery support services such as recovery community organizations and peer-based mutual aid groups such as 12-step programmes or SMART Recovery, hold tremendous value for the accumulation of recovery capital, but the field has not adequately considered the broader community to examine the role that other resources or people in the local community can play, or alternatively how community systems, processes, and activities can act as a barrier to recovery.

The domains of recovery capital

Robert Granfield and William Cloud introduced the concept of recovery capital in 1999, defining it as: '… the sum of one's total resources that can be brought to bear in an effort to overcome alcohol and drug dependency' (1999, 179). They go on to argue that 'recovery capital refers to the convergence of resources subsumed under three major classes of capital: social, physical and human' (1999, 179), following Coleman's (1990) articulation in which social capital arises when social relationships facilitate action; physical capital is entirely tangible and material; and human capital intangible in the form of skills and knowledge.

We know that the quality and quantity of recovery capital is a predictor of recovery outcomes (White and Cloud, 2008; Yates, 2014) and helps us to understand why some individuals are more successful in their recovery journeys than others (Connolly and Granfield, 2017). With this in mind, we must seek to better understand how individuals can be supported to build each component of recovery capital, and how the three recovery capital domains interact in supporting recovery journeys. This was the basis for the second attempt at categorizing domains of recovery capital by Best and Laudet (2010), who combined their learnings from recovery studies in the UK and US to suggest a model of recovery capital based on three domains:

1. Personal recovery capital referring to those internal qualities and characteristics like self-esteem, resilience, coping skills, self-efficacy, and positive communication skills.
2. Social recovery capital which relates to the depth and quality of social relationships and social identity that can support recovery journeys.
3. Collective (later referred to as community) recovery capital referring to access to those resources accessible within the community that can support recovery journeys. Embedded in community recovery capital

was the concept of cultural capital although this also overlaps with the social domain.

Central to this model was the core idea that there was a continuous dynamic interplay between the domains of recovery capital and a putative model (Best, 2019) assuming that social and community capital provided the 'scaffolding' around the individual for personal recovery capital resources to emerge over the course of the recovery journey. One of the key themes that will be discussed in the later part of this chapter is around how specific populations, such as women, minority ethnic groups, and specific cultural groups, have needs and resources that may impact their accrual of community capital and therefore approaches to building community capital must be person-centred, albeit embedded within a set of generic community principles.

Our understandings of community capital have further evolved and been moulded by its relationship and overlap with cultural capital. In previous categorizations of recovery capital, there has been confusion as to where cultural capital lies (Best and Hennessy, 2022). In White and Cloud's (2008) framework for example, this is a foundational pillar of community capital, and a core component of identifying what the appropriate type and intensity of support should be. In contrast, Best and Laudet (2010) described cultural capital as 'values, beliefs and attitudes that link to social conformity and the ability to fit into dominant social behaviors' (Best and Laudet, 2010, 4), as the basis for the operationalization and measurement of the concept. For Best and Laudet, attitudes of the community at large have a direct influence on the individual's ability and willingness to become engaged with their local community (this issue is further considered in Tim Leighton's chapter, Chapter 8 in this volume). Cultural capital cannot be ignored, as it determines what is available and accessible for individuals and is a determinant of the environment in which recovery can happen (Patton, Best, Pula, and Hollandy, 2023). It is therefore crucially important that cultural resources are integrated into community capital framing, and multiple cultures, related as they are to intersectionality, will coexist within all communities, with a resultant impact on recovery journeys.

Thus, community is not a consistent resource across geographic locations or among different populations and groups. Inequality within communities and society are at play here. In light of this, there is an important role and need for specialist support organizations that are responsive to a range of needs, groups, and characteristics that are culturally sensitive. The unintended consequence of creating separate and specialist organizations is that this can sometimes lead to the creation of silos and a sort of segregation of groups. To address this issue, a network of generic and specialist groups and services may be required at a practical level, while cultural needs and issues are an essential component of any measurement of community capital.

One of the central assumptions of this chapter (and the underlying model) is that the recovery community should not sit in its own silo, irrespective of the safety net or cocoon that it may provide to people in early recovery as a buttress against external hostile forces. A core hypothesis of this chapter (and essential for recovery to flourish as a social movement) is that recovery groups are integrated into local community activities and resources. To be a part of the fabric of the wider community and for recovery to be visible and accessible, it must not only interact with the wider community but should ideally contribute to the well-being and civic processes of that community. In this way, not only do the individuals in recovery benefit, but the community at large will do so as well. This concept can be referred to as 'reciprocal altruism'. Imagine a spider web which spans across a community – each thread bridging together places and people of the locale. Over time, the web will become so tightly spun that when an individual needs support, pathways into appropriate support are already built, making a variety of supports available and accessible. The web will also grow, not only in size but in the complex interweaving of its nodes and links.

This is a core concept of Inclusive Recovery Cities (which, along with Recovery Oriented Systems of Care are described and defined towards the end of this chapter). We also argue that this should be extended to other kinds of resources – not just recovery community centres and meetings, but also to public resources like neighbourhood groups and libraries, and to a diverse range of professional supports and services, such as primary healthcare, psychological services and family supports, education pathways, employment opportunities, and affordable, good quality housing. The benefit of engagement with such resources is well documented (Dingle et al, 2015a; 2015b; Best et al, 2016; Collinson and Best, 2019), but assessing the influence of engagement with wider community resources has not been explored in the same depth. The next section of the chapter will examine the methods used to both identify community recovery capital and to engage with it before embedding these approaches within the framework of Recovery Oriented Systems of Care and Inclusive Recovery Cities.

Mapping access to community resources: The role of ABCD

Given that access to community capital is often afforded through engagement with community resources, it is important to pay attention to approaches to identifying (that is, by systematically mapping) and mobilizing these. Asset Based Community Development (ABCD: Kretzmann and McKnight, 1993) is an approach to building on the 'assets' of a community, thought of in terms of places and people within the locale. ABCD has been defined as the process through which 'communities can drive the development process themselves by identifying and mobilizing existing, but often unrecognised assets. Thereby responding to challenges and creating local social improvement and economic development' (Nurture Development, 2023). This occurs through a process of collecting local stories, then gathering together a core group to map the gifts, capacities, and assets in the local community, and finally, finding local connectors in the community who will help to develop a vision and map. This then forms the basis for mobilizing the local assets and working collectively to achieve that vision.

Kretzmann and McKnight (1993) focused on the indigenous resources within a community and suggested that communities often contained the solutions to their own problems in the form of individuals, informal groups and associations, and institutions that could be mobilized to address local challenges and to meet local needs. The resulting ABCD model is, in essence, an attempt to coalesce local resources and to mobilize them for the benefit of communities, to stop professionals trying to problem-solve for communities they do not belong to. However, as McKnight and Block (2010) argued, the identification of assets is only the starting point and a key group of individuals, called *community connectors*, are required to mobilize the identified assets. While the ABCD model was not developed with addiction recovery as its focus, the mobilization of peer recovery specialists as community connectors meant that this model was easily applied in the context of recovery communities and their local impact.

While the ABCD framework has gained much traction (Brooks and Kendall, 2013; Bull, Mittelmark, and Kanyeka, 2013; Friedli, 2013), the challenge is to make the shift from traditional needs-based approaches in which a community is defined by its deficits to a strengths-based approach which recognizes that communities should be built on its capacities (Kretzmann and McKnight, 1993; 1996; Kretzmann et al, 2005). This is entirely consistent with the capital-based model outlined in this chapter (and indeed throughout the book), in which a strengths-based approach means both socially focussed and community-based. It also translates the location of action (and solutions) from professionally-run centres to more informal and fluid locations within and across a community.

This is not to disregard problems that may exist within a community, but instead to use the strengths of the resources available locally to underpin collective action and to create a common cause. If a community is able to identify its own assets, then its citizens will begin to view the locale in light of these strengths (Haines, 2009; Kretzmann and Russel, 2018) and will increasingly look to the community to find solutions to problems as they arise. Further, as this approach produces success, it will lead to increased collective efficacy within the community as the community develops greater confidence in its ability to solve its own problems, and its citizens come to trust each other more as a consequence of this process (Sampson, 2017). This will also encourage communities to invest their energy in further developing the assets that already exist and so a community starts to build strength on strength, and the spider web grows in size and strength.

While mapping assets initially enables a community to take stock of its strengths, the identification and mobilization of the networks associated with these is critical (McKnight and Block, 2010). For example, simply knowing about a local recovery running group holds limited value, but when layered with knowledge of or a connection to the host of the running group and then to its membership, the likelihood of engaging effectively with it, not only to run but also to engage in other community activities, is significantly strengthened (Collinson and Best, 2019). This may not only benefit the individual but the networks around them as knowledge is shared and connections are passed on within a radius of trust. The role of the community connector is therefore twofold – to identify and engage with positive assets and then to act as the human bridge to encourage people in recovery to engage with those assets and groups. This may require a process known as 'assertive linkage' (Manning et al, 2012, described in detail later) to actively support and encourage engagement on the part of individuals who may be initially hesitant or reluctant to become a part of community groups and activities.

ABCD is valuable as a framework for the identification and mobilization of assets, as a means of strengthening communities and the well-being of its residents (Cassetti et al, 2020, 1). That said, simply mapping alone lacks methodological clarity (Blickem et al, 2018) and fails to acknowledge how challenging this process can be for those who have experienced stigmatization or marginalization. A community may have an abundance of resources, but these resources may not be accessible or desirable to engage with (Best and Savic, 2015) and may only be available to small and select groups within the community. Accessing these resources and engaging in community organizations can be particularly challenging for those who are socially excluded and face a myriad of issues including stigma, self-exclusion, lack of access, lack of trust, and unclear pathways into positive community resources.

Best and Savic (2015) deployed the ABCD method in supporting a magistrates' court in the south-east suburbs of Melbourne, Australia, in an attempt to address antisocial behaviour by young people in the local area. Pricked by the failure of traditional criminal justice disposals, the magistrates sought alternative approaches that offered hope to disaffected young people in the area, and ABCD was selected as the way of engaging the local community – consisting of concerned citizens, local community groups, and larger organizations and institutions – in addressing the problem of youth antisocial behaviour using a community strengths model. They hosted a series of afternoon tea events for local businesses and community groups as a result of which 99 organizations or groups signed up to be trained as community connectors in the local area, resulting in a diverse range of activities being made available to and ultimately engaged in by the local young people. Not only were there reductions in antisocial behaviour, but the initiative also helped to generate community pride and new resources and assets were generated through emerging relationships and practices that stemmed from the initial engagement processes. What is crucial is that the working group from the ABCD exercise effectively emerged as a new community asset in its own right.

In a similar initiative, partnering with the Salvation Army on the Central Coast of Australia, Best et al (2014) attempted to address the problem of isolation for residents of two therapeutic communities by attempting to create 'communities without walls'. There were two perceived issues for the participating therapeutic communities:

1. The therapeutic communities were located in rural deprived areas in a well-resourced rehabilitation centre, yet made little contribution to overall community well-being.
2. Graduating residents had developed strong bonds inside the therapeutic community (bonding social capital, Putnam, 2000), but they had little of the bridging or linking social capital that would be needed after they left the therapeutic community to successfully engage in their communities. This was particularly salient for those residents who chose to remain in the local area on completion of the treatment programme rather than to return to their home area following completion of the programme.

For that reason, we started the initiative by creating a coalition of four groups – current residents, graduates of the programme who were still engaged, staff (many of whom were themselves in recovery), and family members. With this initial coalition in place, the first task was to engage the local community about what was missing in the community that could be addressed by the emerging ABCD coalition. This newly formed group then set out a strategy to create a model that we refer to as 'Reciprocal Community Development' (Best et al, 2014) with the aim of using the resources of the therapeutic communities – including things like equine therapy, a community café, and aqua golf – to support the local community, but also of engaging residents in the third (and final) stage of the therapeutic community programme in external community engagement work. This had the twin effect of providing support and resources to the community but also in creating new relationships, connections, and a sense of community belonging to the residents who were about to return to the community following the completion of the programme. The project became a core component of the third ('emergence') phase of the therapeutic communities involved but also provided new relationships, community activities, and pathways for the residents during and after their treatment programmes. But crucially, the project also increased the range of accessible community resources for members of the community while reducing social distance and social exclusion of residents.

An equivalent programme in the UK was funded by the Health Foundation to promote community engagement in Sheffield (Edwards, Soutar, and Best, 2018). In partnership with the main treatment providers in the city, the initial aim was to recruit and train a group of community connectors who would work together to open doors to community resources to support people early in their recovery journeys. The group of people trained – our 'community connectors' – were primarily people with considerable recovery experience but also included a more diverse group of community members. Their work was astonishing in that, as well as bonding as a group and coproducing their own ways of working and supporting each other, they were able to identify and engage with 135 community assets in Sheffield. Those assets were classified into four types of categories: (1) peer-led or mutual aid recovery groups; (2) sports, arts, and recreation clubs and associations; (3) employment, training, and education opportunities; (4) professional services.

While limited research funding and changes within the treatment provider meant that the project was unable to look at long-term impact, this project provided a clear method for the first two key stages of the process – the identification of assets and the generation of a human resource to bridge to those assets in the form of community connectors. An emerging element of the training of community connectors was in their internal governance and their related sense of empowerment. The connectors worked out their own rules and processes for engaging with both the people in early recovery they were working with and with the community assets, as well as providing each other with peer support and guidance. This is another example of a new asset (in this case, the community connectors group) emerging from an ABCD process.

The importance of the second stage of the process, the recruitment and training of connectors to bridge people to community assets, was elucidated in a randomized controlled trial conducted in London (Manning et al, 2012). This trial focused on different methods to support effective engagement in community groups and resources. In the study, 153 patients were admitted to an emergency in-patient treatment ward for acute drug and alcohol problems with a predicted stay of ten days on the ward and were randomly assigned to one of three conditions (see Table 7.1) to attempt to encourage attendance at 12-step mutual aid meetings during their time in the hospital and to see which method might be most effective.

In the assertive linkage condition, there was more meeting attendance while residing on the ward, more meeting attendance in the three months after discharge, and lower levels of alcohol and drug use in the three months

Table 7.1: Three conditions for assertive linkage (Manning et al, 2012)

Standard referral	Given out leaflets specifying the times and locations of meetings
Physician referral	Physician involved in the admission recommended attendance and provided information about the meeting locations
Peer-based 'assertive linkage' condition	Person with lived experience would meet the patient, talk to them about the meetings and offer to take them to a meeting. This peer would offer to meet them afterwards to talk through the meeting and help explain what had happened

Figure 7.1: Three key components of the assertive linkage process

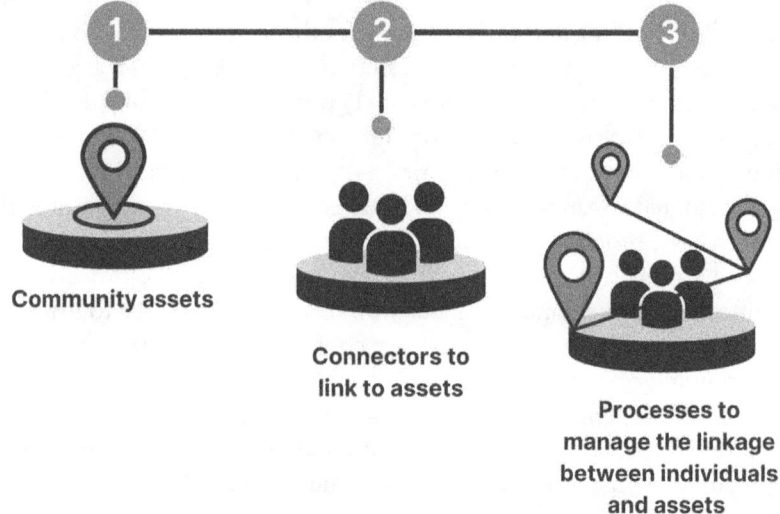

after discharge. The key conclusion is that assets alone are not enough. It is essential that there is an assertive linkage mechanism that brings together the individual and the community asset, and much of our evidence would suggest that it is those with their own lived experience who are best placed to be that connector. In effect, there are three component parts involved in this process (see Figure 7.1).

However, with the focus in the addictions field on individuals and their pathologies, ABCD remains an underfunded and under-utilized model, and one where there is limited research or even agreement on what the appropriate success indicators would be. The next section of the chapter will outline a further elaboration of this model, and in the conclusion we will come back to questions of how the science of ABCD can be advanced within an emerging research agenda around community recovery capital.

Asset Based Community Engagement

Earlier work by the authors (Collinson and Best, 2019) introduced the Asset Based Community Engagement (ABCE) framework. Drawing on the origins of ABCD but attentive to its challenges, they proposed a six-stage model for local recovery communities to systematically map community resources and assertively link individuals to resources to support their recovery. The visual in Figure 7.2 depicts stages 1–4 of the model which are integral to the asset mapping method itself. Stages 5 and 6 however are more widely related to its intended use within recovery practice and rather than being included in the figure are explained in further detail later.

Stage 1: Identifying current levels of community engagement through asset mapping

The ABCE workbook (see Collinson and Best, 2019) begins with the need to identify opportunities for engagement in the local community. It highlights four domains, key to adding a more systematic approach to mapping and engaging with community resources. These are: 1. professional services; 2. peer support and mutual aid; 3. sports, recreation, and arts; and 4. education, employment, and training.

Stage 2: Gain a better understanding of each asset

Once the assets have been mapped, the unique characteristics of these are explored, with each asset rated in relation to its accessibility (for example, location, transport links, opening times), affordability, and its associated social network (for example, are others who attend in recovery or not). For those early in their recovery journey, there may be a preference to access assets that are recovery-specific. Engagement in non-recovery-centric assets, however, is likely to support community integration and long-term recovery growth, and as such, differentiation between the networks associated with each asset is useful.

It is suggested that assets are explored and subsequently rated using a traffic light system, with assets rated green, amber/yellow, or red. This would indicate an asset was 'very accessible' (green), 'fairly accessible' (amber/yellow), or 'not accessible' (red). Although this approach is somewhat subjective for the individual rating the assets, its simplicity makes it understandable and easy to interpret by the individual and implement within practice. Think of this as a 'Trip Advisor' style approach, in which assets are rated and recommended on a peer-to-peer basis.

Figure 7.2: Stages 1–4 of the Asset Based Community Engagement framework

Stage 3: Explore the personal interests of the individual

In the ABCE approach, the person doing the mapping should spend time with the individual to understand what their skills, passions, and hobbies are. This empowerment approach helps the individual to shape their own journey and reflect on what matters to them, and therefore to identify the profile of community resources that are most likely to be suitable to their needs at that particular stage in their recovery journey.

Stage 4: Identify barriers to community engagement

Acknowledging barriers to engagement at a micro, meso, and macro level is a unique aspect of ABCE, and both resources and barriers can occur at the local community level but also at the national (structural) level in terms of policies, laws, norms, and cultural conventions. This section of the ABCE framework draws influence from both addiction recovery and wider community participation, including, but not limited to, barriers such as simply not knowing enough about what exists within the local community; resources not being gender or culturally appropriate; lacking confidence or motivation to engage with such resources; or other constraints such as work or family or transportation. That is not to say these barriers can all simply be 'overcome', but it takes a step towards recognizing what these are and the impact they have on an individual's engagement, or lack of engagement. By doing so, individuals can be supported in a more person-centred manner.

Stages 5 and 6 are relevant once the mapping process has occurred, as these are focused on assertively linking individuals to these resources, should they desire to become further engaged in their community. Ideally, this process is done on a one-to-one basis, for example, between the individual in recovery and their recovery worker or community connector, but it has also been done in a group setting among stakeholders from the community. While this approach allows for knowledge of the locale to be shared in real time, it is important to do more than simply list a directory of assets but instead to pay attention to what is actually utilized and the connections that exist into the resources identified. Without doing so, disconnection may arise between what professionals in a community may be aware of and list, and what is actually being sought out and utilized by the target groups, based on perceived barriers for both the individual and for the group.

With regard to community capital, the ABCE framework operates according to two dominating principles. First, it is a process that helps identify the extent to which community capital exists – both the resources a community has and the capability individuals possess to access these. The knowledge derived from this process also acts as a mechanism to build recovery capital at a larger level, as individuals are supported to engage in new resources, and through this process new resources and connections emerge, strengthening the overall community capital reserves in that location. The impact of ABCE results from the community driving this process itself (for example, those in recovery and currently engaged in resources that are supporting their recovery), so knowledge of local resources is built and shared on a peer-to-peer basis, creating new dynamism and energy in community groups and increased opportunity for each new generation of people undertaking recovery journeys. However, this takes place within a fluid and dynamic context, with reductions in community capital possible as well as gains, depending on the processes of group evolution and success. In other words, the process of undertaking the ABCE work creates new connections and empowerment in communities and increased participation in community resources extending well beyond the initial target groups. Typically, the coordinating group becomes a new community asset in itself and will have a central role to play in community development work.

Collinson (2021) has more recently began to explore the relationship between community engagement (as captured through the four domains of the ABCE workbook) and the impact this has on individual recovery pathways (assessed through use of the REC-CAP; Cano et al, 2017). These data, while only drawing on a small sample (n=50) of individuals in recovery in Sheffield, UK, begin to shed light on this dynamic process. Key findings from this preliminary work are highlighted in the breakout box.

Box 7.1: Key findings from ABCE in practice (Collinson, 2021)

1. *Engagement across multiple domains is important.* Individuals who were engaged in at least one resource involving each of the categories of peers and mutual aid; sports, recreation, and arts; and education, employment, and training had significantly better outcomes six months into their recovery journeys than those who did not. This finding is supportive of the 'social cure' literature (Jetten et al, 2012) which recognizes the value of identification with multiple groups, and the Social Identity Model of Recovery (Best et al, 2016) as engagement in a diverse range of groups are likely to support the formation of new social identities which are supportive of an individual's recovery. The process of social identity change is likely to begin when an individual becomes engaged in pro-social assets, supportive of their sobriety (Frings and Albery, 2015) and involvement in multiple groups is likely to support not only recovery identity but is indicative of active citizenship and ability to engage with community assets and resources.
2. *A shift from 'recovery centric' engagement to 'wider community' engagement is needed.* When individuals' primary health needs are met (for example, substance use or mental health challenges), the need for professional services is reduced significantly and it is engagement in the other domains (as mentioned earlier) which leads to more positive outcomes at six months. Individuals who do this are effectively extending their community capital beyond the recovery community and accessing a more diverse range of community recovery resources.
3. *There is no one size fits all approach.* Engagement must suit the individuals' own needs, interests, skills, and passions and other demographic factors such as gender, race, age, and so on matter. In this study (Collinson, 2021), while levels of engagement were not dependent on gender, the type of engagement was. In particular, women were more likely to be engaged in different community resources and favoured shifting from recovery-centric to wider-community resources at an earlier stage (Collinson and Hall, 2021). Moreover, barriers to further engagement also differed by gender. An example of this was that male participants were more likely to report not knowing enough about what existed in their community, perhaps signifying differences in how they tapped into their social networks to leverage or share knowledge of the locale.

Integrating ABCD and ABCE into conceptual models of recovery capital

ABCD and ABCE are both frameworks intended to support the growth of recovery capital by maximizing the resources available to the individual in recovery and generating residual social and community capital as a result of the process. However, as with the Reciprocal Community Development model outlined in Best et al (2014), the aim is to ensure that the community as a whole benefits, creating new social ties and reducing barriers and social exclusion for people both in recovery and in active addiction, and also for other excluded and marginalized groups in the community. The relationship with social capital is central to this: individuals with higher levels of social capital will generally have greater access to community capital and so have enhanced opportunities to build the resources needed for sustained recovery (Best et al, 2016). If individuals with depleted stocks of social capital, resulting from either membership of excluded groups or social isolation, can successfully be linked into pro-social, meaningful resources it is not only their ability to access community capital that is enhanced, but recovery capital as a whole, through new social networks and the resulting impact on social identity and positive feelings of citizenship. But this should be from a position of equality where both the assumption and the reality is that the person in recovery both benefits from and contributes to the effectiveness of the community group or resource.

The models of ABCD and ABCE are both predicated on the assumption that, through leveraging existing resources (such as the skills and assets of the people and place), and creating a culture that is nurturing and healing, we can look not only to increase the 'stocks' of recovery capital that individuals in recovery must have to prosper, but more broadly strengthen community cohesion and create nurturing, inclusive communities. This is where the contagion of recovery and hope can ripple throughout the locale and individuals are provided with the opportunity not only to embrace recovery but to truly prosper so the processes of ABCD and ABCE are both catalysts of mobilization and incubators for new pathways and new emerging assets.

Recovery as a systems concept

While there have been some impressive anecdotal stories about the effectiveness of ABCD, and some growth in research rigour through the ABCE model, the quantity of scientific evidence remains limited and its implementation inconsistent. There are two particular concerns – one around communities where resources are highly depleted, or highly dispersed, as in rural communities, and second, the actual and perceived accessibility of community resources to disadvantaged populations. The next section examines systemic approaches to building community capital – in the form of Recovery Oriented Systems of Care and Inclusive Recovery Cities – which may offer some solutions to the limited impact and evidence of the asset-based approaches. Further, by viewing them through the lens of recovery capital, they may offer clearer metrics around impact assessment and effectiveness.

In 2008, William White produced an initial monograph on Recovery-Oriented Systems (ROSC) of care (White, 2008) based on the concept that recovery is most effectively delivered where specialist services are integrated. White described the ROSC as 'the complete network of indigenous and professional services and relationships that can support the long-term recovery of individuals and families and the creation of values and policies in the larger cultural and policy environment that are supportive of these recovery processes' (2008, 28). Sheedy and Whitter (2009) extended this concept by listing what their review of the evidence summarized to be the core components of a ROSC, namely that it had the following attributes:

- Person-centred; inclusive of family and other ally involvement; involved individualized and comprehensive services across the lifespan; based on systems anchored in the community.
- The delivery of services involved continuity of care and partnership–consultant relationships (replacing expert–patient power imbalances) that were both strength-based and culturally responsive.
- The commitment to personalization is reflected in requirements of responsiveness to personal belief systems, commitment to peer recovery support services, and through the inclusion of the voices and experiences of recovering individuals and their families.
- All of these are brought together through integrated services that offer system-wide education and training, with ongoing monitoring and outreach, driven by outcomes, research based, and adequately and flexibly financed.

Exciting and innovative examples of ROSCs from the United States were subsequently described in a book called *Addiction Recovery Management* edited by two key figures in the recovery field, William White and John Kelly, and published in 2011. These case studies showed that recovery can be contagious in systems as well as in individuals and that the emerging Recovery Oriented Systems build on the existing strengths and resources in communities. As a result, each ROSC is unique to its location (and its temporal placement) as a core component of what they achieve is predicated on existing community recovery capital and how these resources can be coordinated and mobilized.

It is essential for ROSCs to offer support to individuals at all stages of their substance use careers and recovery journeys – through prevention, intervention, treatment, and post treatment. This is a beneficial shift, recognizing that it is not reasonable to assume recovery will occur solely while in treatment (Skogens and von Greiff, 2014). Instead, support must be flexible, offering autonomy to the individual to choose a recovery pathway which is suited to their own needs and is not time-limited (Sheedy and

Whitter, 2009). Ensuring a continuum of care is readily available (Bassuk et al, 2016) has become a favoured approach among service commissioners and funders (McLellan et al, 2000; Humphreys and Tucker, 2002), as it acknowledges the complexity of recovery and recognizes this as a personalized and individual journey. A significant benefit that comes from the growth and recognition of ROSCs is that access to community resources (which has a direct impact on the accumulation of community capital) is central to maximizing the impact of ROSCs. While individuals may 'get sober' in treatment or recovery-centric spaces, they truly begin to flourish in the broader community. Therefore, supporting integration and engagement at a broader, more holistic level is critical, typically through pathways to integrated support and access to jobs, friends, and houses.

Also originating in the US, 'The Phoenix: A sober active community', has emerged as another recovery-focused initiative applying similar principles to building community capital in a way that not only benefits the individual themselves, but the community at large. The Phoenix is a non-profit that provides free, meaningful activities and social events (such as CrossFit, running clubs, meditation, and sober spaces at music festivals, among other things) in-person and online to anyone with 48 hours of continuous sobriety.

Some of the key principles outlined in this chapter are also echoed in the approach taken by The Phoenix. For example, their membership base includes both those in recovery from substance use or mental health, but also those choosing to live a sober life and supporters of these individuals, including family or affected others. This community-wide approach seeks to challenge perceptions of addiction recovery, stigma, and exclusion, while mainstreaming healing, so that the community at large is afforded access to the process of community engagement as a means to promote better outcomes. This also supports the transition from 'recovery centric' to 'non-recovery centric' community engagement, given the broader community comes together to engage in meaningful activities as one (that is, those in recovery alongside those who are not).

Additionally, The Phoenix's meaningful activities and social events are born out of the passion and interests of their members and volunteers, as well as leveraging what is available within the communities. This integrates recovery into the soil of local communities and increases its visibility. Finally, through bringing other partners (such as CCAR, Recovery Dharma, SheRecovers, and more) into their online platform, The Phoenix are building an ecosystem or 'marketplace' of recovery communities, events, and wider resources. These mutually beneficial partnerships build bridges within the recovery community, that can support the long-term recovery and transformational growth of individuals, all accessible through the tap of a button.

In Europe, a subsequent iteration of the ROSC model has been Inclusive Recovery Cities (IRC; Best and Colman, 2018). In essence, the IRC model takes the ROSC concept and extends it to ensure that it addresses community recovery capital with three very clear goals:

1. Reducing stigma and exclusion through active and positive interactions between the recovery community and the wider community.
2. Actively contributing to civic activities by arranging public-facing events that promote and champion connection.
3. Increasing the bridges between the recovery community and the wider community generating mutual and reciprocal benefit.

Following initial successes in Gothenburg in Sweden, Ghent in Belgium, and Doncaster in the UK, the model has grown extensively through its implementation across 14 municipalities in the Balkan region. This approach is strongly linked to a 'reciprocal altruism' model in which recovery communities are valued as equal partners in community participation and citizenship and where recovery is characterized as both inclusive and integral to the well-being of the wider community. In effect, this model is about creating the conditions in which community recovery capital can proliferate and where its implementation has wider civic benefit. There are also now ten UK Inclusive Recovery Cities that have committed to working together to create a model that is effectively enacting public celebrations of recovery that contribute to citizenship and community well-being. This creates loose partnerships based on city-specific innovations and strengths but united by a common vision and purpose of championing recovery as something positive that becomes entrenched and entwined in wider community well-being.

Conclusion: Community capital is restorative, transformative, and liberating for the community

There is a growing recognition that recovery is an individualized, personal journey but one that takes place on a complex stage involving multiple actors and a set and setting that are highly influential in changing the direction and the trajectory of the journey, through support and through systems and structures that can enable and frustrate in equal measure.

The language of recovery capital has provided the foundations for a metric for recovery progress that has largely been operationalized at an individual level with a number of measures developed in the last decade characterizing where the individual rates or scores on that journey. While there has been a recognition – through scoring personal experiences of social and community capital – that the individual's journey is shaped by the 'who' and 'what' they encounter on the path, there has yet to be a similar operationalization of what constitutes a 'recovery-supportive' or a 'recovery-restrictive' community.

Asset-Based Community Development (ABCD) and Asset-Based Community Engagement (ABCE) have moved the field forward in providing frameworks for understanding the role of community and in offering potential mechanisms for intervention at that level, with the latter also providing some additional measurement methods around assessing impact. However, the science and resulting generalizability of these approaches remains limited and the argument advanced here is that they need to be framed within a community recovery capital measurement approach and embedded within broader and more ambitious community engagement models.

The emergence of Recovery-Oriented Systems of Care and, in particular, Inclusive Recovery Cities, not only brings the scenery to the front of the stage, it also affords us the opportunity to start measuring and mapping what components of context – number of mutual aid groups, availability of affordable housing, accessible pathways to employment – constitute the pathways that people in recovery walk, and how they can be enhanced to create the optimal conditions for recovery growth. But not only for recovery growth, but for how that generates a symbiotic relationship with community engagement, well-being, and collective efficacy.

References

Ashford, R.D., Brown, A., Brown, T., Callis, J., Cleveland, H.H., Eisenhart, E., et al (2019) 'Defining and operationalizing the phenomena of recovery: A working definition from the recovery science research collaborative', *Addiction Research and Theory*, 27(3): 179–88.

Bassuk, E.L., Hanson, J., Greene, R.N., Richard, M., and Laudet, A. (2016) 'Peer-delivered recovery support services for addictions in the United States: A systematic review', *Journal of Substance Abuse Treatment*, 63: 1–9.

Best, D. (2019) *Pathways to Desistance and Recovery: The Role of the Social Contagion of Hope*, Bristol: Policy Press.

Best, D. and Laudet, A. (2010) *The Potential of Recovery Capital*, RSA Projects, Royal Society for the Arts.

Best, D. and Savic, M. (2015) 'Substance abuse and offending: Pathways to recovery', in R. Sheehan and J. Ogloff (eds) *Working Within the Forensic Paradigm: Cross-Discipline Approaches for Policy and Practice*, Abingdon: Routledge, pp 183–5.

Best, D. and Colman, C. (2018) 'Let's celebrate recovery. Inclusive cities working together to support social cohesion', *Addiction Research and Theory*, 27(1): 55–64.

Best, D. and Hennessy, E.A. (2022) 'The science of recovery capital: Where do we go from here?', *Addiction*, 117(4): 1139–45.

Best, D., Beckwith, M., Haslam, C., Haslam, A., Jetten, J., Mawson, E., and Lubman, D. (2016) 'Overcoming alcohol and other drug addiction as a process of social identity transition: The Social Identity Model of Recovery (SIMOR)', *Addiction Research and Theory*, 24(2): 111–23.

Best, D., Byrne, G., Pullen, D., Kelly, J., Elliot, K., and Savic, M. (2014) 'Therapeutic communities and the local community: Isolation or integration', *Therapeutic Communities Journal*, 35(4): 150–8.

Best, D., McKitterick, T., Beswick, T., and Savic, M. (2015) 'Recovery capital and social networks among people in treatment and among those in recovery in York, England', *Alcoholism Treatment Quarterly*, 33(3): 270–82.

Betty Ford Consensus Panel (2007) 'What is recovery? A working definition from the Betty Ford Institute', *Journal of Substance Abuse Treatment*, 33(3): 221–8.

Blickem, C., Dawson, S., Kirk, S., Vassilev, I., Mathieson, A., Harrison, R., and Lamb, J. (2018) 'What is asset based community development and how might it improve the health of people with long-term conditions? A realist synthesis', *SAGE Open, BMC Health Service Research*, 8: 1–13.

Brooks, F. and Kendall, S. (2013) 'Making sense of assets: What can an assets based approach offer public health?', *Critical Public Health*, 23(2): 127–30.

Bull, T., Mittelmark, M.B., and Kanyeka, N.E. (2013) 'Assets for well-being for women living in deep poverty: Through a salutogenic looking-glass', *Critical Public Health*, 23(2): 160–73.

Cano, I., Best, D., Edwards, M., and Lehman, J. (2017) 'Recovery capital pathways: Modelling the components of recovery wellbeing', *Drug and Alcohol Dependence*, 181: 11–19.

Cassetti, V., Powell, K., Barnes, A., and Sanders, T. (2020) 'A systematic scoping review of asset-based approaches to promote health in communities: Development of a framework', *Global Health Promotion*, 27(3): 15–23.

Cloud, W. and Granfield, R. (2008) 'Conceptualising recovery capital: Expansion of theoretical construct', *Substance Use and Misuse*, 42(12): 1971–86.

Coleman, J. (1990) *Foundations of Social Theory*, Cambridge: Harvard University Press.

Collinson, B. (2021) *What is the Role of Community Engagement in Developing Women's Recovery Capital*, PhD thesis, University of Derby, Available from: https://repository.derby.ac.uk/item/981w4/what-is-the-role-of-community-engagement-in-developing-women-s-recovery-capital

Collinson, B. and Best, D. (2019) 'Promoting recovery from substance misuse through engagement with community assets: Asset based community engagement', *Substance Abuse: Research and Treatment*, 13, 1178221819876575.

Collinson, B. and Hall, L. (2021) 'The role of social mechanisms of change in women's addiction recovery trajectories', *Drugs: Education, Prevention and Policy*, 28(5): 426–36.

Connolly, K. and Granfield, R. (2017) 'Building recovery capital: The role of faith-based communities in the reintegration of formerly incarcerated drug offenders', *Journal of Drug Issues*, 47(3): 370–82.

Dingle, G., Cruwys, T., and Frings, D. (2015a) 'Social identities as pathways into and out of addiction', *Frontiers in Psychology*, 6: 1–12.

Dingle, G.A., Stark, C., Cruwys, T., and Best, D. (2015b) 'Breaking good: Breaking ties with social groups may be good for recovery from substance misuse', *British Journal of Social Psychology*, 54(2): 236–54.

Edwards, M., Soutar, J., and Best, D. (2018) 'Co-producing and re-connecting: A pilot study of recovery community engagement', *Drugs and Alcohol Today*, 18(1): 39–50.

Friedli, L. (2013) '"What we've tried, hasn't worked": The politics of assets based public health', *Critical Public Health*, 23(2): 131–45.

Frings, D. and Albery, I.P. (2015) 'The social identity model of cessation maintenance: Formulation and initial evidence', *Addictive Behaviors*, 44: 35–42.

Granfield, R. and Cloud, W. (1999) *Coming Clean: Overcoming Addiction Without Treatment*, New York: New York University Press.

Haines, A. (2009) 'Asset-based community development', in R. Phillips and R. Pittman (eds) *An Introduction to Community Development*, London: Routledge, pp 38–48.

Humphreys, K. and Tucker, J. (2002) 'Toward more responsive and effective intervention systems for alcohol-related problems', *Addiction*, 97(2): 126–32.

Jetten, J., Haslam, A., and Haslam, C. (2012) *The Social Cure; Identity, Health and Wellbeing*, Hove, UK: Psychology Press.

Kelly, J. and White, W. (eds) (2011) *Addiction Recovery Management*, New York: Humana.

Kretzmann, J. and McKnight, J. (1993) *Building Communities from the Inside Out: A Path Toward Finding and Mobilising a Community's Assets*, Skokie, IL: ACTA Publications.

Kretzmann, J. and McKnight, J.P. (1996) 'Assets-based community development', *National Civic Review*, 85: 23.

Kretzmann, J.P. and Russel, C. (2018) *The Four Essential Elements of an Asset-based Community Development Process. What is Distinctive About an Asset-based Community Development Process?*, ABCD Institute.

Kretzmann, J.P., McKnight, J., and Puntenney, D. (2005) *Discovering Community Power: A Guide to Mobilizing Local Assets and Your Organization's Capacity*, Evanston, IL: Asset-Based Community Development Institute, School of Education and Social Policy, Northwestern University.

Manning, V., Best, D., Faulkner, N., Titherington, E., Morinan, A., Keaney, F., et al (2012) 'Does active referral by a doctor or 12-step peer improve 12-step meeting attendance? Results from a pilot Randomised Control Trial', *Drug and Alcohol Dependence*, 126(1): 131–7.

Martinelli, T.F., Nagelhout, G.E., Bellaert, L., Best, D., Vanderplasschen, W., and van de Mheen, D. (2020) 'Comparing three stages of addiction recovery: Long-term recovery and its relation to housing problems, crime, occupation situation, and substance use', *Drugs: Education, Prevention and Policy*, 27(5): 387–96.

McLellan, A., Lewis, D., O'Brien, C., and Kleber, H. (2000) 'Drug dependence, a chronic medical illness: Implications for treatment, insurance, and outcomes evaluation', *JAMA*, 284(13): 1689–95.

McKnight, J. and Block, P. (2010) *The Abundant Community: Awakening the Power of Families and Neighbourhoods*, San Francisco: Berrett-Koehler Publishers Inc.

Nurture Development (2023) Asset Based Community Development (ABCD) – Nurture Development, https://www.nurturedevelopment.org/asset-based-community-development/ [Accessed 31 January 24].

Patton, D., Best, D., Pula, P., and Hollandy, Y. (2023) 'The culture of recovery: An antidote to coloniality', *Addiction & Criminology*, 6(5): 166.

Putnam, R.D. (2000) 'Bowling alone: America's declining social capital,' In *Culture and Politics: A Reader*, New York: Palgrave Macmillan US, pp 223–34.

Sampson, R.J. (2017) 'Collective efficacy theory: Lessons learned and directions for future inquiry', in Francis T. Cullen, John Paul Wright, and Kristie R. Blevins (eds) *Taking Stock*, England: Routledge, pp 149–67.

Sheedy, C.K. and Whitter, M. (2009) *Guiding Principles and Elements of Recovery Oriented Systems of Care*, Rockville, MD: SAMHSA.

Skogens, L. and von Greiff, N. (2014) 'Recovery capital in the process of change – differences and similarities between groups of clients treated for alcohol or drug problems', *European Journal of Social Work*, 17(1): 58–73.

Substance Abuse and Mental Health Services Administration (2012) *SAMHSA's Working Definition of Recovery*, Substance Abuse and Mental Health Services Administration.

Timpson, H., Eckley, L., Sumnall, H., Pendlebury, M., and Hay, G. (2016) '"Once you've been there, you're always recovering": Exploring experiences, outcomes, and benefits of substance misuse recovery', *Drugs and Alcohol Today*, 16(1): 29–38.

White, W. (2008) *Recovery Management and Recovery-Oriented Systems of Care: Scientific Rationale and Promising Practices*, North-East and Great Lakes Addiction Technology Transfer Center: University of Wisconsin–Madison, Center for Health Enhancement, Wisconsin, United States.

White, W.L. (2009) 'The mobilization of community resources to support long-term addiction recovery', *Journal of Substance Abuse Treatment*, 36(2): 146–58.

White, W. and Cloud, W. (2008) 'Recovery capital: A primer for addictions professionals', *Counselor*, 9(5): 22–7.

Yates, R. (2014) 'Recovery capital, addiction theory and the development of recovery communities', *The Turkish Journal on Addictions*, 1: 96–112.

8

A Realist Perspective on Recovery Capital: Agents, Structures, Contexts, and Mechanisms

Tim Leighton

Overview

The main argument of this chapter emphasizes the need to progress from measuring and specifying recovery capital to explaining more completely how it operates as a medium of exchange, building on the valuable body of work that has already moved in this direction.

The first section of the chapter will argue that it is difficult to analyse and address the acknowledged gaps in the science of recovery capital (Best and Hennessy, 2022) without considering the historical arc of its development against a longstanding and continuing ideological conflict, which has itself transformed into a new shape over the past 30 years. It will then move to considering how the understanding of components of recovery capital have changed over time and the implications of this for research.

I will then suggest that one significant way of moving forward is to adopt a critical realist approach. Realism, including critical realism, holds that the world has an existence independent of our knowledge of it, and that it is possible to develop scientific knowledge about unobservable structures and mechanisms that cause events in the world. In particular, critical realism enables the scientific study of emerging social structures and their mutually transformative relationship with human agency. This opens the possibility of explaining more fully how the landscape of recovery is created and sustained or hindered.

Critical realism proposes that a context of facilitating and constraining mechanisms activate or hinder recovery mechanisms, which produce outcomes both at the individual level and also at the level of emerging social structures. In this chapter, I argue that the realist conception of contexts and mechanisms improves the field's current understanding of recovery mechanisms, usually investigated by identifying mediators of outcomes via statistical models. In particular, the need to include the role of reasoning in the analysis, in a broad sense that includes values and emotions, and volition, will be emphasized.

This framework will help to clarify the 'ambiguity about how best to separate the domains of Recovery Capital to understand them as entities in the real world' (Best and Hennessy, 2022, 1142). It will also help illuminate how the field of addiction recovery is both reproduced and transformed in the relationship between individual and corporate agents and the social and cultural structures of recovery.

Background

When William Cloud and Robert Granfield published their study of people who had achieved 'natural recovery' from addictions (Cloud and Granfield, 1994; Granfield and Cloud, 1996, 1999; and see Chapter 2 in this volume), their findings were framed as a challenge to the current orthodoxy about addiction in the United States. This held that durable remission required the acceptance of addiction as a chronic, incurable condition, entailing life-long attention to recovery, which could never be completed as there was an ever-present danger of the disease reinstating itself. The belief that professional treatment was required to initiate recovery was also widespread, and their 1994 paper, 'Terminating addiction naturally: post-addict identity and the avoidance of treatment', presented their study participants as 'black swans' whose existence (together with many more who had been identified by researchers and addiction experts) clearly called into question the orthodox view. The authors made a strong argument that challenges to the dominant view were resisted because of vested interests who had created a lucrative and booming industry, based on marketing the imperative for treatment.

The evidence for natural remission without treatment or mutual aid support was so substantial that the black swans transmuted into an 'elephant that no one sees' (Granfield and Cloud, 1996). These early papers focused on what the authors described as a hidden population of middle-class addicts. The majority of these created a 'post-addict identity' that tended to marginalize or eliminate the experience of addiction as a component of current self-concept, in contrast to the 'engulfment in the addict identity' or the adoption of an addict identity with 'master status' (Brown, 1991). Moreover, many participants articulated an active avoidance of treatment and mutual aid based on strong disagreement with the ideology, which they saw as counterproductive and demeaning. Many regarded the culture of mutual aid groups as fostering dependency, and some felt that associating with others who had a history of addiction was risky and unhealthy. These participants seemed to emphasize an individualistic outlook and an uneasiness with a communitarian concept of recovery. This was one of the challenges the study raised to the then current orthodoxy in the US, which held that 12-step mutual aid was essential for secure recovery.

Indeed, Granfield and Cloud's 1999 book, *Coming Clean: Overcoming Addiction Without Treatment,* was welcomed by strong critics of the treatment industry and the disease model of addiction, such as Stanton Peele, who wrote an effusive foreword to the book. However, a closer look produces a more nuanced picture. Despite what the authors term critical differences, they say 'many of our untreated remitters engaged in activities that are functionally equivalent to effective treatment and 12 Step group participation' (Granfield and Cloud, 1999, 26). They describe many examples of finding new meaning in activities and relationships, in which participants typically displayed 'focused immersion' and an intensity comparable to the relationship with the addiction. This often produced 'improvements in their level of attachment to and involvement in society', which in turn produced strong satisfactions and rewards (Granfield and Cloud, 1999, 95). This appears to be a reciprocal process in which opportunities for involvement support desistance of substance use, but being addiction-free in turn increases the enthusiasm and enjoyment of the involvement.

The term recovery capital was not used in the early articles, but the book introduces the concept and elaborates its usefulness, in particular for practitioners to adopt lessons from the experience of natural recovery (Granfield and Cloud, 1999, 179–90). A clear model is presented in which the availability of resources permitted the use of strategies which supported continued desistance from uncontrolled substance use. The most important and commonly used strategies were the development of alternative activities, developing relationships with non-using people, and avoidance of drug-using people and situations. The focus of natural recovery as presented in the book is on remaining free from addiction, but it is clear that other commonly cited components of recovery, such as personal well-being, life-satisfaction and social involvement, are also supported and produced by the availability of resources.

So at the stage when Granfield and Cloud were publishing their book and early articles, the ideological tension was between a model of addiction and recovery predicated on the chronic and incurable disease model, which insists on the need for treatment and long-term association with other recovering addicts, and one which stresses individual mastery, personal autonomy, and choice of associations. It also positions both addiction and recovery within a social context. The former is characterized by its critics as representing vested interests and bad science and as a tool of social control, creating dependency, while the latter is seen by disease model advocates as being in denial of the true nature of addiction. The advocates of natural recovery see it as having many advantages including cost savings, less disruption, and less stigma, as well as supporting empowerment, choice, and self-efficacy (Granfield and Cloud, 1999, 162–72).

Strategies and mechanisms

However, the actual mechanisms which produce recovery in both models have considerable overlap. There is a certain irony in the interesting and important finding by Kelly and colleagues that the three most important mechanisms of recovery in Alcoholics Anonymous are increasing self-efficacy, the changes in social network entailed in reducing contact with people who use alcohol problematically, and increasing relationships with those who are sober (Kelly et al, 2011). These are identical to those identified as effective strategies by those in Granfield and Cloud's study, together with conversion to highly meaningful life activities, both religious and secular (Granfield and Cloud, 1999, 80–4). It perhaps should be noted that the participants in Project MATCH (Babor and Del Boca, 2003), data from which Kelly et al used to perform mediational analysis, most likely possessed a fair quantum of recovery capital, especially the 'out-patient sample' who responded to newspaper ads and similar recruitment invitations to enter the study. This may be contrasted with the 'aftercare sample' who entered Project MATCH via a stay in a residential treatment centre. The latter, while still benefitting from the same mechanisms as the other cohort, also significantly benefitted from increasing spiritual practices and from relief from depression (Kelly et al, 2011). The Project MATCH participants generally achieved very good outcomes with quite a minimal intervention both in intensity (for the outpatients) and duration. This may indicate they are closer to Granfield and Cloud's participants in social positioning and access to support than to the often very socially disadvantaged clients of typical community-based drug services. These are likely to need an extended period of recovery capital building before they are able to find stability, security, and full autonomy.

In two papers published in 2001, Granfield and Cloud reintroduce the term recovery capital and provide several examples of mechanisms – that is, how access to human, physical, and social capital provide benefits which support or sustain recovery (Granfield and Cloud 2001). They also introduce the term 'negative social capital' and describe deficits in human capital. The example of negative social capital given is of a man who maintains social contact with drug-using friends, so that while these relationships form part of his social capital, they are potentially or actually detrimental to his programme of recovery (Cloud and Granfield, 2001, 99). The concept of negative recovery capital was elaborated in a later paper (Cloud and Granfield, 2008). We must return to this concept later as it is an issue that complicates the scientific understanding of recovery capital and is a potential source of confusion.

The rise of the new Recovery Movement

The first decade of the 21st century saw a crucially important set of changes which affected the conceptual development of recovery capital. Following increasing momentum in the 1990s, what William White (2005) has called a 'renaissance of recovery as an organizing construct' manifested in a flurry of political initiatives, advocacy, and activism in the United States. During this decade, a new recovery movement became visible, together with an emerging recognition of a recovery community (White, 2008). Mutual aid societies, such as SMART Recovery and Lifering Secular Recovery, founded in the 1980s and 1990s as alternatives to the 12-step fellowships, acquired a higher profile and systematic research into their membership and effectiveness began. Institutes in the US and the UK published definitions of or consensus statements about addiction recovery, generally in a tripartite form including durable control or cessation of addictive use, improved well-being and quality of life, and social participation (Betty Ford Institute Consensus Panel, 2007; UKDPC, 2008).

Another development was the gradual (if limited) acceptance of a plurality of versions of recovery, including those who were not totally abstinent, or who were managing their recoveries with the aid of opiate substitution treatment (for example, White and Mojer-Torres, 2010).

The 2000s saw new advocacy based on public testimony about addiction and recovery, and an increase in community-based recovery organizations led and staffed for the most part by people with lived experience of addiction and offering a range of services and resources. The Center for Substance Abuse Treatment (CSAT) changed the focus of its Recovery Community Services Program in 2002 from education and policy change to active support for peer-led community projects. As a result, this was a key step in the professionalization of recovery and lived experience. The emergence of a community dedicated to people in recovery provided by people in recovery, offering opportunities for recreation, social support, sport, training, education, and work made an extension of the recovery capital concept necessary. This emergence into public and academic consciousness of a recovery community marks a break from the early publications of Cloud and Granfield. Although their participants relied on social, physical, and human capital, both to protect themselves from the more dire consequences of their addiction and to initiate, develop, and sustain their recoveries, almost all made a distinct choice not to enter a communal venture based on association with other people who had quit substance use. Their social capital consisted of relationships and connections within the family and the general community.

They tended to keep their addiction histories private and tightly rationed, and their current personal and social identities minimized the significance of their addiction experience.

The appearance and definition of community capital

Two further related ideas blended into this progression. One was the contagious nature of recovery – the visible community of recovery created more recovery opportunities and benefits for the community. The other was the recognition that collectives such as families and neighbourhoods also suffered deleterious effects as a result of addiction and that they were also deserving of recovery for themselves (Best and Laudet, 2010).

This eventually led to the coining of a new domain of recovery capital: community capital (White and Cloud, 2008; Best, Musgrove, and Hall, 2018). This was both an advance and problematic, leading to similar conceptual confusions as had been pointed out by Portes when the term social capital had begun to be applied by sociologists to communities as well as to individuals. It becomes unclear whether community capital inheres in community assets themselves or in the relationships of connection to those resources, which activate personal and corporate agency. Just as Marx defined capital as a social relation (Shaikh, 1990) concerned with the making of profit, so too is recovery capital, though with a different set of concerns.

Moreover, with the growth of recovery advocacy as a social justice initiative, interest in recovery was expanding beyond the middle-class participants of Granfield and Cloud's study sample to encompass disadvantaged sections of society and minority communities, who were widely acknowledged as bearing the worst impacts of addiction, experiencing marginalization and stigma at a greater scale, and having fewer opportunities through formal structures and supports to develop recovery capital. Granfield and Cloud had themselves foreseen this – from their earliest articles they had urged that the lessons of natural recovery be extended to treatment practitioners and to other social groups with lower recovery capital. It could be said that the study of recovery capital moved from examining the routes out of addiction by those who possessed it, to enquiring how recovery capital is built by, with, and for those who lack it. In practice, an example would be using measures such as the Assessment of Recovery Capital (ARC) to identify areas of recovery strength and threat, and to create recovery plans prioritizing areas of low strength and high threat (for example, Best, 2010).

The paradigm shift and its subsequent tensions

In 2007, William White published an article announcing what he saw as a major paradigm shift, from what he called 'pathology and intervention paradigms' (that is, on a medical model) to a 'solution-focused recovery paradigm' and invited research to shift from the aetiology of addiction and the effectiveness of treatment to the lived experience of recovering people. White followed this paper with a substantial quantity of monographs, commentaries, practitioner primers, and historical analyses. Both in the US and the UK, researchers began to include measures of recovery capital in their studies.

The ideological tension shifted in this decade. Instead of a polarization between the disease model and its mandated abstinence versus mastery and control of addictive behaviour, two other polarizations emerged into focus (although they were not new). Both become relevant to the argument of this chapter that the historical context cannot be ignored in analysing the gaps in research into recovery capital.

In a very British debate, a subset of recovery advocates and policy makers who were labelled the 'New Abstentionists' (Ashton, 2008) were viewed by advocates of harm reduction as conducting a moral crusade based on abstinence (Best et al, 2010). This dispute was mainly about treatment effectiveness and the merits of residential rehabilitation versus methadone maintenance. It is important to our argument as it concerns power, money, and the distribution of resources (Best, Groshkova, and McTague, 2009).

In the UK, resources for drug services are allocated by the government in line with the current 'Drugs Strategy'. From the mid-1990s the emphasis had been on scaling up access to opioid substitution treatment, partly as a response to public perception of 'drug-related crime' (Stevens, 2007). The Drugs Strategies published prior to 2010 did not mention the word recovery at all, but after that the word erupts into multiple occurrences in both English and Scottish strategies and policy papers. It is clear that in this new discourse being in 'recovery' or 'full recovery' and being on prescribed treatment are considered distinct categories. One consequence of this was the failure to provide or even recognize the need for substantial recovery resources for those on opioid substitution treatment, even though attempts were made to make such treatment 'recovery oriented' (NTA, 2012). This may partly explain why in research by Best and colleagues those in maintained recovery (that is, on a methadone prescription) 'were more anxious about using heroin and had lower self-efficacy, worse physical health, poorer quality of life, and more peer group members still using' (Best et al, 2011), and why 'heroin users in abstinent recovery generally reported better functioning than those in maintained recovery' (Best et al, 2012). Rather than being an inherently inferior type of recovery, it may be that maintained recovery is tougher due to the lack of recovery capital provision. After all we have many examples of people achieving sustained life success and recognition while maintained on methadone (White and Mojer-Torres, 2010).

As to how recovery capital comes to be provided, resources need to be built with corporate agency by people who *care enough*, whether those be advocates with lived experience, or professionals, civil servants, or others. The 'provision' results from exchange of personal, social, and community capital. Some people can do this on their own but it usually requires corporate agency and bounded solidarity. Examples of this are the emergence of the 12-step fellowship Methadone Anonymous and more recently Medication-Assisted Recovery Anonymous (MARA), which aim to mitigate the stigma experienced by many in traditional mutual aid fellowships (Gilman, Galanter, and Dermatis, 2001; Ginter, 2016; White et al 2013).

The second polarization, even more relevant to the gaps in our knowledge and still ongoing, echoes the earlier argument about the necessity of treatment for recovery as well as White's paradigm shift. This, in the UK at least, concerns whether recovery (from a political point of view mainly in the form of relief from social ills and healthcare costs) springs most fruitfully from professional intervention on traditional lines, supported by state funding and commissioning, or whether it derives from community activism and is created by the recovering community itself. Of course, both of these may create great benefit and both may be needed (Granfield and Cloud stressed that not everyone is a good candidate for natural recovery), but the division here is driven by a struggle for support, recognition, and funding between traditional treatment providers who began to offer recovery support services, and Lived Experience Recovery Organisations (LEROs, similar to RCOs in the US). Alcoholics Anonymous and the 12-step movement could be said to have switched sides. Previously associated with the disease model and adopted by many treatment programmes as a central philosophy, it was now recognized as an exemplar of community recovery. A well-known addiction professional, Mark Galanter, wondered in 2016 whether 'the volunteerism established in AA can be extended so that 12 step members can provide a protective environment without a professional driven format' (Galanter, 2016, 153).

In the UK at least, the recovery community was and is divided as to whether community recovery organizations should seek funding and commissioning on an equal basis to and independent from traditional treatment providers, or whether they should remain 'off-grid' and self-fund and self-generate their activities, somewhat in the spirit of AA being 'fully self-supporting, declining outside contributions' (Livingston, private communication, 2023). It has been argued that the British government was at one point persuaded that 12-step mutual aid, being free and presented to them as kind of 'magic bullet', would relieve them of some of the need to fund treatment (Ashton, 2008). Similarly, the willingness of volunteers to run and staff LEROs/RCOs for free or for very little has perhaps hampered their recognition and their access to financial support provided to traditional treatment agencies.

Relevance to the research programme

I argue that the historical, ideological, and political context must be taken into account in guiding research. This is because, as outlined later, recovery research is not and should not be a value-neutral activity. It is not a disinterested search for abstract knowledge, but a means to encourage and facilitate social change.

The central argument of this chapter is that we need to understand not only how to describe and categorize recovery capital and how to measure it, though these are vital foundations. We need to understand recovery capital as a process of potential and actual exchange. Building and exchanging are processes, and processes involve mechanisms, which are usually not directly observable.

In the following sections I will lay out some of the issues that still need addressing, while recognizing the huge value of research already carried out. I suggest that a scientific realist approach, deriving from the theoretical and field research of Margaret Archer, an influential British sociologist and philosopher in the tradition of critical realism, and from the work on evidence-based policy and realist evaluation by Ray Pawson and Nick Tilley, offers a strong way forward.

In particular, this is because scientific realism contends that physical and social reality are structured, and that causal processes (generative mechanisms) take place at a level below that of the observable. What occurs at the observable level are events produced by the activation of causal mechanisms in a particular context. Mechanisms exist as potentials that may or may not be actualized (for example, recovery capital always has potential to be exchanged for benefit, but it may or may not be, depending on context). A great deal of natural science accepts this as a matter of course. Scientific and critical realism have developed methods for identifying and describing mechanisms and explaining their action.

This perspective is of great value in understanding the variation and complexity of the experience of addiction and recovery and the differential response of individuals and groups in the face of interventions and resources.

Concretely, it may help to explain why individuals high in recovery capital and with many opportunities fail to achieve recovery and how groups of disadvantaged people find ways to transcend these disadvantages and achieve well-being, meaning, and solidarity. It also allows understanding of how new pathways and forms of recovery can be created and sustained.

The current state of knowledge

The following sections aim to suggest how the research community should develop programmes to illuminate what recovery capital is and how it works. This requires some analysis and critique of research that has already been done, and a proposal that a realist perspective will augment and integrate the knowledge that has so far been accrued. The literature on recovery capital has been comprehensively reviewed by Hennessy (2017), and recently Best and Hennessy (2022) surveyed the existing research and asked 'Where do we go from here?'.

They pointed out that research on recovery capital to date had been unsystematic, that there was little agreement about the concept or about the components of recovery capital. They explain that many of the studies depend on self-report measures using a plethora of different questionnaires, which is a significant limitation. The six questionnaires they mention had expanded to ten by the time of the recent review by Bunaciu and her colleagues. And these included no less than 41 separate constructs (Bunaciu et al, 2023). Hennessy had drawn attention in her review to other ways of assessing recovery capital, including analysing social networks and peer support, and the relationship of these to well-being and quality of life. This proliferation of measures is a clear indicator of the lack of consensus and coordination in the field, particularly as while there is some overlap in the constructs measured by the questionnaires, there are also significant differences, for example in attention to social networks.

Cultural capital

Hennessy's review of the literature is replete with insight. Both she and Best are aware of the value of quantitative and qualitative methods and the need for both (Hennessy, 2017; Best and Hennessy, 2022). Her approving commentary on the change in the meaning of 'cultural capital' is important in pointing out that what is valuable in the lives of recovering people in different social and cultural conditions is broader and more varied than simple economic prosperity. But her comments also highlight some of the conceptual confusion, especially concerning the location of social and cultural capital. Cultural capital, as it appeared in the earlier work of Cloud and Granfield, was somewhat close to Bourdieu's conception. Bourdieu was insistent that cultural capital, while it was provided by families by way of their physical capital (by affording private school fees, for example), was a possession of the individual actor. He saw it as a form of human capital 'defined as the habitus of cultural practices, knowledge, and demeanors learned through exposure to role models in the family and other environments' (Bourdieu, 1979, cited in Portes, 1998). Bourdieu also stressed the fungibility of social and cultural capital – they could be exchanged for wealth by way of increased human capital. Granfield and Cloud saw the possession of cultural capital in the form of pro-social attitudes and taking on conventional norms and values as giving access to some of the necessities of recovery, including economic and social stability.

However, the description of cultural capital in White and Cloud's (2008, 3) primer for addictions is something very different: '*cultural capital* is a form of community capital. It constitutes the local availability of culturally-prescribed pathways of recovery that resonate with particular individuals and families'. Depending on how 'availability' is read, this appears to locate the capital itself in the community. This is one of the confusions flagged up by Portes (1998). He says that it is 'important to distinguish the resources themselves from the ability to obtain them by virtue of membership in different social structures', because to do so risks a circular argument. Defining social (or cultural) capital as equivalent to the resources obtained therefrom 'is tantamount to saying that the successful succeed' (Portes, 1998, 5). In addition to distinguishing the resources themselves, Portes advises that it is also important to distinguish the possessors of social capital (who make claims) from the sources (who provide the benefits).

These are very important points. There is no good reason why the components of recovery capital and the labels attached to them have to remain faithful to their original meaning in Bourdieu or Coleman. But if a change in meaning leads to a change in the understood location of the conceived entity, that is likely to create confusion. However, what Portes omits to analyse, in the case of an emergent recovery community, is how those who make claims may join together to form *corporate actors* (for example, to create a LERO), and thus become themselves the creators of resources and the providers of benefits.

The assignment of components of recovery capital to different levels, for example, individual, micro, and meso, does not really help by itself as there is a danger that these end up as areas rather than levels, in the service of measurement, that is, characterized by a 'flat ontology', limited to the empirical domain.

What this means is that the vast majority of research in our field depends on measuring and counting things which can be observed (the empirical), and then applying statistical analysis to establish whether these sets of events (for example, individuals receiving an intervention and reduced drug use by these people later on) can be linked mathematically. Everything that is included in the statistical analysis consists of numbers derived from observations. This level of observations excludes underlying unobserved events, and also the causal mechanisms that underly those events. That is why research of this kind that restricts itself to observations is said to have a 'flat ontology'.

Moreover, to isolate what events caused the results, statistical models and research designs attempt to 'control' for other possible factors that might have affected the outcomes. The problems with this in trying to understand human behaviour are various, but the two main ones from a realist point of view are, first, that human beings and their organizations consist of 'open systems' which have such a range of variables and inherent uncertainty that isolating the ones being researched is essentially impossible, and second, these methods cannot offer any explanation for the causal effects, or illuminate why these effects vary in different contexts.

There is no attempt in an experimental design to explore the mechanisms of change, which hampers our understanding if our aim is to improve opportunities for recovery and to maximize the range of people who could benefit from, and contribute to building, recovery resources in the community. This statement may come as a surprise to those familiar with the increasing use of the term 'mechanisms' in addiction treatment and recovery research. But it is a central part of the realist critique of statistical research that what are revealed typically as mediators in a causal chain are not the mechanisms themselves (for example, Kazdin, 2007; Tryon, 2018). What are referred to as mechanisms are really a kind of measured input that is correlated with an output and, as Bunge (2004, 201) comments, 'observable inputs and outputs ... explain nothing'.

What is the way forward? As we explore the concept of recovery capital, it is clear that the key questions are 'What is it?' and 'How does it work?'. These are not questions that can be answered just by measuring things, nor just by inviting people to talk about their recovery experience (qualitative research), although both of these play an indispensable role in building an explanatory model.

Clearly recovery capital is in some way related to social structures and also related to individual (or corporate) agency. This is expressed with some vagueness by Coleman (1988); is it possible to clarify it? Both Bourdieu and Coleman see social capital as different from human and physical capital because 'it inheres in the structure of relations between actors and among actors' (Coleman, 1988, S98). A relational model supported by an appropriate ontology is required both 'to understand the domains as entities in the real world' and to clarify how these entities are related. It is this relational aspect which has the potential to transform our knowledge and realign our research about recovery.

Reflexivity and transformation

To clarify what is meant here I will provide some illustrations. A central insight of a realist perspective is that people encounter the world as it is, but also have the power to transform it. People act in society according to established routines which often unconsciously guide their actions (what Bourdieu calls habitus), but they are also able to create, build on, subvert, and transform social structures. Archer (2007, 2012) holds that what mediates between people and social structures is *reflexivity*, meaning the ability to attend to one's internal conversation. As society becomes more complex and unpredictable, reflexivity becomes ever more important, and people's reliance on habitus to navigate the world becomes much less adequate. To make one's way successfully requires reflexivity to enable good choices and to progress one's identity project.

She identifies modes of reflexivity which are more and less successful in making one's way in the world. She shows that people tend to have a dominant mode of reflexivity but that they may evolve in the direction of others. What I wish to do here is to connect reflexivity to recovery capital, as shown in Table 8.1.

To illustrate the interactions and exchanges of recovery capital, including the use of reflexivity, here is a vignette. Some assert that a community provides recovery resources and that those in need access these or fail to do so. But imagine the process of a person starting their recovery in an area where there are no Narcotics Anonymous (NA) meetings. They have access to transportation

Table 8.1: Archer's modes of reflexivity and their relation to recovery capital

Margaret Archer's modes of reflexivity (characteristics from Goodman, 2017)		
Reflexivity mode	Characteristics	Hypothesized relation to recovery capital
Communicative reflexivity	Our inner conversations require confirmation and communication with others before we act. A person who predominantly uses communicative reflexivity will consider what their peers are thinking and will want to act in such a way as to fit in.	Need for a supportive recovery-focused friendship group – social capital invested in mutual aid participation.
Autonomous reflexivity	Our inner conversation requires no confirmation with others, they are self-sustained and lead directly to action. Here we have a 'lone inner dialogue' which leads to action.	High self-efficacy and self-determination (personal capital). May have less need for a recovery-focused support network. Social capital invested in a wider range of beneficial relationships. Better placed to innovate recovery resources where there are few or none.
Meta-reflexivity	Our inner conversation is subjected to our own criticism. We may then critique whether effective action is possible before we act. This is about self-monitoring, our thinking about how we think, and when dominant results in self-questioning.	This mode can help or hinder action. It may be connected to what pragmatic recovery participants regard as overthinking or intellectualizing. But as personal recovery capital it can be converted into innovation and creativity.
Fractured reflexivity	Our internal conversations intensify the disorientation and distress we already feel and this leads to inaction.	Clearly lacking in personal capital, reduced confidence and trust. Diminished social capital due to difficulty maintaining supportive relationships.

to travel to meetings in other areas (physical/financial capital) where they make friends (social capital) and learn how NA meetings work (cultural capital). Their evolving value system promotes a wish to start a meeting locally, both to improve their own recovery support and to distribute it to others. It is via reflexivity that this person can understand what is required to start a local meeting. They make phone calls to local churches, meet a minister, agree to rent the hall weekly. They make posters and get them put up in the local doctors' surgery. They commit to weekly attendance to open and lead the meeting. The new meeting is advertised in other NA meetings. Established members commit to visiting and speaking to support the meeting. A few newcomers venture in, and some stay. Within a few years there are several NA meetings in the area. For each involved person, new friendships offer support, and constructive mutual interactions build self-confidence and self-esteem. The clarity of the NA service structure (a pre-existing cultural structure also created over time and in various places via analogous mechanisms) shores up the new meetings and ensures that members encounter a secure and predictable environment that is also welcoming and inclusive. The meetings become real entities, sustained by people's commitment but independent of any specific actor.

It will also be the case that some people will not succeed in integrating into this support structure. This will be a result of constraining mechanisms, for example the negative recovery capital described earlier, an emotional investment in relationships that are not conducive to integration into a 12-step recovery. Alternatively, they may hold strong beliefs, as did many of Granfield and Cloud's participants, that are incompatible with the 12-step philosophy (Granfield and Cloud, 1999, 107–20). These mechanisms ultimately act through the person's reasoning (not simply rationality), what Archer refers to as the internal conversation, which is an articulation of that person's concerns and values. This can lead to failure to recover, but, crucially, it can also lead to developing or identifying alternative recovery social support systems, such as secular mutual aid groups.

Traditional mutual aid groups leave significant social needs unmet, such as work or training opportunities, recreational activities, social support for groups of people who do not benefit from established mutual aid, support and building of recovery capital for those who have not yet decided to embark on abstinence or who wish to base their recovery on moderated use or on the assistance of prescribed medication.

The LERO/RCO as corporate actor

In each of these cases, initiatives have emerged to begin to meet these needs. Once more the core mechanisms involve individuals recognizing a need and a potential solution, usually banding together to form what is known as a 'corporate actor'. Once again human, social, and cultural capital are made use of to start building new entities, such as recovery clubs and Lived Experience Recovery Organisations (LEROs), which in turn allow people who encounter and participate in them to thereby transform themselves. The strengthening of these entities and the activity of their participants produces what Best has called community capital. The activities and purposes of LEROs in the UK have a wide range, from sports and recreational clubs, hill-walking groups, and drop-in centres for support, advice, and friendship, to training opportunities and study groups, linkage to detoxification and rehab, and micro-businesses such as bakeries, coffee shops, catering services, and restaurants. Each of these has evolved via the exchange of recovery capital.

These entities do not emerge in a vacuum, they have a pre-existing social and cultural *context* which may facilitate, augment, or hinder their development. Once again, it is imperative to understand the mechanisms by which the context affects the success or otherwise of recovery resources. This context may be rather complex and multi-stranded, but it is possible to identify the key mechanisms. The way the alcohol and drug treatment, and larger healthcare and policy environment, view the needs of people in and yet to be in recovery and how individual treatment programmes and agencies support the growth of community capital are important mechanisms, as are the ways by which funding is secured to pay for rented spaces, equipment, expertise, and eventually salaries. A kind of corporate habitus sustains the tendency of commissioners to commission what they know (traditional treatment) and being subject to 'evidence-based' guidance makes it hard to get support for new recovery-oriented initiatives. Once again this may be transcended by individual commissioners who develop a value-driven interest and understanding of recovery and start to support recovery organizations actively and directly, in which their volition and reflexivity are crucially implicated.

The point here is that to understand recovery capital we need to go beyond measuring it as a quantity. We need to study how it actually works. In 2012, Best and colleagues wrote:

> The hypothesis emerging is that personal and social recovery capital are mutually generative in that engaging with peers in recovery is part of a process of community engagement and immersion in meaningful activities that build a positive identity and protect against relapse. The associations reported between meaningful activities, quality of life, psychological well-being and improved health are a dynamic process of change mediated by social experiences and that generates recovery capital. (Best et al, 2011, 6)

As will be explained later, the use of terms such as 'mutually generative' is strongly suggestive of a realist perspective.

By 2022, Best and Ivers were welcoming 'an opportunity to examine the interactions and dynamic relationships between internal and contextual factors' (Best and Ivers, 2022, 156). They go on to say that Best (2019a) suggested that 'assertive linkage to community resources and ongoing positive role models and peer advocates represent the conditions through which personal capital can be nurtured'.

The emerging hypothesis referred to in the earlier comments cannot be elaborated into an explanatory theory by measuring quantities. The elaboration will come from understanding mechanisms. How exactly do encounters with positive role models nurture personal capital, for example? Very likely through mechanisms various and complex, but also comprehensible and useful. Activities become meaningful via the socially mediated internal conversation of the actor, but what actually makes an activity meaningful? Using a realist context-mechanism-outcome framework (to be discussed later) we can research how this happens and how participation in meaningful activity enhances personal identity, perceived quality of life, and well-being.

What is going on when a person in early recovery meets positive role models? Is it the learning of 'cultural practices, knowledge, and demeanors' as Bourdieu (1979, 3–6, cited in Portes 1998) would have it? Well, in some cases probably yes. But also through being accepted by admired others who have longer recovery time might well increase hope and self-esteem. These increases in personal and cultural capital make possible further contributions to community recovery resources and thus to the stock of community capital.

It should be clear that these processes are not determined but context dependent. The context also includes the possibility of constraining recovery mechanisms. It is equally important to understand these to find ways to mitigate and circumvent them.

How can a realist approach help, and what does realist research look like?

The two orthodox research paradigms in the addiction and recovery field are the quantitative 'positivist' approach based on statistical analysis of measured quantities, and the qualitative paradigm, represented by a range of approaches, but generally considered 'contructivist' or 'hermeneutic/ interpretivist' (attempting to discover meaning). Constructivism holds that people construct their own knowledge of the world and more radical forms of social constructionism hold that reality is created entirely socially.

Quantitative studies measure things while qualitative studies (usually) collect interviews with participants and analyse the content and structure of these to discover themes, connections, and meanings. Both of these have made valuable contributions to the study of recovery capital, but each leaves us a step or two away from understanding how recovery capital actually 'works' in the world. Combining the two in 'mixed methods' studies may reveal a range of perspectives but often in practice, the rigorous approaches to mixed methods (for example, data triangulation) are not followed and there is a lack of thorough integration for new knowledge generation.

Realism offers a solution in that it does not discount the value of empirical testing, nor does it fall into the relativism of social constructivism (Greenwood, 1992). Realism accepts that our knowledge of the world is largely socially constructed but that it refers to entities that are objectively real and exist independent of our epistemology. A realist perspective can help to understand the relationship between the reasoning of people acting in the world and the social conditions they encounter, and how human action can transform social reality. It offers a distinctive version of the relationship between agency and structure which avoids both an oversocialized conception of people and the opposite position whereby social manifestations are reduced to the actions of individuals.

A critical realist perspective also allows us to include a recognition of the value-laden nature of social change and research into it. Dennis Wrong (1961) pointed out that social research tends to become disconnected from the questions that we are asking. Research into recovery capital is predicated on questions about how individuals and society can be made better, in particular how the recovering community might expand and become more inclusive, and this 'critical' dimension must not be ignored, else we end up with what Wrong calls a 'one-sided view of reality'. He also points out that the goal of social research cannot be reduced to 'the creation of a formal body of knowledge satisfying the logical criteria of scientific theory set up by philosophers and methodologists of natural science' (Wrong, 1961, 183). A related point is made by Margaret Archer who says, commenting on the range of opinions about social change, 'nobody is wrong, but everybody is exercising selective perception. The selectivity of folk wisdom is matched by academic approaches that are equally selective. This is the source of the conundrum – and it is rooted in empiricism.' (Archer 2013, 1).

This is not an empty or irrelevant academic argument. Because of this perspectival selectivity, social change and its components are inevitably contested at the empirical level; as a result, ideological conflicts have real effects on how recovery and recovery capital are conceived and what we ought to do to progress our goals. What counts as recovery affects what will be acknowledged as recovery capital. Recovery capital research has the potential to illuminate how these conflicts hinder or facilitate the growth of recovery in individuals and communities. Rather than discounting measurement there is a need to clarify how 'measurement tools' such as REC-CAP (Cano et al, 2017) make a practical difference as they are used to inform care planning and community engagement, and as they help a person make new choices via their reflexivity (in other words filling out a REC-CAP and discussing it can shift the way someone reasons and makes choices).

This integration of a person's reasoning into the understanding of their response to social and cultural resources they encounter is a crucial advantage of a realist approach. As Ray Pawson has pointed out,

> Social programmes ... offer resources (material, social, cognitive) to subjects, and whether they work depends on the reasoning of these individuals. Subjects may seek out programmes (or not), volunteer for them (or not), find meaning in them (or not), develop positive feelings about them (or not), learn lessons from them (or not), apply the lessons (or not), talk to others about them (or not). It is within this interpretative process – or mechanism – that the causal powers of programmes reside. Any method of systematic review that omits such a vital agent from its core hypotheses automatically sets up a depleted inquiry. (Pawson, 2006, 45)

This applies just as much to recovery resources and the programmes or less formal social initiatives that provide them.

And crucially involved in this process is the building and deployment (or not) of recovery capital. If social capital, for instance, consists of usable personal connections, the possessor of this capital may deploy it, or not, to the advantage or disadvantage of their recovery, and whether they do depends on the person's reasoning. (It is important to point out here that a realist account of reasoning certainly includes personal values and the emotions arising from them, it is not simply 'rational choice'.)

But these personal values are not static, they are influenced and transformed within social relationships. The actions resulting from a person's reasoning are thus dependent on context. And all of these, outcomes, mechanisms, and context, are processes not static situations.

So, a realist approach can help construct a (testable) account of how personal values and priorities both change as a result of encountering social and cultural structures but also potentially transform them in turn. It explains how groups of people with common interests and 'bounded solidarity' become 'corporate agents' with increased power to transform and develop social and cultural resources. It can also show how pre-existing structures and corporate agents, such as using and dealing networks, can inhibit such development. Drug using and drinking (at least for young males in particular) are profoundly social activities, and they offer social roles to occupy, which helps explain why finding alternative social connections and roles is predictive of recovery.

In summary, a realist approach, by using a context > mechanisms > outcomes framework, can illuminate how recovery capital is generated, and how it is deployed, including its exchange into other forms. With a focus on reflexivity as a key mechanism that mediates between persons and social structures, there is a huge opportunity, to be discussed later, to improve the participation of people with lived experience of addiction and recovery in a collaborative research process.

Complexity and ambivalence – an example

A realist approach allows us to address complexity and ambivalence in recovery capital research. As might be expected, most strategies adopted to initiate and sustain recovery have pros and cons, in that the same strategy may have both positive and negative effects on recovery capital.

An example of this is shown in an elegant study by De Maeyer et al (2011). While the paper does not reference recovery capital directly, it is clearly of relevance to the concept. People who were using methadone long-term to help manage their recoveries were interviewed about their quality of life and the impact that methadone had on this. A thematic analysis produced five themes: having social relationships, psychological well-being, having an occupation, being independent, and having a meaningful life. Each of these was composed of a set of subthemes. Very usefully, the impact of being on methadone is discussed for each theme. Very often this impact is on accessibility of social resources, opportunities to participate in society and receive reward from that, and to develop autonomy and meaningfulness. These are clearly central aspects of recovery capital. Using methadone had positive and negative effects for each theme, for instance the stigmatization of methadone users constrained social relationships and the quality of available jobs (depleting social capital), but the stability and more normal functioning it engendered allowed smoother social integration and better work performance (increasing social capital). The stabilizing effect of methadone on emotions was felt to be both positive in that it improved coping and reduced anxiety (increasing personal capital), and negative in that it was felt to attenuate authentic experiencing (depleting personal capital). Methadone supported independence financially and behaviourally, but constrained independence by producing reliance on supply and making travel difficult.

What does a realist perspective add?

The different ways that one form of treatment both built and hampered different forms of recovery capital will be clear to most readers. How does a realist perspective deepen the explanation?

A realist focus on identifying contexts, mechanisms, and outcomes will clarify how building recovery capital is assisted or impeded, in this case for people who use methadone maintenance to support their recovery. For example, some of the positive mechanisms of methadone include reducing craving for street heroin, stabilization of daily routine, reducing emotional lability and intensity. Whether these mechanisms produce outcomes such as employment, better parenting, improved self-image, and so on depends on contexts. Contexts can include other mechanisms such as the effect of a support group or mentor, or opportunities to avoid other drug users. In all of these examples, personal reflexivity is involved in choice-making or transforming opportunities.

Conversely, contexts such as social stigma or exclusion from traditional mutual aid work against the mechanisms of methadone producing good outcomes. There are also a set of less positive mechanisms at work, say, emotional flattening. The negative outcomes of this could and often are mitigated by other contexts, such as help to reduce the dose or by developing emotional awareness. The use of emotional awareness to change one's experience involves reflexivity. Research into and analysis of contexts, mechanisms and outcomes can really clarify these interlocking mechanisms and shed light onto how things actually work, particularly if the mediating role of volition and the internal conversation is included in the analysis.

Realist research

How might a realist research programme build on existing recovery capital research? Here are some possibilities.

As Ray Pawson has said about social programmes, 'In fact, it is not programmes that work but the resources they offer to enable their subjects to make them work. This process of how subjects interpret the intervention stratagem is known as the programme 'mechanism' and it is the pivot around which realist evaluation revolves' (Pawson, 2002, 342).

This focus is very suitable for recovery capital research as the growing recovery community involves people encountering resources that are variously located and which all have a potential and sometimes a declared aim of building recovery capital. We can see recovery capital as an *outcome*, and explore the mechanisms and contexts that produce it, and we can also see the deployment or exchange of recovery capital as a *mechanism*, with recovery benefits, both personal and social, as the outcome.

All programmes or initiatives will (implicitly or explicitly) have a programme theory or theories. This is also true of entities that offer recovery resources. A typical set of rationales might be 'if we offer an accessible programme of recreational activities to people in recovery they will experience alternative rewards which will make return to drug use less likely, OR they will make supportive friendships OR they will find meaning or increased confidence by participating'. These theories may be implicit and not fully articulated, and they may explain the way the programme builds recovery capital, or it may be mistaken (much interesting realist research has revealed that what programme designers and practitioners think their programme's 'aims and objectives' are may be very different from how participants actually use the resource and how it changed their attitudes, reasoning, and outlook; for example, Duguid et al, 1996).

A realist review of studies in the literature which explicitly enquire into recovery capital or implicitly include it (as with the study by De Maeyer et al described earlier) is likely to have considerable explanatory value. De Maeyer's study might be combined and compared with similar studies, which either explore the same or different recovery strategies. As with conventional systematic review, realist review (or synthesis) can include both quantitative and qualitative studies, but the integration of these is achieved by the light shed on mechanisms in each case.

There is much scope for realistic evaluation of recovery resources and their participants, for example looking at the functioning of LEROs would address important questions such as 'what works, for whom, in what circumstances, and how?' (Pawson and Tilley, 1997, 65). Of particular interest are the emergent processes whereby the primary agency of people who have interests in common, by means of joint goal setting and active organization, forms corporate agency. Understanding these processes will help foster and nurture developing LEROs.

Using reflexivity with participants and researchers

Individuals will also have theories about what helps and hinders their recovery, and will be a vital resource in developing the theory of recovery capital. So far research that has included individuals with lived experience has mainly been done using quantitative thematic analysis or survey methods. However, recovery capital research has been enriched with creative and innovative qualitative methods such as photovoice, community-based participatory action research, social identity mapping, and social media scraping (for example, Nieweglowski et al, 2018; Beckwith et al, 2019; Best, 2019b; Van Steenberghe, Vanderplasschen, and De Maeyer, 2021)

To build on this rich knowledge base, not only is there scope for realist synthesis to bring much of this into a unified framework, but also realist research has developed ways not only of hearing and recording the voices of those with lived experience but also explicitly inviting them to consider the researcher's theory and to assist actively in improving and developing it. An early example was Pawson's 'theory-driven interview' in which participants were invited to critique the supposed aims and methods of a prison education programme, reflecting on their own motivations and experience and comparing these with the explicitly presented 'programme theory'. What this revealed was that participants had various well-articulated reasons for participating in prison education courses but none of them undertook them for the purported purpose of reform through increased awareness. This interview method has been developed and improved (Hamilton-Smith and Hopkins, 1998), moving further from the limitations of forced choice in considering how experience relates to theory.

It is not difficult to see how this focus on theory would augment knowledge of recovery capital and how it works. A very useful addition to the context–mechanism–outcome framework was offered by Dalkin et al (2015) in a study of practitioner decision making in palliative care for older adults. Recognizing that many social interventions involve stakeholders' volition, both in implementation and take-up, they recommended separating the mechanism into resources and reasoning.

This framework used in a series of theory-driven interviews could be used to deepen understanding of a) how recovery capital is built and b) recovery capital use as a volitionally activated mechanism. There is much original and enlightening research that could be augmented using this kind of analysis, including studies that do not refer explicitly to recovery capital. Three examples are Kelly and Greene's (2014) article on the mechanisms by which increased spiritual practices sustain recovery, Kelly, Levy, and Matlack's (2024) study of why people choose to attend different types of mutual aid and what they get out of attending, and Zemore and colleagues' (2023) article about shared meaning in recovery.

There is also great scope in this framework for confirmation and development of models such as the Inkspots and Ice Cream Cone model (Best and Ivers, 2022), by mobilizing the reflexivity of people with lived experience. It is of great importance to emphasize that recovery capital and its 'expenditure' has a critical role not just in sustaining individual recovery but also in the creation of recovery resources and the transformation of communities.

Conclusions

The chief argument of this chapter has been that research into recovery capital requires attention to the cultural and historical context, that recovery science cannot and should not be 'value-free', and that despite enormous progress in research from both quantitative and qualitative designs, there seems to be a stuck point in our knowledge which is important to overcome. I suggest that one problem is an inadequate conception of the generative mechanism, despite an increasing attention to mediators and causal chains in addiction research generally, and the burgeoning appearance of the term mechanism in seminal studies. I contend that a realist approach, underpinned by the theoretical and field work of Margaret Archer and others in the critical realist tradition, offers one way forward.

Critical realist theory is complex and vigorously debated and can seem intimidating and difficult to approach. I agree with Jan Karlsson (2019) that Archer's models of structure, agency, identity, and social change are the most fruitful currently in social science and 'the best we have access to' (Karlsson, 2020, 3). Recently, guides to critical realist method, including how to identify and describe generative mechanisms, have appeared written by and for early years researchers (for example, Maisuria and Banfield, 2022). I am optimistic that more researchers into recovery and the processes of recovery capital will become interested in using critical realist methods in their studies.

A key idea I wanted to emphasize was recovery capital as a process of exchange. Understanding how recovery capital is or is not deployed and in what contexts it is exchanged for benefits seems to me to be a new area of enquiry, albeit building on important work by others. Some have compared recovery capital to financial capital in the form of a bank balance, but I feel that, rather than expenditure, a better analogy is with investment, as the exchange of recovery capital seems to produce returns for both provider and beneficiary, particularly in the context of a lived experience recovery organization based on mutuality. This process is potentially genuinely morphogenetic (Archer, 2013), leading to a transformation of social conditions for the better.

References

Archer, M.S. (2007) *Making our Way through the World: Human Reflexivity and Social Mobility*, Cambridge, UK: Cambridge University Press.

Archer, M.S. (2012) *The Reflexive Imperative in Late Modernity*, Cambridge, UK: Cambridge University Press.

Archer, M.S. (2013) 'Social morphogenesis and the prospects of morphogenic society', in M.S. Archer (ed) *Social Morphogenesis*, Dordrecht: Springer, pp 1–22.

Ashton, M. (2008) 'The new abstentionists', *Druglink*, January (Special Insert).

Babor, T.F. and Del Boca, F.K. (eds) (2003) *Treatment Matching in Alcoholism*, Cambridge: Cambridge University Press.

Beckwith, M., Best, D., Savic, M., Haslam, C., Bathish, R., Dingle, G., et al (2019) 'Social identity mapping in addiction recovery (SIM-AR): Extension and application of a visual method', *Addiction Research & Theory*, 27(6): 462–71.

Best, D. (2010) *Establishing a Recovery Philosophy in Drug Treatment Services and Systems*, Paisley: University of the West of Scotland.

Best, D. (2019a) *Pathways to Recovery and Desistance*, Bristol: Policy Press.

Best, D. (2019b) 'What do you need to recover? Jobs, Friends and Houses', in *Pathways to Recovery and Desistance*, Bristol: Policy Press, pp 49–66.

Best, D. and Laudet, A. (2010) *The Potential of Recovery Capital*, London: Royal Society of Arts.

Best, D. and Hennessy, E.A. (2022) 'The science of recovery capital: Where do we go from here?', *Addiction*, 117(4): 1139–45.

Best, D. and Ivers, J.H. (2022) 'Inkspots and ice cream cones: A model of recovery contagion and growth', *Addiction Research & Theory*, 30(3): 155–61.

Best, D., Groshkova, T., and McTague, P. (2009) 'The politics of numbers', *Druglink,* September/October, 16–17.

Best, D., Musgrove, A., and Hall, L. (2018) 'The bridge between social identity and community capital on the path to recovery and desistance', *Probation Journal*, 65(4): 394–406.

Best, D.W., Groshkova, T., Sadler, J., Day, E., and White, W.L. (2011) 'What is recovery? Functioning and recovery stories of self-identified people in recovery in a services user group and their peer networks in Birmingham England', *Alcoholism Treatment Quarterly*, 29(3): 293–313.

Best, D., Gow, J., Knox, T., Taylor, A., Groshkova, T., and White, W. (2012) 'Mapping the recovery stories of drinkers and drug users in Glasgow: Quality of life and its associations with measures of recovery capital', *Drug and Alcohol Review*, 31(3): 334–41.

Best, D., Bamber, S., Battersby, A., Gilman, M., Groshkova, T., Honor, S., et al (2010) 'Recovery and straw men: An analysis of the objections raised to the transition to a recovery model in UK addiction services', *Journal of Groups in Addiction & Recovery*, 5(3–4): 264–88.

Betty Ford Institute Consensus Panel (2007) 'What is recovery? A working definition from the Betty Ford Institute', *Journal of Substance Abuse Treatment*, 33(3): 221–8.

Bourdieu, P. (1979) 'Les trois états du capital culturel', *Actes de la Recherche en Sciences Sociales*, 30(1): 3–6.

Brown, J.D. (1991) 'Preprofessional socialization and identity transformation: The case of the professional ex', *Journal of Contemporary Ethnography*, 20(2): 157–78.

Bunaciu, A., Bliuc, A.M., Best, D., Hennessy, E.A., Belanger, M.J., and Benwell, C.S. (2023) 'Measuring recovery capital for people recovering from alcohol and drug addiction: A systematic review', *Addiction Research & Theory*, 32(3): 225–36.

Bunge, M. (2004) 'How does it work? The search for explanatory mechanisms', *Philosophy of the Social Sciences*, 34(2): 182–210.

Cano, I., Best, D., Edwards, M., and Lehman, J. (2017) 'Recovery capital pathways: Modelling the components of recovery wellbeing', *Drug and Alcohol Dependence*, 181: 11–19.

Cloud, W. and Granfield, R. (1994) 'Terminating addiction naturally: Post-addict identity and the avoidance of treatment', *Clinical Sociology Review*, 12(1): 13.

Cloud, W. and Granfield, R. (2001) 'Natural recovery from substance dependency: Lessons for treatment providers', *Journal of Social Work Practice in the Addictions*, 1(1): 83–104.

Cloud, W. and Granfield, R. (2008) 'Conceptualizing recovery capital: Expansion of a theoretical construct', *Substance Use & Misuse*, 43(12–13): 1971–86.

Coleman, J.S. (1988) 'Social capital in the creation of human capital', *American Journal of Sociology*, 94: S95–S121.

Dalkin, S.M., Greenhalgh, J., Jones, D., Cunningham, B., and Lhussier, M. (2015) 'What's in a mechanism? Development of a key concept in realist evaluation', *Implementation Science*, 10: 49.

De Maeyer, J., Vanderplasschen, W., Camfield, L., Vanheule, S., Sabbe, B., and Broekaert, E. (2011) 'A good quality of life under the influence of methadone: A qualitative study among opiate-dependent individuals', *International Journal of Nursing Studies*, 48(10): 1244–57.

Duguid, S., Hawkey, C., and Pawson, R. (1996) 'Using recidivism to evaluate effectiveness in prison education programs', *Journal of Correctional Education*, 47(2): 74–85.

Galanter, M. (2016) *What Is Alcoholics Anonymous? A Path from Addiction to Recovery*, Oxford, UK: Oxford University Press.

Gilman, S.M., Galanter, M., and Dermatis, H. (2001) 'Methadone Anonymous: A 12-step program for methadone maintained heroin addicts', *Substance Abuse*, 22(4): 247–56.

Ginter, W. (2016) 'Methadone Anonymous and mutual support for medication-assisted recovery', in Jeffrey D. Roth, William L. White, and John F. Kelly (eds) *Broadening the Base of Addiction Mutual Support Groups*, London: Routledge, pp 117–29.

Goodman, B. (2017) 'Margaret Archer, modes of reflexivity: The structured agency of nursing action', *Nurse Education Today*, 48: 120–2.

Granfield, R. and Cloud, W. (1996) 'The elephant that no one sees: Natural recovery among middle-class addicts', *Journal of Drug Issues*, 26(1): 45–61.

Granfield, R., and Cloud, W. (1999) *Coming Clean: Overcoming Addiction Without Treatment*, New York: NYU Press.

Granfield, R. and Cloud, W. (2001) 'Social context and "natural recovery": The role of social capital in the resolution of drug-associated problems', *Substance Use & Misuse*, 36(11): 1543–70.

Greenwood, J.D. (1992) 'Realism, empiricism and social constructionism: Psychological theory and the social dimensions of mind and action', *Theory & Psychology*, 2(2): 131–51.

Hamilton-Smith, N. and Hopkins, M. (1998) 'Theory-driven interviewing: From theory into practice', *Bulletin of Sociological Methodology/Bulletin de Méthodologie Sociologique*, 60(1): 80–105.

Hennessy, E.A. (2017) 'Recovery capital: A systematic review of the literature', *Addiction Research & Theory*, 25(5): 349–60.

Karlsson, J.Ch. (2019) 'Social structures and human agency', in B. Danermark, M. Ekström, and J.Ch. Karlsson (eds) *Explaining Society Critical Realism in the Social Sciences* (2nd edn), London: Routledge.

Karlsson, J.Ch. (2020) 'Refining Archer's account of agency and organization', *Journal of Critical Realism*, 19(1): 45–57.

Kazdin, A.E. (2007) 'Mediators and mechanisms of change in psychotherapy research', *Annual Review of Clinical Psychology*, 3(1): 1–27.

Kelly, J.F. and Greene, M.C. (2014) 'Toward an enhanced understanding of the psychological mechanisms by which spirituality aids recovery in Alcoholics Anonymous', *Alcoholism Treatment Quarterly*, 32(2–3): 299–318.

Kelly, J.F., Levy, S., and Matlack, M. (2024) 'A systematic qualitative study investigating why individuals attend, and what they like, dislike, and find most helpful about, smart recovery, alcoholics anonymous, both, or neither', *Journal of Substance Use and Addiction Treatment*, 161, 209337.

Kelly, J.F., Hoeppner, B., Stout, R.L., and Pagano, M. (2011) 'Determining the relative importance of the mechanisms of behavior change within Alcoholics Anonymous: A multiple mediator analysis', *Addiction*, 107(2): 289–99.

Livingston, private communication, July 1, 2023.

Maisuria, A. and Banfield, G. (eds) (2022) *Working with Critical Realism: Stories of Methodological Encounters*, Abington: Routledge.

National Treatment Agency (2012) *Medications in Recovery: Reorientating Drug Dependence Treatment*, London: NTA.

Nieweglowski, K., Corrigan, P.W., Tyas, T., Tooley, A., Dubke, R., Lara, J., et al (2018) 'Exploring the public stigma of substance use disorder through community-based participatory research', *Addiction Research & Theory*, 26(4): 323–9.

Pawson, R. (2002) 'Evidence-based policy: The promise of realist synthesis', *Evaluation*, 8(3): 340–58.

Pawson, R. (2006) *Evidence-based Policy: A Realist Perspective*, London: Sage.

Pawson, R. and Tilley, N. (1997) *Realistic Evaluation*, London: Sage.

Portes, A. (1998) 'Social capital: Its origins and applications in modern sociology', *Annual Review of Sociology*, 24(1): 1–24.

Shaikh, A. (1990) 'Capital as a social relation', in J. Eatwell, M. Milgate, and P. Newman (eds) *Marxian Economics*, London: Palgrave Macmillan UK, pp 72–8.

Stevens, A. (2007) 'When two dark figures collide: Evidence and discourse on drug-related crime', *Critical Social Policy*, 27(1): 77–99.

Tryon, W.W. (2018) 'Mediators and mechanisms', *Clinical Psychological Science*, 6(5): 619–28.

UKDPC (2008) *The UK Drug Policy Commission Recovery Consensus Group: A Vision of Recovery*, London: UK Drug Policy Commission.

Van Steenberghe, T., Vanderplasschen, W., and De Maeyer, J. (2021) *Recovery Pathways: Day-to-day Life of Women with a Drug Use History*, Ghent: Owl Press.

White, W. (2005) 'Recovery: Its history and renaissance as an organizing construct', *Alcoholism Treatment Quarterly*, 23(1): 3–15.

White, W. (2008) 'The culture of recovery in America: Recent developments and their significance', *Counselor*, 9(4): 44–51.

White, W. and Cloud, W. (2008) 'Recovery capital: A primer for addictions professionals', *Counselor*, 9(5): 22–7.

White, W. and Mojer-Torres, L. (2010) *Recovery-oriented Methadone Maintenance*, Chicago, IL: Great Lakes Addiction Technology Transfer Center.

White, W.L., Campbell, M.D., Shea, C., Hoffman, H.A., Crissman, B., and DuPont, R.L. (2013) 'Coparticipation in 12-step mutual aid groups and methadone maintenance treatment: A survey of 322 patients', *Journal of Groups in Addiction & Recovery*, 8(4): 294–308.

Wrong, D.H. (1961) 'The oversocialized conception of man in modern sociology', *American Sociological Review*, 26(2): 183–93.

Zemore, S.E., Ziemer, K.L., Gilbert, P.A., Karno, M.P., and Kaskutas, L.A. (2023) 'Understanding the shared meaning of recovery from substance use disorders: New findings from the What is Recovery? study', *Substance Use: Research and Treatment*, 17, DOI: 10.1177/11782218231199372.

9

The Role of Specialist Substance Use and Addiction Treatment in Building Recovery Capital

Wouter Vanderplasschen, Florian De Meyer, Clara De Ruysscher, Aline Pouille, and Deborah Louise Sinclair

Introduction

How we look at addiction, treatment, and recovery has changed over time. Globally, a wide range of interventions and treatment options are available to deal with substance use problems. From a historical and cross-cultural perspective, various approaches to addiction and its treatment can be distinguished, some of which have endured (van den Brink, 2005; West, 2006). Moral theories of addiction point to the lack of willpower of individuals, suggesting harsh (treatment) methods for behaviour change (for example, boot camps, corporal punishments, and even the death penalty in some countries). Pharmacological theories situate the problem of addiction in the substance, resulting in the Prohibition Act (1920–33) and a War on Drugs in the United States (1980– ...) and other countries. The disease model of addiction, supported by Alcoholics Anonymous and other 12-step facilitated programmes (for example, the Minnesota Model), starts from the assumption that some individuals have an innate deficit that is best managed by lifelong abstinence (van den Brink, 2005). Some psychological theories view addiction as a symptom of an underlying personality disorder, requiring treatment of its root causes (for example, long-term treatment in therapeutic communities). At the same time, behaviourist approaches primarily see substance use as learned (coping) behaviour that can be reversed by, for example, cue exposure. In recent decades, more comprehensive and integrative theories have been developed including the bio-psycho-social model of addiction (treatment) and the prevailing view of addiction as a chronic, relapsing brain disorder

(Heilig et al, 2021). Although non-exhaustive and despite the limitations of most of the aforementioned theories, this brief overview illustrates that dominant views of addiction determine how policies, treatment, and support for individuals with substance use problems are shaped. Currently, prevention, harm reduction, treatment, and recovery support are regarded as valuable public health measures to decrease the impact of substance use and related problems (UNODC, 2018; WHO, 2020). In this chapter, we aim to assess the role of treatment and recovery support services in building recovery capital and to explore how recovery capital is related to enduring treatment outcomes based on available research. This knowledge can help us to develop and optimize treatment programmes that contribute to growth in recovery capital and the reduction of negative elements that may impede addiction recovery.

Addiction recovery and recovery pathways

Addiction recovery can be considered a non-linear, deeply personal process of change involving various life domains, in particular, control over substance use (or sobriety), improved health and well-being, social participation, and active citizenship (Betty Ford Institute Consensus Panel, 2007; UK Drug Policy Commission, 2008). Under the impetus of the personal recovery movement in mental health, leading a productive and meaningful life and striving to reach one's full potential are now central elements of what addiction recovery entails (Ashford et al, 2019).

Several studies have shown that recovery is an idiosyncratic process with multiple pathways, which are chosen based on contextual, cultural, personal, and momentary needs and aspirations (Substance Abuse and Mental Health Services Administration & Office of the Surgeon General, 2016; Dekkers et al, 2021; Bellaert et al, 2022; Day et al, 2023). The recent international REC-PATH study distinguished at least five mechanisms of behaviour change/recovery pathways, including (1) 12-step mutual aid groups; (2) other types of peer-based recovery support; (3) outpatient, community-based treatment (including medically assisted treatment); (4) residential and therapeutic community treatment; and (5) unassisted or natural recovery, without support or involvement from specialist treatment services or peer-based mutual aid (Best et al, 2018; Vanderplasschen and Best, 2021). In this work, Best, Vanderplasschen, and colleagues demonstrated that what we often consider distinct and separate recovery pathways are frequently combined. That is, 41 per cent of persons in addiction recovery in the UK, Belgium, and the Netherlands participated in mutual aid groups as well as in- and outpatient treatment, with another 38 per cent using at least two recovery pathways (Martinelli et al, 2021).

The effectiveness of substance use and addiction treatment has been extensively studied and the evidence for specific interventions has been synthesized in a myriad of systematic reviews and meta-analyses, usually demonstrating small to moderate effect sizes (Miller and Wilbourne, 2002; Beaulieu et al, 2021). Abstinence rates – the primary outcome indicator measured – usually vary between 10 and 50 per cent, depending on the objectives, study design, time window, and quality of the intervention (Hubbard et al, 2003; Johannessen et al, 2019; Vanderplasschen et al, 2019). Although the efficacy and efficiency of treatment are debated due to high relapse and drop-out rates after treatment, length of stay and treatment retention have repeatedly been identified as the most robust predictors of positive treatment outcomes (rather than treatment orientation or type of intervention) (Vanderplasschen et al, 2013). Additionally, the quality of the client-counsellor/therapist relationship, which promotes retention and provides continuing care and support, has been associated with better treatment outcomes (Vanderplasschen et al, 2010; Blodgett et al, 2014). Yet, no single intervention or treatment modality stands out as the 'best' or 'most effective'. It is generally accepted that treatment effectiveness and the extent to which specialist treatment contributes to an individual's recovery process does not solely depend on the quality of an intervention, but also on the person, the point in the addiction/recovery journey, the surrounding support network, and the broader context. The US Surgeon General's Report on Alcohol, Drugs, and Health (2016) outlined multiple pathways to addiction recovery and presented compelling evidence for 12-step mutual aid groups and 12-step facilitated treatment (see also Kelly et al, 2020; Martinelli et al, 2021), as well as substantial support for educational settings and approaches (for example, therapeutic communities, recovery high schools) and recovery housing (for example, recovery residences, Oxford or halfway houses). Treatment is a highly diverse and broad construct and not the only pathway to recovery. Models of recovery and recovery capital have shown a range of alternative (positive) outcome goals and indicators that were not traditionally part of outcome evaluations but can be robust predictors of post-treatment success and recovery (for example, mutual aid participation, subjective well-being, and diversity of social support networks).

Recovery capital and addiction treatment

Granfield and Cloud (1999) introduced the concept of 'recovery capital' to represent the accumulation of internal and external resources that individuals can draw upon to initiate, facilitate, and sustain recovery processes. Commonly, three types of recovery capital are distinguished on multiple ecological levels (Best and Laudet, 2010), namely, personal (for example, self-efficacy and material resources), social (for example, non-using friends and family bonds), and community capital (for example, substance use treatment services and housing options). In contrast, factors that inhibit recovery have been formulated as negative recovery capital or barriers to building recovery capital. These barriers refer to the absence of some types of recovery capital (for example, personal capital: low self-esteem or few communication skills; social capital: lack of family support) or impeding elements that may refrain from building recovery capital (for example, friends or a partner who use drugs; having a criminal record) (Cloud and Granfield, 2008; Patton et al, 2022). Recovery capital is dynamic (positive resources can be added, negative elements can be removed) and can be exhausted or accumulated throughout life. It varies in response to specific conditions and circumstances (Best and Hennessy, 2022). In recent years, there has been a shift away from the traditional focus of treatment on achieving abstinence towards maximizing recovery capital (Laudet and White, 2008; Cloud and Granfield, 2008; Groshkova et al, 2012; Vilsaint et al, 2017). That is, the addiction treatment and recovery fields have emphasized moving away from acute 'cure' and problem resolution to a focus on holistic, enduring recovery with outcomes beyond abstinence (McLellan et al, 2000; Laudet, 2008; Koob and Volkow, 2016; American Society of Addiction Medicine, 2019; Volkow, 2020).

White (2002) has posited that 'most clients entering addiction treatment have never had much recovery capital or have dramatically depleted such capital by the time they seek help' (p 30). While recovery capital can be present when persons who use substances or have substance use disorders initiate specialist treatment, it may also be acquired or retrieved during specialist treatment (White and Cloud, 2008; Parlier-Ahmad et al, 2021). Davidson and colleagues (2010) have stated that, although people who have substantial recovery capital may either recover on their own or with formal help, those who have lost or never possessed sufficient recovery capital will first have to acquire internal and external resources to achieve recovery. Consequently, service providers should offer service users particular conditions for recovery based on their recovery capital (Davidson and White, 2007; Best et al, 2010). By identifying recovery assets and barriers, addiction specialists can be better equipped to provide tailored support across the various stages of the recovery process (Cloud and Granfield, 2008; Laudet and White, 2008; Hibbert and Best, 2011; Skogens and von Greiff, 2014). When working within the conceptual framework of recovery capital, service providers apply a strengths-based approach and will seek to proactively build capacity rather than attending to immediate problems only (a reactive approach) (Topor et al, 2018).

Aims of this chapter

The role of recovery capital is increasingly recognized as central to individuals' recovery processes, growing with more time in recovery but also amenable to change by treatment and recovery support mechanisms. The assessment of recovery capital is a strengths-oriented analysis of personal and environmental resources that support addiction recovery and encompass various elements such as substance use and sobriety, health, citizenship, meaningful activities, coping, and social support (Groshkova et al, 2012). Therefore, this chapter aims to provide an overview of recent studies on recovery capital in relation to the role of specialist treatment and various types of recovery support (for example, peer support, recovery housing) that have been published since the publication of Cloud and Granfield's (2008) landmark paper. A wide range of studies were retrieved, which we have clustered into the following topics:

- quantitative studies of recovery capital in treatment populations and the impact on various functioning outcomes (for example, substance use, quality of life, and employment);
- quantitative studies of the impact of recovery capital on diverse treatment-related outcomes (for example, treatment access, retention, and completion);
- qualitative studies of recovery capital and service providers' related experiences and perspectives;
- qualitative studies of recovery capital as perceived by service users and persons in recovery.

Studies are described in chronological order and a summary of core findings follows each cluster of studies. We conclude this chapter with some general observations and recommendations and discuss ways forward for future research.

1. Recovery capital, treatment, and functioning outcomes

In an early study of recovery capital among 323 individuals with alcohol use disorders in inpatient treatment in Pennsylvania (US) (Sterling et al, 2008), a measure of recovery capital was developed that was administered at treatment intake and three-month post-admission. The authors found modest relationships between the amount of recovery capital and abstinence efficacy and lower recovery capital was related to more alcohol craving.

In an attempt to quantify recovery capital, Groshkova and colleagues (2012) developed the Assessment of Recovery Capital (ARC), a comprehensive measure with acceptable psychometric properties, and consisting of 50 items assessing recovery strengths within ten sub-scales of five items each. The ARC covers a broad range of domains that are critical to recovery at successive stages of the process and is applicable to various recovery pathways including, but not limited to, treatment. The ARC is regarded as a useful complement to deficit-based assessment and monitoring instruments for individuals with substance use disorders in and out of treatment.

Based on the ARC, the REC-CAP instrument has been developed as a holistic tool to assess recovery capital and was first used among individuals in recovery residences in Florida (US) (Cano et al, 2017). The findings indicated that recovery capital grows with spending more time in the residence ('retention') and with increased participation in meaningful activities (education, community engagement, employment). More recovery capital was also associated with a reduction in barriers to recovery and unmet needs which, in turn, promote recovery capital and positive well-being. The authors concluded that it is important to focus on building recovery capital in treatment through offering meaningful activities that can help develop new skills and resources that make the time in treatment valuable and meaningful. A prolonged length of stay is important to reduce recovery barriers and negative recovery capital (Cano et al, 2017).

In an international study (REC-PATH), Martinelli and colleagues (2021) examined the relationship between mutual aid group participation and recovery capital, social network involvement, and commitment to sobriety among persons in drug addiction recovery (n=367) in the UK, the Netherlands, and Belgium. The study findings revealed that participation in mutual aid groups was strongly associated with greater levels of recovery capital (assessed with the Brief Assessment of Recovery Capital, BARC-10; Vilsaint et al, 2017), changes in social networks, and stronger commitment to sobriety. The findings highlight how mutual aid support may complement specialist addiction treatment in building recovery capital. Subsequent analyses of this dataset demonstrated that overall recovery capital was high among this study cohort but reduced slightly over the 12-month observation period (Bellaert et al, 2025). Higher levels of recovery capital at baseline were associated with better quality of life scores and more perceived social support. The study further indicated that recovery capital was significantly higher among persons in sustained (one to five years) and stable (>5 years) recovery compared to persons in early recovery (<1 year).

As part of a larger study, Gilbert (2022) examined the relationship between recovery capital and recovery success among a sample of individuals in addiction recovery involved in community recovery organizations. The study findings affirmed the centrality of recovery capital in participants' recovery efforts in early recovery (<1 year). While treatment and 12-step meetings developed and promoted crucial support relationships modelling an abstinence-based lifestyle, fostering spiritual development, and nurturing self-efficacy, using recovery capital as a theoretical framework helped to reveal potential harms – that is, relationships in treatment and at meetings that could impede recovery (recovery barriers) – in the first months of individuals' recovery trajectories.

Bormann and colleagues (2023b) examined whether service users' recovery capital improved as a function of attending an addiction medicine clinic with active case management (n=136). The study sought to establish whether changes occurred in criminality and concurrent alcohol and methamphetamine use. The ARC scale was used to measure recovery capital and ARC scores increased from 34.1 to 40 during the study. The odds of engaging in criminal activity or using methamphetamine and alcohol were significantly lower when ARC scores were higher.

The same authors (Bormann et al, 2023a) also assessed the relationship between recovery capital and self-reported drinking days in persons seeking opioid use disorder treatment and demonstrated that increases in recovery capital were strongly associated with increased odds of alcohol abstinence, even in the absence of a specific intervention targeting alcohol use.

Best and colleagues (2023) used the REC-CAP measure to predict retention in a large sample of individuals in recovery residence settings (n>2000) in Virginia (US) and measured changes in recovery capital and barriers to recovery at admission and at 90-day intervals thereafter. The study showed gradual improvements in recovery capital over time that were primarily related to reductions in recovery barriers and unmet needs, as well as to increases in recovery group participation. The authors concluded that addressing sobriety and risk-taking, acute accommodation concerns, and mental health issues were strongly related to retention in recovery residences and building recovery capital, as was the degree of social integration in these recovery houses (Jason et al, 2021). The REC-CAP tool was further used by the same authors among adult prisoners who engaged in a transitional therapeutic community programme in Virginia (US) and then engaged with local recovery residences (Best et al, 2024). The results suggest positive effects of this programme on both retention and recovery capital growth and a crucial continuity of care effect when engaging in subsequent recovery housing. These findings are highly supportive of a so-called 'bridging' effect, indicating that continuity of care is associated with continuing growth in recovery capital following the transition to a recovery residence after a prison therapeutic community programme and with positive changes in multiple recovery capital domains.

In addition to being studied as a predictor variable or correlate, recovery capital has also been employed as a treatment outcome indicator. For example, MacDonald and colleagues (2023) assessed the impact of an exercise programme – integrating elements of gymnastics, strongman training, Olympic lifting, sprints, and callisthenics – on individuals undergoing substance use treatment. Compared with non-recipients, participants in the exercise programme exhibited more positive trends in their well-being, including reduced feelings of hopelessness and depression, as well as enhanced energy levels and improvements associated with leading fulfilling and meaningful lives without substance use (measured with the BARC-10) (MacDonald et al, 2023).

Similarly, Belanger and colleagues (2024) evaluated a pilot intensive recovery support intervention for individuals in recovery residences in Virginia (n=175) and found that this novel recovery support, which integrates assertive community linkage and enhanced recovery coaching, outperformed outcomes of the standard recovery housing programme in terms of treatment engagement, retention and recovery capital growth (as measured with the REC-CAP). In this sample, the biggest gains in recovery capital were observed between 90 and 180 days after entering recovery housing, suggesting a period of acclimation and relationship-building to the housing prior to seeing large growth.

Summary

Overall, studies focusing on persons with substance use problems in inpatient and outpatient treatment settings demonstrate growth of recovery capital during and after treatment, which is, in turn, associated with improved substance use outcomes (for example, higher abstinence rates, reduced substance use and craving, and improved self-efficacy; Sterling et al, 2008; Bormann et al, 2023b; Gilbert, 2022) and improved functioning in other domains (for example, having supportive relationships, no criminal involvement, health and well-being, and participation in recovery groups; Bormann et al, 2023b; Gilbert, 2022; MacDonald et al, 2023; Best et al, 2024). Similar observations have been made among persons attending mutual aid group meetings (Martinelli et al, 2021) and individuals in recovery residences (Best et al, 2023; Belanger et al, 2024). In particular, more time spent in recovery residences is related to increased recovery capital, which goes hand in hand with participation in meaningful activities and experiencing fewer recovery barriers and unmet needs (Cano et al, 2017; Best et al, 2023). The combination of (prison therapeutic community) treatment and recovery housing may provide a crucial bridge to accumulating recovery capital and making positive changes, as recently demonstrated by Best and colleagues (2024). While findings from these studies are congruent, the number of studies that have used recovery capital as an outcome predictor or indicator is limited and diverse (even unstandardized) measures have been used to assess recovery capital.

2. Recovery capital and treatment-related outcomes

Treatment drop-out has been extensively described in the addiction literature and has been estimated to be between 20 and 50 per cent in a recent meta-analysis (Lappan et al, 2020). According to Headid and colleagues (2024), persons who do not complete substance use treatment have similar outcomes to persons who do not receive treatment. Addressing drop-out and enhancing treatment completion are therefore crucial in improving functioning outcomes post-treatment (see earlier discussion).

Based on a large sample of persons attending substance use treatment in the US (Sánchez, Sahker, and Arndt, 2020), it was shown that higher recovery capital at baseline (measured by the ARC) was associated with being married and employed and having higher levels of education and secure housing, while having co-occurring mental health problems and higher addiction severity were associated with less recovery capital. Importantly, the likelihood of treatment completion increased with higher levels of recovery capital in an almost linear way (Sánchez et al, 2020), indicating the need for identifying treatment and recovery barriers and providing interventions to increase recovery capital during treatment.

Recovery capital has also been measured among persons in non-abstinent recovery, participating in medically-assisted treatment in India. Parlier-Ahmad and colleagues (2021) used the BARC-10 to measure recovery capital among men and women in outpatient opioid use disorder treatment with buprenorphine. They found high levels of recovery capital among this sample, comparable to that of persons who resolved an alcohol or drug problem, indicating that the degree of recovery capital affects treatment entry and those with lower levels of recovery capital do not identify the need for nor enter treatment easily. A core recommendation of this study was to include assessments of recovery capital in harm reduction services to tailor available services to individuals' specific needs.

Employment is a facet of recovery capital that supports long-term recovery. It is unclear whether employment is an antecedent of recovery in providing structure, basic needs, social relations, and agency, or whether addiction recovery creates the preconditions for working and leading a contributing and satisfying life. Employment serves many benefits in recovery and may be crucial in maintaining stable recovery (Sahker et al, 2019). The presence of recovery capital was assessed among a large sample of persons with substance use problems in Iowa (US), indicating that various forms of human recovery capital related to employment (that is, having an occupation, employment history, and income) had an impact on treatment completion, but not on actual substance use six months after starting treatment. What primarily affected substance use outcomes was growth in employment behaviours/ outcomes during treatment (that is, number of months employed and the number of days abstinent) (Sahker et al, 2019).

Similarly, Fernandez and Peters (2023) assessed the relation between employment-related human recovery capital and treatment completion among individuals with a cocaine use disorder in the US 2020 Treatment Episode Data Set. They explored the potential for employment and primary payment sources to predict the completion of outpatient/residential treatment. Treatment completion was significantly higher among persons who were employed upon discharge and with those with private insurance.

Recently, Headid and colleagues (2024) demonstrated – without using a standardized instrument – that recovery capital at baseline did not differ between programme graduates and non-graduates among residents in recovery houses in South Carolina. However, graduates reported significantly higher scores on all recovery capital indicators at graduation, suggesting an accumulation of recovery capital during their residence that is associated with improved retention and completion rates.

Summary

Treatment retention and completion have been identified as crucial mediators of treatment outcomes and some recovery capital studies have looked at differences in recovery resources and barriers among persons entering and leaving treatment. Preventing drop-out is central to yielding the benefits conferred by treatment and to building recovery capital. While one may assume that persons seeking substance use treatment have depleted their recovery capital and that the amount of baseline recovery capital is not predictive of programme completion, studies in treatment settings (Sánchez et al, 2020) and recovery residences (Headid et al, 2024) have shown that programme completion is strongly related to growth in recovery capital when compared to those leaving the programme prematurely. Measuring recovery capital is also strongly recommended in harm reduction programmes, as it may help to identify strengths in disadvantaged populations and inform person-centred treatment (Parlier-Ahmad et al, 2021). Employment facets of human recovery capital (for example, having an occupation, income, and employment history) and its growth have been shown to impact treatment completion (Sahker et al, 2019), suggesting the inclusion of employment-promoting activities as a mechanism for building recovery capital during treatment (Fernandez and Peters, 2023).

3. Service providers' perspectives and experiences around supporting recovery capital development

Recovery has been described as a profoundly individual journey and can be challenged by cooccurring problems such as mental health issues. Based on interviews with experienced professionals in Sweden (Topor et al, 2018), access to different forms of recovery capital was considered a core element in individuals' recovery processes. In particular, self-distrust and lack of trust in others were associated with low (personal) recovery capital and a lack of helpful social networks. Distrust is considered a consequence of a life characterized by mental health and substance use problems, situations created by the different aims, agendas, and cultures of diverse services and insufficient material conditions for leading a normal life. If professionals are not accepted as trustworthy agents, it will be challenging to induce change, trust oneself, and develop new social networks. Consequently, coproductive approaches based on individuals' agendas and improving basic daily conditions (housing and finances) are needed for initiating and securing addiction recovery (Topor et al, 2018). Moreover, recovery should be seen as a deeply social and relational process, involving other persons and contextual factors, besides the importance of developing a positive sense of self and hope based on experiences of acceptance and agency.

Hennessy and colleagues (2023) tested the implementation of a tool for assessing recovery capital (using the REC-CAP system) in two drug treatment courts in the US, as these clients usually face several barriers to recovery and treatment. An online survey and focus groups suggested that drug court staff felt that the REC-CAP assessment provided additional important information about clients' strengths and barriers and suggested specific next steps for staff to guide their clients. Given that many individuals experiencing substance use problems are involved in the criminal justice system, it is recommended to identify recovery capital in this population and intervene to extend their recovery capital. According to the authors (Hennessy et al, 2023), the philosophy underpinning the drug treatment court model strongly aligns with recovery capital theory. Consequently, assessment of recovery capital and related planning and monitoring offers great potential to be adapted and integrated into the drug court system and other diversion practices.

Osborne and Kelly (2023) explored the role of physical health on recovery trajectories and the role physical recovery capital may play in augmenting integrated care through interviews with service providers (n=13) and service users (n=20) across New South Wales, Australia. Interviewees reported that recovery was compromised when health issues – particularly those linked to pain and hopelessness – were unaddressed. In contrast, when individuals' physical health improved, recovery barriers (mental health symptoms, boredom, and isolation) decreased. More specifically, it emerged that when physical health care was incorporated into treatment, it supported recovery assets through learning and skill development, increased independence, deeper engagement, and enjoyment. The study showed that improved physical health created benefits for the building of cultural capital (improved physical appearance) and social capital (through social connections).

Summary

Studies of service providers' perceptions and experiences of recovery (capital) and the role of treatment illustrate the need for more personalized, strengths-based, and coproductive approaches, and for securing basic needs and conditions (that is, housing, food, finances, and physical health) to make recovery possible (Topor et al, 2018). Strengths-based approaches may also have great potential in drug treatment courts and other diversion settings that traditionally apply punitive and risk reduction strategies starting from the assessment of risks, disorders, and danger (Hennessy et al, 2023). Providing physical health care and increasing physical recovery capital may help initiate recovery and build social and cultural recovery capital (Osborne and Kelly, 2023).

4. Recovery capital and service users' experiences and perspectives

In an early study in northern England, Duffy and Baldwin (2013) conducted 45 semi-structured qualitative interviews to explore perceived barriers or facilitators of sustained recovery post-treatment. Most participants had high levels of recovery capital and were engaged in aftercare services. Supported housing was considered critical for recovery. A leading source of social support was the recovery community and participants were motivated to rebuild family relationships, especially with their children. Attending to human recovery capital (that is, underlying issues and internal factors) instilled confidence in the possibility of an enduring recovery, while addressing physical and social capital (that is, family relationships and having a 'normal life') was motivating for most participants.

Skogens and von Greiff (2014) explored service users' perceptions of treatment outcomes and contextual factors that have shaped their recovery trajectories, with particular attention to 'socially integrated' and 'marginalized' groups. While the marginalized group developed certain facets of recovery capital in treatment (for example, acquiring a job, and building new social networks), this type of recovery capital tended to already be present in members of the integrated group. As persons in marginalized situations have less robust recovery capital, extended post-treatment support is likely necessary for promoting recovery. In a later study, the same authors (Skogens and von Greiff, 2016) compared male and female service users' perceptions of the necessary conditions for change, using recovery capital as their analytic framework. They found that respondents from marginalized groups reported more changes related to employment, housing, and the existence of a stable social network. In contrast, the integrated groups' recovery capital changed more in terms of personal development and relationships. The authors also found that gender stereotypes, which differed by social status, impacted service users' recovery efforts.

In Ireland, Morton and colleagues (2016) evaluated service users' change processes during a 20-week-long substance use treatment programme that incorporated fitness and education using focus groups midway through and upon completion of the programme. Findings demonstrated the importance of fitness and education for building personal and social recovery capital and education in reducing substance use and its impact on families to increase recovery capital. During the programme, participants acquired health-related skills, lifestyle changes (for example, cooking and healthy eating), and improved relationships with family, which provide important sources of recovery capital.

A study in the Philippines (Castillo and Resurreccion, 2019) used a case study design to explore the lived experiences of those using services following treatment, examining their recovery capital, stress factors, and personal views on recovery and addiction. The post-treatment phase was marked by managing the stress of reintegrating into society, repairing relationships, and restoring social functioning (becoming gainfully employed and meeting responsibilities). Factors that were influential in maintaining recovery and building recovery capital were social support, having connections, and engagement in recovery-supportive activities.

A case study of a peer-based recovery support model in Cumbria (UK) that uses a hub and spoke method to create visible recovery while actively engaging with and supporting community growth, provided several examples of creating recovery pathways for vulnerable populations (Best et al, 2021). Through building personal recovery capital by engaging with recovery coaches and behavioural health companions (for building social recovery capital), and the utilization of recovery hubs to build community partnerships and pathways to meaningful activities (community recovery capital), lived experience recovery organizations can facilitate addiction recovery and the accumulation of recovery capital.

A qualitative study of a sample of 25 persons in addiction recovery in Belgium who used assisted and unassisted recovery pathways (Dekkers et al, 2021) identified recovery supportive environments (for example, specialist treatment, recovery groups, but also home environments or drug-free wings in prison) and 'time' as main elements for change and building recovery capital during their recovery process, which contributed to 'a (new) sense of self' and a 'sense of future' (sources of personal recovery capital).

Patton and colleagues (2022) focused on the management of negative recovery capital (the pains of recovery) during recovery trajectories based on the narratives of 30 men and women in addiction recovery. They found that the pains of recovery are common in early recovery and rarely lead to positive changes. According to the authors, negative recovery capital needs to be managed effectively (eliminated/reduced) to allow for the accumulation of recovery capital, especially in the early phases of recovery. On the other hand, a range of pull factors (recovery capital) were identified that created and promoted positive changes (for example, identity change and finding purpose) and were often associated with mutual aid participation and other types of recovery support (Patton et al, 2022).

In a study of three individuals with complex problems ('triple diagnosis': SUD, intellectual disability, and cooccurring mental health conditions) in inpatient addiction treatment, Pars and colleagues (2023) explored the viability of the concept of recovery capital. Drawing on case files and interviews, recovery capital was found to be a feasible alternative framework to the medical model and a supplement to the bio-psycho-social model, enabling the charting of barriers and assets in this population. Participants prioritized individual skill development over other recovery domains during treatment and a strengths assessment allowed for evaluating critical factors for recovery in complex cases. The authors suggest that knowledge of these elements can help service providers to tailor interventions accordingly.

Qualitative interviews around personal strengths and assets with persons in addiction recovery in and out of treatment in Quebec (Canada) revealed the importance of focusing on what is going well (Beaulieu et al, 2023). This approach is regarded as an important alternative to the predominant deficit-oriented focus in substance use treatment. Developing recovery capital is a complex, cumulative process, involving the improvement of intrinsic qualities and skills and learning through relational and treatment experiences. The authors conclude that various dimensions of recovery capital are linked and mutually influence one another.

Summary

Based on a wide range of qualitative studies of service users' experiences and perspectives, it appears that social support and engagement in recovery-supportive environments and activities (for example, treatment and attending mutual aid groups) help to initiate recovery and strengthen recovery capital (Castillo and Resurreccion, 2019; Dekkers et al, 2021; Patton et al, 2022). Attending to underlying (mental) health and family issues and addressing the development of personal and social recovery capital facilitate addiction recovery according to persons in recovery (Duffy and Baldwin, 2013; Morton et al, 2016). The pains of recovery need to be managed particularly in early recovery, along with accessing recovery resources and experiencing positive changes (Patton et al, 2022). Skogens and von Greiff (2014) found that for persons with substance use problems who were marginalized in society, treatment provided the vehicle for access to aspects of recovery capital that were already present among more 'socially integrated' persons. Similarly, recovery can be enhanced for vulnerable populations by making recovery visible in the community and actively supporting community growth, building on persons with lived experiences of addiction (Best et al, 2021). The recovery capital framework offers an alternative model for identifying strengths and 'what goes well', particularly among individuals with complex problems (Beaulieu et al, 2023; Pars et al, 2023).

Conclusion and ways forward

Recovery capital is understudied in treatment research, where it can aid in assessment and planning (Sánchez et al, 2020). Extant studies demonstrate that strong recovery capital at the outset of treatment predicts abstinence, lower relapse rates, and treatment completion (Groshkova et al, 2012; Sánchez et al, 2020). Furthermore, associations have been found between elevated levels of recovery capital and enduring recovery, steady employment, and stable housing (Laudet, 2008; Kelly et al, 2018; Best and Hennessy, 2022). On the other hand, negative recovery capital (for example, no partner support, a social network solely consisting of peers who use substances) has been linked to heightened dropout and minimal motivation to complete treatment (Baker et al, 2020; Keith et al, 2022). Findings diverge by gender such that increases in recovery capital are linked to participation in education and work (that is, meaningful activities) in males, while community engagement and focusing on health have been found to strengthen recovery capital in females (Bormann et al, 2023b). Yet, it is challenging to draw firm conclusions from available studies given the diversity of related study samples, designs, instrumentation, and variables of interest to researchers. More robust and methodological studies of recovery capital are sorely needed to advance its conceptual and empirical development (Best and Henessy, 2022).

While we have primarily focused on recovery pathways that incorporate treatment, various settings, interventions, and strategies can be characterized as recovery supportive; the concept of recovery capital also applies in prisons, drug treatment courts, recovery residences, and mutual aid groups (Dekkers et al, 2021). To support long-term recovery, service users' needs need to be assessed from a recovery capital framework (Kaur et al, 2022). Recovery capital suggests the presence of strengths, assets, and capabilities to foster development and human flourishing (Best and Ivers, 2022). Work and meaningful activities are important sources of recovery capital: by offering structure, making connections with the broader community, and building prosocial relationships, various forms of recovery capital are reclaimed that can, in turn, improve quality of life, reduce cravings, increase happiness and well-being, teach new skills, and enhance self-esteem (Epstein and Preston, 2012; Petry et al, 2014).

Future research

Specific areas for further research identified in this chapter include research on the role of recovery capital in the recovery process beyond the extant focus on its use as a baseline variable or one of several outcome indicators. Relatedly, as the construct of recovery capital has not been applied widely in recovery research, further work is needed on how it relates to other similar concepts such as quality of life and well-being (Bellaert et al, 2024). Further research should also study recovery capital in non-Anglophone countries, including countries in the Global South. Conducting more research in diverse practice settings will elucidate how to practically integrate recovery capital from intake procedures through to aftercare activities. Research exploring coproductive and strengths-based approaches would also benefit practitioners seeking to incorporate recovery capital theory and build trust and rapport (Vanderplasschen et al, 2019). Another area for future research relates to how recovery capital can best be leveraged for use with service users with concurrent addictions (including behavioural addictions), other mental health issues, and complex presentations.

Practice implications

To build recovery capital, treatment and other types of recovery support must be better attuned to the needs of individual service users. Practically, this necessitates in-depth assessment (including strengths and assets) to inform a treatment plan that meets service users' needs and considers service users' unique biopsychosocial risks and barriers in specific domains of recovery capital (for example, Chiauzzi, 1991). Treatment plans are not static but need to be monitored and modified throughout treatment, shifting focus during early and later treatment stages (Chiauzzi, 1991; Flores, 2001; Buga et al, 2017).

Continuous assessment and monitoring may potentially reveal risks to recovery (for example, recovery-endangering friends or partners; need for safe and secure housing; nutritional deficits; unemployment) that can direct treatment activities in outpatient or residential settings. For example, there are various ways in which service users' financial resources may be supported (for example, helping to secure a support grant or preparing for interviews, while in a later recovery stage, discussions could centre on the management of work-related triggers). Collaboratively developing alternative coping strategies for substance use is also critical for enhancing personal recovery capital (Freimuth et al, 2008), including a focus on other addictive behaviours that may arise during recovery (Sinclair et al, 2021). Building social recovery capital entails establishing new relationships, reconnecting with family and others, and repairing existing relationships. Recent research has shown that social network diversity (with some network members who are in recovery, but not all or none) was associated with more recovery capital in early recovery; for those with more time in recovery, closer bonds appeared to be more important than network diversity (Roxburgh et al, 2023). A social network comprised entirely of persons in recovery should be avoided in early recovery and should also include other persons or groups. Community recovery capital can be enhanced by linking service users with sports clubs, volunteer organizations, and recovery support groups such as Narcotics Anonymous or Gamblers Anonymous, particularly if individuals experience or have experienced issues with these or other addictions (Sinclair et al, 2021). Connecting service users to such community resources will establish structures for post-treatment monitoring of addictions, health, and functioning (Sussman and Black, 2008). In conclusion, treatment and other types of recovery support should focus more on optimizing individuals' recovery capital by reducing recovery barriers and increasing positive recovery resources that contribute to abstinence, improved well-being, and enduring recovery.

References

American Society of Addiction Medicine (2019) 'Definition of addiction', *ASAM* [online], Available from: https://www.asam.org/Quality-Science/definition-of-addiction [Accessed 20 March 2024].

Ashford, R., Brown, A., Brown, T., Callis, J., Cleveland, H., Eisenhart, E., et al (2019) 'Defining and operationalizing the phenomena of recovery: A working definition from the recovery science research collaborative', *Addiction Research & Theory*, 27(3): 179–88.

Baker, D.E., Edmonds, K.A., Calvert, M.L., Sanders, S.M., Bridges, A.J., Rhea, M.A., and Kosloff, S. (2020) 'Predicting attrition in long-term residential substance use disorder treatment: A modifiable risk factors perspective', *Psychological Services*, 17(4): 472–82.

Beaulieu, M., Tremblay, J., Baudry, C., Pearson, J., and Bertrand, K. (2021) 'A systematic review and meta-analysis of the efficacy of the long-term treatment and support of substance use disorders', *Social Science & Medicine*, 285, 114289, DOI: https://doi.org/10.1016/j.socscimed.2021.114289.

Beaulieu, M., Bertrand, K., Tremblay, J., Lemaitre, A., and Jauffret-Roustide, M. (2023) 'Personal strengths and resources that people use in their recovery from persistent substance use disorder', *Drugs: Education, Prevention and Policy*, 31(5): 570–83.

Belanger, M.J., Sondhi, A., Mericle, A.A., Leidi, A., Klein, M., Collinson, B., et al (2024) 'Assessing a pilot scheme of intensive support and assertive linkage in levels of engagement, retention, and recovery capital for people in recovery housing using quasi-experimental methods', *Journal of Substance Use and Addiction Treatment*, 158: 209283, DOI: https://doi.org/10.1016/j.josat.2023.209283.

Bellaert, L., Van Steenberghe, T., De Maeyer, J., Vander Laenen, F., and Vanderplasschen, W. (2022) 'Turning points toward drug addiction recovery: Contextualizing underlying dynamics of change', *Addiction Research & Theory*, 30(4): 294–303.

Bellaert, L., Zerrouk, A., Sinclair, D.L., Martinelli, T.F., Best, D., Vander Laenen, F., et al (2025) 'Correlates and stability of recovery capital among persons in long-term recovery from drug addiction in three countries', in M. Florence, W. Vanderplasschen, M. Yu, J. De Maeyer, and S. Savahl (eds) *Handbook of Addiction, Recovery and Quality of Life: Cross-cutting Perspectives from Around the Globe*, Cham: Springer.

Best, D. and Laudet, A. (2010) *The Potential of Recovery Capital*, Cham, Switzerland: Royal Society for the Arts.

Best, D. and Hennessy, E.A. (2022) 'The science of recovery capital: Where do we go from here?', *Addiction*, 117(4): 1139–45.

Best, D. and Ivers, J.H. (2022) 'Inkspots and ice cream cones: A model of recovery contagion and growth', *Addiction Research & Theory*, 30(3): 155–61.

Best, D., Higham, D., Pickersgill, G., Higham, K., Hancock, R., and Critchlow, T. (2021) 'Building recovery capital through community engagement: A hub and spoke model for peer-based recovery support services in England', *Alcoholism Treatment Quarterly*, 39(1): 3–15.

Best, D., Bamber, S., Battersby, A., Gilman, M., Groshkova, T., Honor, S., et al (2010) 'Recovery and straw men: An analysis of the objections raised to the transition to a recovery model in UK addiction services', *Journal of Groups in Addiction & Recovery*, 5(3–4): 264–88.

Best, D., Vanderplasschen, W., Van de Mheen, D., De Maeyer, J., Colman, C., Vander Laenen, F., et al (2018) 'REC-PATH (Recovery Pathways): Overview of a four-country study of pathways to recovery from problematic drug use', *Alcoholism Treatment Quarterly*, 36(4): 517–29.

Best, D., Sondhi, A., Best, J., Lehman, J., Grimes, A., Conner, M., and DeTriquet, R. (2023) 'Using recovery capital to predict retention and change in recovery residences in Virginia, USA', *Alcoholism Treatment Quarterly*, 41(2): 250–62.

Best, D., Sondhi, A., Hoffman, L., Best, J., Leidi, A., Grimes, A., et al (2024) 'Bridging the gap: Building and sustaining recovery capital in the transition from prison to recovery residences', *Journal of Offender Rehabilitation*, 63(1): 21–36.

Betty Ford Institute Consensus Panel (2007) 'What is recovery? A working definition from the Betty Ford Institute', *Journal of Substance Abuse Treatment*, 33(3): 221–8.

Blodgett, J.C., Maisel, N.C., Fuh, I.L., Wilbourne, P.L., and Finney, J.W. (2014) 'How effective is continuing care for substance use disorders? A meta-analytic review', *Journal of Substance Abuse Treatment*, 46(2): 87–97.

Bormann, N.L., Weber, A.N., Arndt, S., and Lynch, A. (2023a) 'Improvements in recovery capital are associated with decreased alcohol use in a primary opioid use disorder treatment-seeking cohort', *The American Journal on Addictions*, 32(6): 547–53.

Bormann, N.L., Weber, A.N., Miskle, B., Arndt, S., and Lynch, A.C. (2023b) 'Recovery capital correlates with less methamphetamine use and crime in the community', *Journal of Addiction Medicine,* 17(6): e361–e366.

Buga, S., Banerjee, C., Zachariah, F., Mooney, S., Patel, P., and Freeman, B. (2017) 'Cross addiction – A case presentation', *Oncolog-Hematolog,* 38(1): 39–42.

Cano, I., Best, D., Edwards, M., and Lehman, J. (2017) 'Recovery capital pathways: Modelling the components of recovery wellbeing', *Drug and Alcohol Dependence,* 181: 11–19.

Castillo, T.C. and Resurreccion, R. (2019) 'The recovery experience: Stress, recovery capital, and personal views on addiction and recovery in posttreatment addiction recovery', *Philippine Journal of Psychology,* 52(1): 103–26.

Chiauzzi, E.J. (1991) *Preventing Relapse in the Addictions: A Biopsychosocial Approach,* Oxford, UK: Pergamon.

Cloud, W. and Granfield, R. (2008) 'Conceptualizing recovery capital: Expansion of a theoretical construct', *Substance Use & Misuse,* 43(12–13): 1971–86.

Davidson, L. and White, W. (2007) 'The concept of recovery as an organizing principle for integrating mental health and addiction services', *The Journal of Behavioral Health Services & Research,* 34, 109–20.

Davidson, L., White, W., Sells, D., Schmutte, T., O'Connell, M., Bellamy, C., and Rowe, M. (2010) 'Enabling or engaging? The role of recovery support services in addiction recovery', *Alcoholism Treatment Quarterly,* 28(4): 391–416.

Day, E., Manitsa, I., Farley, A., and Kelly, J.F. (2023) 'A UK national study of prevalence and correlates of adopting or not adopting a recovery identity among individuals who have overcome a drug or alcohol problem', *Substance Abuse Treatment Prevention and Policy,* 18: 68, DOI: https://doi.org/10.1186/s13011-023-00579-2.

Dekkers, A., Bellaert, L., Meulewaeter, F., De Ruysscher, C., and Vanderplasschen, W. (2021) 'Exploring essential components of addiction recovery: A qualitative study across assisted and unassisted recovery pathways', *Drugs-Education Prevention and Policy,* 28(5): 486–95.

Duffy, P. and Baldwin, H. (2013) 'Recovery post treatment: Plans, barriers and motivators', *Substance Abuse Treatment, Prevention, and Policy,* 8: 6, DOI: https://doi.org/10.1186/1747-597X-8-6.

Epstein, D.H. and Preston, K.L. (2012) 'TGI Monday?: Drug-dependent outpatients report lower stress and more happiness at work than elsewhere', *The American Journal on Addictions,* 21(3): 189–98.

Fernandez, D.E.R. and Peters, B. (2023) 'Employment and primary source of treatment payment: Physical recovery capital as a predictor of cocaine use treatment completion', *Journal of Substance Use,* 29(5): 956–62.

Flores, P.J. (2001) 'Addiction as an attachment disorder: Implications for group therapy', *International Journal of Group Psychotherapy*, 51(1: special issue): 63–81.

Freimuth, M., Waddell, M., Stannard, J., Kelley, S., Kipper, A., Richardson, A., and Szuromi, I. (2008) 'Expanding the scope of dual diagnosis and co-addictions: Behavioral addictions', *Journal of Groups in Addiction & Recovery*, 3(3–4): 137–60.

Gilbert, W.C. (2022) 'Voices from the rooms and programs: Recovery capital speaks', *Journal of Social Work Practice in the Addictions*, 22(1): 53–67.

Granfield, R. and Cloud, W. (1999) *Coming Clean: Overcoming Addiction Without Treatment*, New York: New York University Press.

Groshkova, T., Best, D., and White, W. (2012) 'The Assessment of Recovery Capital: Properties and psychometrics of a measure of addiction recovery strengths', *Drug and Alcohol Review*, 32(2): 187–94.

Headid, R.J., Doane, T.C., Cohen, B.D., Smith, E.C., Redden, D., and Stoner, A.M. (2024) 'Identifying components of recovery capital that support substance use disorder treatment completion', *Addictive Behaviors Reports*, 19, 100538, DOI: https://doi.org/10.1016/j.abrep.2024.100538.

Heilig, M., MacKillop, J., Martinez, D., Rehm, J., Leggio, L., and Vanderschuren, L. (2021) 'Addiction as a brain disease revised: Why it still matters, and the need for consilience', *Neuropsychopharmacology*, 46(10): 1715–23.

Hennessy, E.A., Krasnoff, P., and Best, D. (2023) 'Implementing a recovery capital model into therapeutic courts: Case study and lessons learned', *International Journal of Offender Therapy and Comparative Criminology*, 0306624X231198810.

Hibbert, L.J. and Best, D.W. (2011) 'Assessing recovery and functioning in former problem drinkers at different stages of their recovery journeys', *Drug and Alcohol Review*, 30(1): 12–20.

Hubbard, R.L., Craddock, S.G., and Anderson, J. (2003) 'Overview of 5-year followup outcomes in the drug abuse treatment outcome studies (DATOS)', *Journal of Substance Abuse Treatment*, 25(3): 125–34.

Jason, L.A., Guerrero, M., Salomon-Amend, M., Light, J.M., and Stoolmiller, M. (2021) 'Personal and environmental social capital predictors of relapse following departure from recovery homes', *Drugs: Education, Prevention and Policy*, 28(5): 504–10.

Johannessen, D.A., Nordfjærn, T., and Geirdal, A. (2019) 'Change in psychosocial factors connected to coping after inpatient treatment for substance use disorder: A systematic review', *Subst Abuse Treatment, Prevention, and Policy*, 14, 16, DOI: https://doi.org/10.1186/s13011-019-0210-9.

Kaur, A., Lal, R., Sen, M.S., and Sarkar, S. (2022) 'Comparison of recovery capital in patients with alcohol and opioid dependence – An exploratory study', *Addiction & Health*, 14(2): 105–14.

Keith, D.R., Tegge, A.N., Athamneh, L.N., Freitas-Lemos, R., Tomlinson, D.C., Craft, W.H., and Bickel, W.K. (2022) 'The phenotype of recovery VIII: Association among delay discounting, recovery capital, and length of abstinence among individuals in recovery from substance use disorders', *Journal of Substance Abuse Treatment,* 139, 108783, DOI: https://doi.org/10.1016/j.jsat.2022.108783.

Kelly, J.F., Greene, M.C., and Bergman, B.G. (2018) 'Beyond abstinence: Changes in indices of quality of life with time in recovery in a nationally representative sample of US adults', *Alcoholism: Clinical and Experimental Research,* 42(4): 770–80.

Kelly, J.F., Humphreys, K., and Ferri, M. (2020) 'Alcoholics Anonymous and other 12-step programs for alcohol use disorder', *Cochrane Database of Systematic Reviews,* 3, DOI: https://doi.org/10.1002/14651858.CD012880.pub2.

Koob, G.F. and Volkow, N.D. (2016) 'Neurobiology of addiction: A neurocircuitry analysis', *The Lancet Psychiatry,* 3(8): 760–73.

Lappan, S.N., Brown, A.W., and Hendricks, P.S. (2020) 'Dropout rates of in-person psychosocial substance use disorder treatments: A systematic review and meta-analysis', *Addiction,* 115(2): 201–17.

Laudet, A.B. and White, W. (2008) 'Recovery capital as prospective predictor of sustained recovery, life satisfaction, and stress among former polysubstance users', *Substance Use & Misuse,* 43(1): 27–54.

Laudet, A.B. (2008) 'The road to recovery: Where are we going and how do we get there? Empirically driven conclusions and future directions for service development and research', *Substance Use & Misuse,* 43(12–13): 2001–20.

MacDonald, A., Ingram, R., Ridell, M., and Harp, K. (2023) 'Enhancing long-term recovery from substance use disorder: The impact of an exercise program on recovery capital and overall well-being', *Kentucky SHAPE Journal,* 61(1): 15–24.

Martinelli, T.F., van de Mheen, D., Best, D., Vanderplasschen, W., and Nagelhout, G.E. (2021) 'Are members of mutual aid groups better equipped for addiction recovery? European cross-sectional study into recovery capital, social networks, and commitment to sobriety', *Drugs: Education, Prevention and Policy,* 28(5): 389–98.

McLellan, A.T., Lewis, D.C., O'Brien, C.P., and Kleber, H.D. (2000) 'Drug dependence, a chronic medical illness: Implications for treatment, insurance, and outcomes evaluation', *JAMA,* 284(13): 1689–95.

Miller, W.R. and Wilbourne, P.L. (2002) 'Mesa Grande: A methodological analysis of clinical trials of treatments for alcohol use disorders', *Addiction,* 97(3): 265–77.

Morton, S., O'Reilly, L., and O'Brien, K. (2016) 'Boxing clever: Utilizing education and fitness to build recovery capital in a substance use rehabilitation program', *Journal of Substance Use*, 21(5): 521–6.

Osborne, B. and Kelly, P.J. (2023) 'Substance use disorders, physical health and recovery capital: Examining the experiences of clients and the alcohol and other drug workforce', *Drug and Alcohol Review*, 42(6): 1410–21.

Parlier-Ahmad, A.B., Terplan, M., Svikis, D.S., Ellis, L., and Martin, C.E. (2021) 'Recovery capital among people receiving treatment for opioid use disorder with buprenorphine', *Harm Reduction Journal*, 18: 103, DOI: https://doi.org/10.1186/s12954-021-00553-w

Pars, E., VanDerNagel, J.E., Dijkstra, B.A., and Schellekens, A.F. (2023) 'Using the recovery capital model to explore barriers to and facilitators of recovery in individuals with substance use disorder, psychiatric comorbidity and mild-to-borderline intellectual disability: A case series', *Journal of Clinical Medicine*, 12(18): 5914, DOI: https://doi.org/10.3390/jcm12185914.

Patton, D., Best, D., and Brown, L. (2022) 'Overcoming the pains of recovery: The management of negative recovery capital during addiction recovery pathways', *Addiction Research & Theory*, 30(5): 340–50.

Petry, N.M., Andrade, L.F., Rash, C.J., and Cherniack, M.G. (2014) 'Engaging in job-related activities is associated with reductions in employment problems and improvements in quality of life in substance abusing patients', *Psychology of Addictive Behaviors*, 28(1): 268–75, DOI: https://doi.org/10.1037/a0032264

Roxburgh, A.D., Best, D., Lubman, D.I., and Manning, V. (2023) 'Composition of social networks to build recovery capital differ across early and stable stages of recovery', *Addiction Research & Theory*, 32(3): 186–93.

Sahker, E., Ali, S.R., and Arndt, S. (2019) 'Employment recovery capital in the treatment of substance use disorders: Six-month follow-up observations', *Drug and Alcohol Dependence*, 205, 107624, DOI: https://doi.org/10.1016/j.drugalcdep.2019.107624.

Sánchez, J., Sahker, E., and Arndt, S. (2020) 'The Assessment of Recovery Capital (ARC) predicts substance abuse treatment completion', *Addictive Behaviors*, 102, 106189, DOI: https://doi.org/10.1016/j.addbeh.2019.106189.

Sinclair, D.L., Sussman, S., De Schryver, M., Samyn, C., Adams, S., Florence, M., et al (2021) 'Substitute behaviors following residential substance use treatment in the Western Cape, South Africa', *International Journal of Environmental Research and Public Health*, 18(23), 12815, DOI: https://doi.org/10.3390/ijerph182312815.

Skogens, L. and von Greiff, N. (2014) 'Recovery capital in the process of change – differences and similarities between groups of clients treated for alcohol or drug problems', *European Journal of Social Work*, 17(1): 58–73.

Skogens, L. and von Greiff, N. (2016) 'Conditions for recovery from alcohol and drug abuse – comparisons between male and female clients of different social position', *Nordic Social Work Research*, 6(3): 211–21.

Sterling, R., Slusher, C., and Weinstein, S. (2008) 'Measuring recovery capital and determining its relationship to outcome in an alcohol dependent sample', *The American Journal of Drug and Alcohol Abuse*, 34(5): 603–10.

Substance Abuse and Mental Health Services Administration & Office of the Surgeon General (2016) *Facing Addiction in America: The Surgeon General's Report on Alcohol, Drugs, and Health*, Washington, DC: US Department of Health and Human Services.

Sussman, S. and Black, D.S. (2008) 'Substitute addiction: A concern for researchers and practitioners', *Journal of Drug Education*, 38(2): 167–80.

Topor, A., Skogens, L., and von Greiff, N. (2018) 'Building trust and recovery capital: The professionals' helpful practice', *Advances in Dual Diagnosis*, 11(2): 76–87.

UK Drug Policy Commission (2008) *The UK Drug Policy Commission Recovery Consensus Group: A Vision of Recovery*, London: UKDPC.

United Nations Office on Drugs and Crime (UNODC) and World Health Organization (WHO) (2018) *International Standards on Drug Use Prevention* (2nd edn), Vienna: United Nations Office on Drugs and Crime & World Health Organization.

van den Brink, W. (2005) 'Verslaving, een chronisch recidiverende hersenziekte', *Verslaving*, 1: 47–53.

Vanderplasschen, W. and Best, D. (2021) 'Mechanisms and mediators of addiction recovery', *Drugs: Education, Prevention and Policy*, 28(5): 385–8.

Vanderplasschen, W., Bloor, M., and McKeganey, N. (2010) 'Long-term outcomes of aftercare participation following various forms of drug abuse treatment in Scotland', *Journal of Drug Issues*, 40(3): 703–28.

Vanderplasschen, W., Rapp, R.C., De Maeyer, J., and Van Den Noortgate, W. (2019) 'A meta-analysis of the efficacy of case management for substance use disorders: A recovery perspective', *Frontiers in Psychiatry*, 10, 186, DOI: https://doi.org/10.3389/fpsyt.2019.00186.

Vanderplasschen, W., Colpaert, K., Autrique, M., Rapp, R.C., Pearce, S., Broekaert, E., and Vandevelde, S. (2013) 'Therapeutic communities for addictions: A review of their effectiveness from a recovery-oriented perspective', *The Scientific World Journal*, 427817, DOI: https://doi.org/10.1155/2013/427817.

Van Steenberghe, T., Reynaert, D., Roets, G., and De Maeyer, J. (2020) *Ervaring werkt?! Ervaringskennis cocreatief inbedden in je organisatie*, Acco. *Journal of Social Intervention: Theory and Practice*, 32(4): 102–17, DOI: http://doi.org/10.18352/jsi.801.

Vilsaint, C.L., Kelly, J.F., Bergman, B.G., Groshkova, T., Best, D., and White, W. (2017) 'Development and validation of a Brief Assessment of Recovery Capital (BARC-10) for alcohol and drug use disorder', *Drug and Alcohol Dependence,* 177: 71–6.

Volkow, N. D. (2020) 'Personalizing the treatment of substance use disorders', *American Journal of Psychiatry,* 177(2): 113–16.

West, R. (2006) *Theory of Addiction,* New Jersey: John Wiley & Sons.

White, W. (2002) 'An addiction recovery glossary: The languages of American communities of recovery', in *Let's Go Make Some History: Chronicles of the New Addiction Recovery Advocacy Movement,* Washington, DC: Johnson Institute and Faces and Voices of Recovery, pp 225–88.

White, W. and Cloud, W. (2008) 'Recovery capital: A primer for addictions professionals', *Counselor,* 9(5): 22–7.

World Health Organization (WHO) and United Nations Office on Drugs and Crime (UNODC) (2020) *International Standards for the Treatment of Drug Use Disorders: Revised Edition Incorporating Results of Field-testing,* Geneva: World Health Organization and United Nations Office on Drugs and Crime.

10

Recovery Capital Applications in Policy and Practice

Reed Yearwood, Amy Mericle, and Jessica Best

Background

This chapter examines practical applications of building recovery capital. Using a case study approach involving the implementation of the **REC-CAP** (Cano et al, 2017; Best et al, 2023), we highlight how the results and analyses influenced social policy in the state of Virginia in the United States. The 'REC-CAP assessment', embedded in the Advanced Recovery Management System (ARMS), is used to measure recovery capital and inform personalized recovery plans to guide interventions. This chapter navigates recovery capital in policy and practice by exploring various ways in which it has been applied, documenting existing applications, and discussing its transformative effect on individual behaviour and community capacity. In an attempt to grasp both theory and practical elements of the recovery capital concept, a brief history of the REC-CAP is presented, alongside authentic examples of how the measurement of recovery capital has influenced policies and practices around addiction recovery. Our aim is to fill gaps in the current understanding of recovery capital implementation, with implications toward future research, practices, and policies. The story conveys recovery capital as a transformative change agent among individuals and communities.

For far too long, the behavioural health space has focused on deficits. Individuals struggling with substance use disorder were depicted as incomplete puzzles, defined by their missing pieces and rough misshapen edges. Recovery, if imagined at all, was often perceived as a laborious process of patching up these perceived shortcomings and vulnerabilities, brick by agonizing brick. A shift emerged by a new wave of voices insisting on reshaping the narrative, shining a light on other aspects of self that were present, not just the missing pieces. They argued that by focusing solely on deficits we would neglect the inherent strengths and resourcefulness already embedded into various parts of society (for further discussion of this historical shift, see Granfield and Cloud, Chapter 2, and Best, White, and Hoffman, Chapter 3). Assets inside the individual, community resources, and social networks were waiting to be assembled into a complete and empowering picture.

This is precisely where recovery capital steps in, guiding us like a map, organizing individual components, and labelling the strengths which leverage all the scattered pieces toward a complete puzzle. Recovery capital not only encompasses an individual's personal qualities like resilience, it also encompasses connections made through social networks and community resources. By measuring domains of recovery capital, a deficit-laden diagnosis is replaced with a more holistic understanding of an individual's recovery journey – the completed puzzle of their strengths, resources, and barriers. Recovery capital measurement informs interventions which mitigate problems, build upon existing strengths, and pave the way toward sustained recovery.

Conceptual foundations

Recovery capital can be observed along **micro-, meso-,** and **macro-** levels of social analysis (Ashford et al, 2020). The micro conceptualization of recovery capital entails an individual navigating positive and negative experiences, barriers, and resources associated with their recovery journey. For example, individuals who have experienced incarceration may experience greater barriers to recovery than someone who has not previously been incarcerated (Best et al, 2024). Extrapolating further, barriers to recovery might exist on a broader social level where categories and groups are defined by similarly shared experiences. The greater population of incarcerated individuals, and incarceration itself, acts as a barrier to individual as well as community recovery (Pouille et al, 2021). Meso conceptualization, then, expands to structural components like community capacity (Birgel et al, 2023), categorizing *groups*, and social ordering. This might look like a community or organization. The relationship between micro- and meso-levels of social analyses are continuous, as investigating a micro level reveals how social ordering emerges to create ongoing meaning which spreads throughout wider networks (Serpa et al, 2019). On the meso level, questions can be asked pertaining to *how* and *why* recovery capital affects communities, organizations, and even governments. How is recovery capital managed by larger groups so that more positive recovery can be shared by all? The recovery capital concept translates theory into practice, research into real-world recovery journeys, and unveils its role in the development and implementation of policies and practice.

Of note, the behavioural health scope has largely focused on deficits. 'Recovery', if imagined at all, has consistently represented the laborious process of patching up perceived shortcomings and vulnerabilities. As more and more individuals grapple with challenges associated with addiction, a new wave of voices insisted on reshaping the narrative about the addicted population. This wave sees peers navigating substance use together, disordered or not, and are increasingly healing and discovering (or recovering!) their paths to wellness by identifying strengths that exist among them. A Peer Recovery Specialist (PRS) is a self-identified person with lived experience involving a mental health condition, including addiction, who is in successful and ongoing recovery from challenges associated with or involving the condition (Reif et al, 2014). 'Peers' actively participate in the development of individual, community, and social capital and thus are critical to the flux and components of the recovery capital framework. Peers involve themselves in numerous activities which affect recovery capital on different social levels. Among them are: advocacy, connecting others to recovery support services, developing community relationships, and experiential sharing (Byrne, Mericle, and Litwin, 2023).

Applied sociologists 'aim to produce positive social change through active intervention' (Bruhn, 1999). **Applied Sociology** is used to describe the use of sociological knowledge in answering research questions/social problems defined by specific interest groups, rather than the researcher (Steele and Price, 2007, 4). To encourage specificity, we will use the term **applied recovery capital** to describe such phenomena as it occurs in the addiction and mental health services scope. Applied recovery capital delineates practitioners and organizational elements which use or experience recovery capital theories and methods to produce positive recovery capital transformation, translating recovery capital theory into practice.

How the REC-CAP assessment is used to measure recovery capital

John Lehman, a champion for **certified recovery residences** (CRRs) in Florida, applied recovery capital by reaching out to William White, a renowned name of the recovery advocacy movement. John's ambition was to demonstrate the efficacy of CRRs and to more deeply understand how they could enhance individual recovery journeys. He needed a measurement tool, to quantify progress and demonstrate the vital role of CRRs within a recovery ecosystem, with an overarching goal to shorten devastating cycles of addiction.

William White connected John to Dr David Best, a recovery researcher interested in recovery capital, who was, at the time, developing the REC-CAP assessment, expanding upon the Assessment of Recovery Capital (Groshkova, Best, and White, 2012). David and John oversaw the piloting of the REC-CAP assessment across eight CRRs in Florida. The REC-CAP measures a range of personal, social, and community recovery capital factors as well as barriers and unmet needs of the recovering individual. Barriers to recovery is a section which measures recovery barriers in five key areas: unstable accommodations, substance use, risk-taking, justice system involvement, and lack of meaningful activities. Similarly, unmet needs categorizes potential barriers to stable recovery including lack of basic needs, treatment and healthcare, community services, legal or housing support.

Recognizing the operational challenges of manually collecting and scoring data and overall data management, John Lehman began to build an electronic version of the assessment. Recovery capital expanded with the birth of the Advanced Recovery Management System (ARMS). This was more than just a digital upgrade, it was a huge leap forward in terms of growing the propensity of recovery for an individual by providing instant recovery capital metrics and a direct link to care planning by operationalizing the results. ARMS streamlines the data collection processes, including the REC-CAP assessment, and paves the way for a structured recovery support service known today as Measure, Plan, & Engage (MPE). The REC-CAP was at the forefront of two innovations for recovery capital measurement. First, that the completion was online so results were instantaneous, and second, that, in the tradition of White and Cloud (2008), a score profile was used to direct future recovery action – in this case for recovery care planning and community engagement.

The foundation of the Measure, Plan, & Engage model is the REC-CAP assessment, embedded in ARMS. The REC-CAP represents the 'M', in MPE: to measure. Measurement is the approach which will initiate and drive care and action planning ('P' for 'Plan'). Plan is the next step in the model where individuals engage with peers who help tailor interventions to meet needs and highlight strengths to enhance their recovery journey. The 'E', for 'Engage', completes the MPE process by seeking to actively engage participants/clients by using peer navigators to provide direct linkage to community recovery support services. In this way, MPE understands and accounts for the uniqueness of each recovery journey, charting a personalized course that encourages empowerment, self-efficacy, and resilient recovery. Follow-up assessments are key to ensure continual support and adaptation to fit individual needs. It is a dynamic and cyclical process that monitors progress, adjusts goals, identifies which community-based resources will address those goals, and, whenever possible, assertively links the individual to those resources. The cyclical MPE process is repeated at consistent intervals, with intermittent meetings to review progress and adjust support as needed.

Upon completion of the REC-CAP, ARMS automatically generates and displays a data visualization to help identify strengths and highlight areas that need attention. A 'traffic-light' system guides the way: strengths are displayed in green, while areas that warrant careful monitoring but do not require immediate intervention are displayed in yellow. These domains are kept under observation while focus is directed toward more urgent needs, or those areas in need of immediate intervention, displayed in red. Visual cues empower individuals and professionals to make informed decisions about priorities and resource allocation. The digital version of REC-CAP, embedded within the ARMS platform, went beyond the boundaries of traditional assessments and offered immediate guidance to transform the data into actionable insights. Figure 10.1 shows an example of the ARMS visual display and unique colour-code system.

Notes on the colour-code scheme: HIGH (Green): a list of the assets that the client has that should be used to help to build their recovery capital and to meet their personal goals. MEDIUM (Yellow): these groups are neither strengths nor problems and will only become the focus once goals are met and there are no more red areas on the client's summary results. LOW (Red): these areas are to be addressed as soon as possible, ideally using any strengths that have been identified, but may also need additional assertive linkage from the programme to other community-based resources.

Measuring recovery capital on an individual basis signalled a wave of policy makers across the globe to spring into action. The next section describes how recovery capital was adopted as an organizing framework in one particular area in the US.

Transforming the landscape: Applied recovery capital in the Commonwealth of Virginia

Part of what makes the conceptualization of recovery capital so powerful is the way it can be applied to individual and systems-level change. Recovery capital observed on a *macro* level implores questions as to how our concept associates with those whose job it is to develop health parity laws, policies, and organizational procedure. This is precisely what began to unfold in the Commonwealth of Virginia as it navigated implementation of the REC-CAP assessment in its beginning stages, putting into practice its initial platform on ARMS, which exemplified how government structures can influence, and be influenced by, recovery capital. In our case example, the Virginia Association of Recovery Residences (VARR) increased access to nearly 1,000 certified recovery housing beds, a 36 per cent increase in equitable access, at the same time doubling its certified bed capacity (Best et al, 2023). To get a better sense of how this came about, we completed a series of interviews with individuals at various 'levels' using the ARMS system and engaging with MPE data. This started with Anthony Grimes, who played a critical role of applying recovery capital to translate data to state representatives as executive director of the VARR.

Figure 10.1: REC-CAP assessment summary results screen: Data visualization of the recovery capital indices

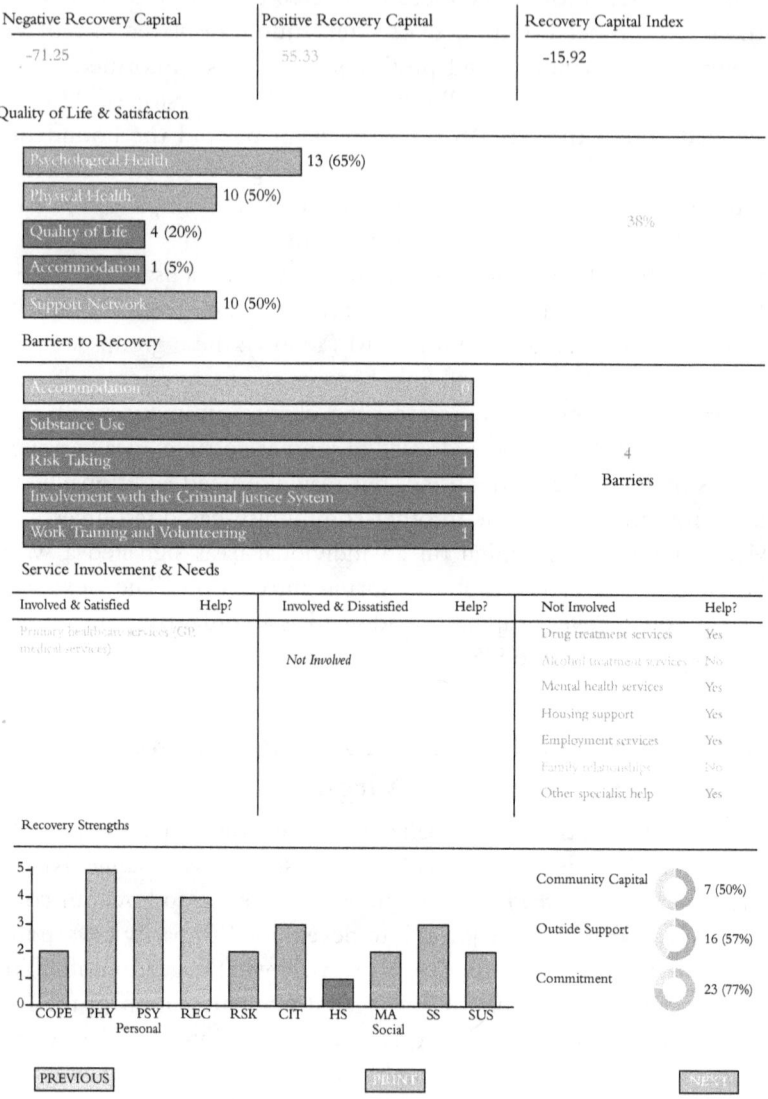

Source: Recovery Outcomes Institute, 2024.

We would argue that the systematic measurement of recovery capital enables two main activities: (1) to measure recovery capital accrued (that is, personal transformation over time) and (2) to analyse the role it plays in *social ordering*, or the extent to which recovery capital can be categorized and grouped among individual, community, and societal levels. If recovery capital is not unlike its capital counterparts, then it can be classified as *durable*. This would mean that the intrinsic value of recovery capital at any given point in time is not the same as the value of an individual's retention or ability to attain it. This concept alone encourages further study under the pretence that economical laws might then apply. If such were the case, similar instances will occur where financing struggles to meet demanded need, and while durability is congruent to standing the test of time, financing durable assets is generally scrutinized. In finance, durability affects the actual cost of any given asset and therefore the overall financing need, with the constant net effect of impeding financing (Rampini, 2019).

VARR played a critical role in advancing the application of recovery capital measurement in policies and practice. Formally inaugurated in 2012 as a 'state affiliate' for the National Alliance of Recovery Residences (NARR), VARR adopted NARR national standards to certify and regulate recovery housing (CRRs) (NARR, 2018). In a personal interview between the authorship team and VARR executive director Anthony Grimes, who identifies as being a person in long-term recovery from substance use disorder, Grimes discussed how his exposure to and refinement of recovery capital took hold on a macro-sociological scale.

VARR began receiving small increments of limited funding ($\approx$ $30,000 USD) through a partnership with the Commonwealth of Virginia Department of Behavioral Health & Developmental Services (DBHDS) to provide recovery support services (RSS) throughout the region. This partnership was established to facilitate State Opioid Response (SOR) grant funding to VARR. By 2018, VARR, with direct support by regional representatives, had introduced a legislative bill to their state House of Representatives.

With the passing of *House Bill 2045*, DBHDS (the department) began granting more funding to include capacity expansion for recovery support among the Commonwealth, as well as indigent bed funding. By September 2019, the organization was ready to hire an executive director, Anthony Grimes, who set to work as an advocate for unified recovery support services. The first REC-CAP dashboards became operational by late 2019 and Grimes, on behalf of VARR, proceeded to promote the efficacy and usage of the REC-CAP assessment to the department. Almost immediately, VARR and research analysts at the Recovery Outcomes Institute identified disparities among the population served by residences in the VARR network (see Figures 10.2 and 10.3). Funding went from around $30,000 to $250,000 within two years from a senator budget amendment, and then to $10 million, an outcome of providing data-driven summaries of recovery capital changes among CRR residents.

The **accrued recovery capital** afforded VARR the opportunity to continue the expansion of recovery support services. Near the middle of 2020, amidst the COVID-19 pandemic, VARR had increased its capacity to 650 certified beds among recovery housing operators across Virginia.

Figure 10.2: VARR network admissions (by ethnicity) (ROI, 2019)

ADMISSIONS BY ETHNICITY FOR VARR NETWORK PROVIDERS

2020	White	Non-White	Period Total	%White	%Non-White
Qtr1	234	56	290	80.7%	19.3%
Qtr2	439	199	638	68.8%	31.2%
Qtr3	345	177	522	66.1%	33.9%
Qtr4	253	127	380	66.6%	33.4%
2021	White	Non-White	Period Total	%White	%Non-White
Qtr1	316	178	494	64.0%	36.0%
Qtr2	376	225	601	62.6%	37.4%
Qtr3	500	295	795	62.9%	37.1%
Qtr4	413	251	664	62.2%	37.8%
2022	White	Non-White	Period Total	%White	%Non-White
Qtr1	399	321	720	55.4%	44.6%
Qtr2	398	228	626	63.6%	36.4%
Grand Totals	**3,673**	**2,057**	**5,730**	**64.1%**	**35.9%**

Figure 10.3: Admissions diversity by per cent (%) VARR network providers (ROI, 2023)

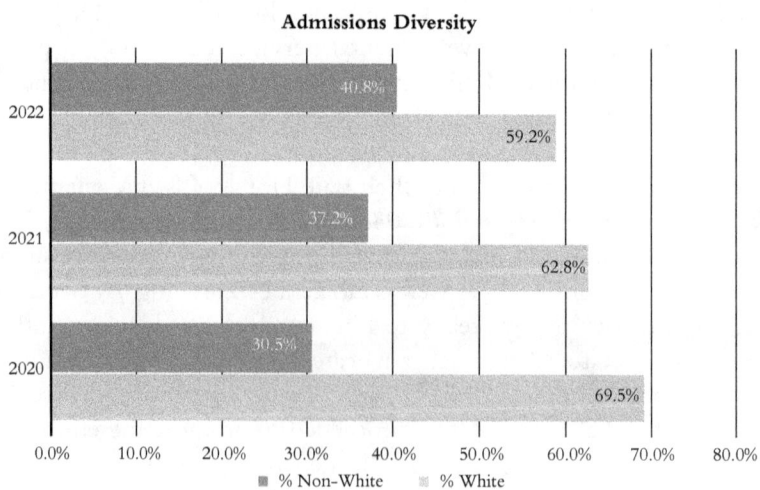

As capacity grew, so did data compiled by the REC-CAP assessment. Figures 10.2 and 10.3 show how metric analysis by John Lehman and the Recovery Outcomes Institute (ROI) were used in presentations supporting VARR's petitions for funding.

Admissions by ethnicity were analysed among VARR network providers and indicated disparity among non-White groups ($p<0.0001$, OR 3.36, 95 per cent confidence interval [CI]). In the first quarter (Qtr1) of 2020, White admissions totaled 234 individuals compared to 56 non-White individuals, indicating a disparity of 61.4 per cent. Approximately two years later, when quarter one (Qtr 1) was measured in 2022, the disparity gap had closed by more than 50 per cent (50.6 per cent) with 399 White individuals and 321 non-White admissions. Figure 10.3 shows how confidential information was de-identified and translated in presentation. A horizontal bar graph highlights noticeable differences between White and non-White groups.

VARR's enterprise dashboard displays aggregate data, allowing for macro-analysis which enabled VARR to aggressively demand state funding, coinciding with a growth in admissions by non-White groups over the subsequent years. VARR executive director Anthony Grimes claims the funding was directly responsible for shrinking the disparity among race in admissions by VARR network providers. He explained that by examining [de-identified] REC-CAP data, VARR applied recovery capital by translating to Virginia policy makers that minority populations' equitable access to recovery housing was limited by insufficient funding toward recovery support services, including critical infrastructure like recovery housing. On VARR's end, a DEIA model (diverse, equitable, inclusive, and accessible) was created to foster minority housing expansion and ownership. VARR exhibited applied recovery capital operating as a catalyst for social change, establishing a connection between recovering individuals and their respective state governments by their mutual affinity for recovery capital.

Interview 1: VARR Executive Director

According to Mr Grimes, VARR's immediate goal was to consolidate funding streams that were allocated by using REC-CAP data to provide empirical justification to:

(1) continue indigent bed funding;
(2) continue funding employment transition programmes for recovering individuals; and
(3) evidence the inherent value of peers with lived experience who may also be guided by the evidence-based system.

As he stated,

> When you implement an acute care model [upon society], you have more resources but are exceedingly constrained by an overburdened system. All the data in the world says individuals' biological and social lives transform at five years of continuous recovery ... The true value is that by enacting a funding stream, VARR enables its operational capacity to serve people who have never previously been served.

The VARR experience illustrates how recovery capital can play a pivotal role in shaping behavioural health addiction and recovery support service policies. It influences the design of programmes and services aimed at helping individuals reach sustained recovery from addiction. The authorship team also interviewed individuals from various strata among the VARR system of recovery support to reduce bias in these claims. Interviews included peer recovery navigators who use the REC-CAP assessment to provide care planning for their participants, as well as other directors of service providers who use REC-CAP data to assess internal and external infrastructure. The method of these interviews was to increase visibility of a spectrum of recovery capital. Individuals served by the VARR network represent micro-level strata which are affected by large infrastructure enhancements, that is, funding by organizations that develop standards to practice, like VARR. To better grasp our concept, organizations that operate as a vessel for recovery capital represent the middle ground; those individuals and groups which represent a stratum entirely of its own called the meso level, referring to aggregate components affected by both ends of the spectrum.

Exploring the role of recovery capital at a provider/meso level

Recovery capital measured and assessed using the REC-CAP platform has had a powerful impact on providers. To capture this, we spoke with Matthew Conner, assistant director at VARR, and an enterprise champion of the ARMS system, having utilized its capabilities to its fullest and awarded accolades within the training system. The interview illustrates his personal experience with using the ARMS system to assess recovery capital, the challenges and triumphs encountered in its implementation, and its potential to influence decision making and practice.

Interview 2: ARMS REC-CAP Enterprise Specialist

Matt's journey with recovery capital began around 2018 during his recovery at the McShin Foundation, a treatment provider and recovery community organization. There, he encountered the concept through a peer leadership training programme and was immediately drawn to its simplicity and practicality. He recalls using a paper-based system to assess resources and develop recovery plans, a precursor to the more formalized tools available today in the ARMS system. '*We [VARR] had something like a database system of the RDP, [Recovery Data Platform]*' Matt explains, '*It had different measurements and it had the BARC-10, it had the ARC, like the long form, all of it. It was a lot. It was a lot! I do remember that.*' While the initial focus was on data collection, the lack of clear direction on using it for recovery planning left him contemplating: '*What's the rhyme or reason of just doing it with people if there's no follow-up to it?*'

Matt's role provides technical support to organizations and helps facilitate the Measure, Plan, and Engage process. In his interview he emphasized the importance of education, not just about recovery mechanics but also the bigger picture – how, in his experience, the REC-CAP assessment was empowering residents, benefitting operators, and ultimately contributing to a macro data set that informs policies and resource allocation. He recognized the importance of promoting a unified system of recovery support services from within his role at an organization which provided oversight and standards of practice. He expressed a major feat in translating that information to providers served by VARR. Rather than starting from a place of '*this is something that needs to be done and you all need to do it,*' Matt explained that he even uses a strengths-based approach to assist with implementation and adoption of data collection to VARR network providers.

A significant hurdle Matt encounters is the lack of familiarity of recovery capital terminology among operators. He bridges this gap by helping translate recovery capital concepts and demonstrating how recovery capital aligns with their current recovery efforts through regular technical support meetings and fielding questions through the VARR office in real time.

One of the more common challenges Matt faces is scepticism from operators who question the purpose of REC-CAP assessment and MPE data collection. '*Why are we doing all this work for someone else's research?*' Matt recalls is a frequent concern. He continues to address this by relying on recovery capital, its current scientific foundation, and attempts to paint a picture to VARR operators that better data has yielded positive results for the entire recovery ecosystem. '*So, again, I paint that picture of how this trickles down and how it trickles up.*' Matt inspires personal recovery journeys by communicating the meaning behind cultivating recovery capital. He conceded that his role is to translate this information as easily as possible to operators within the VARR network of recovery support services, explaining how they can enhance their own deliverables simply by having a process to assess recovery capital and using the results to create recovery plans. Matt has stayed vigilant in communicating that the entire system contributes to a large data set which in real time has had a profound effect on structural policy and practice, which they (VARR) have hoped will lead to more resources. '*It's like painting a big picture about how all these things connect; from resident, to the operator, to an affiliate, to policy makers and what that ecosystem looks like,*' Matt concluded.

Matt's insight provides examples of the positive impact of the REC-CAP assessment. He recounts a situation where a resident's declining recovery capital score triggered a crucial conversation between resident and provider, revealing how the synergetic system of care planning works.

They actually ended up sharing. They really had been struggling, some things had happened in their life and they were thinking about using [substances], and until taking the assessment they hadn't put any information like that into the universe. It was pretty cool to be able to use the REC-CAP assessment as their pivot point to really address where someone's at and steer a conversation with that.

The Measure, Plan, and Engage process improves delivery of services within recovery residences. By requiring regular assessments and plan reviews, it ensures consistent support for all residents, not just those who are new. MPE fosters a holistic approach by facilitating linkages to external services like community resources. Matt continued,

the REC-CAP assessment and the timed intervals of engagement with recovery planning, and review that takes place in between – it helps people not fall into the fray. As long as you live in this recovery residence, you know, at these times, you're going to have engagement with a navigator, and a house leader or another navigator is probably going to be frequently checking in with you.

Matt's thoughts on the REC-CAP tool within the ARMS system highlights the potential recovery capital data has to build a strong foundation for recovery support services, ultimately leading to better resource allocation and informed decision making. He was not alone in his perspective, as many of these ideas were reinforced by another provider.

Interview 3: Director of Operations – True Recovery RVA

Chris Waugh's first encounter with recovery capital wasn't expressed as love at first sight. As a house manager at True Recovery RVA, he viewed the concept curiously but lacked clarity. His interest was piqued by the potential to quantify and measure recovery. '*My introduction to the concept of recovery capital came from my mentor David Rook, who used to own True Recovery RVA. He was the first person I ever heard speak about recovery capital, and that was about 2019. I wouldn't describe it as something that I immediately gravitated to.*'

Today, Chris is Director of Operations at True Recovery RVA and a passionate advocate for the REC-CAP and MPE process. His perspective reflects common shifts to a data-driven approach that he says is now embedded throughout their business culture. The REC-CAP assessment is integrated from day one. '*We've put a lot of work into changing our culture,*' Chris explains. New residents are introduced to REC-CAP and the MPE process during intake. The intake process transitioned from a formal process to a conversation designed to understand each resident's unique story.

Chris emphasized the importance of communication. Intake emails have been revamped to include narratives informed by baseline REC-CAP results. '*These insights help us identify any "red flags" early on,*' Chris says, '*allowing for interventions that boost engagement and chances of success.*' Chris explained the insights help to prompt swift interventions to bolster engagement, retention, and chances of success for their residents.

Chris shared with us that every three weeks, True Recovery RVA holds a community meeting where the efficacy of care planning through MPE is promoted. '*We celebrate successes, offer encouragement, and transparently share data-driven insights.*' He described a community meeting where progress is celebrated, challenges are addressed openly, and accountability is fostered. Their culture creatively rewards individuals in their programme: a gift card is awarded to their 'most engaged' resident. '*What I personally like the most,*' Chris enthusiastically shared, '*is being able to see where we [the company] were and then set goals.*' The interview revealed an instance of recovery capital data informing policy changes and programme development for business operations. '*We come up with an idea and see outcomes reflected in the numbers.*' He argued, 'the *REC-CAP is fact-based, data-driven, and the gold standard* [in Virginia].' He confirmed he does all he can to promote the efficacy of sound data collection. True Recovery RVA's story exemplifies recovery capital transforming recovery support service systems.

Interview 4: Recovery navigator

Claudia, Certified Peer Recovery Specialist (CPRS), is programme coordinator at WAR Foundation, another recovery residence operator. She shared how the use of the REC-CAP assessment has significantly impacted her ability to support individuals in their recovery journey by helping her to better understand residents' strengths and areas which need improvement. Claudia explained her own use of the REC-CAP assessment to formulate personalized recovery care plans based on assessment responses. She shared that it allows her to focus on specific areas that require attention, which she believes enhances her ability to provide support for the unique needs of each individual she guides toward sustained recovery.

'*The discovery map has been really essential for me,*' Claudia highlighted. '*Explaining to them, like, hey, we've got to get this foundation together. This is important for us to produce the things that we really want to produce here.*' Figure 10.4 shows the discovery map, an easy to digest bridge of REC-CAP results in a format that is meant to help facilitate a collaborative recovery planning process. Together, peers and their recovery navigator deliberate REC-CAP results and 'produce recovery plans.'

Figure 10.4 shows what Claudia is referring to. The apples in the five 'strengths trees' represent subdomains of each positive capital domain. She

THE HANDBOOK OF RECOVERY CAPITAL

Figure 10.4: REC–CAP discovery map (ROI, 2023)

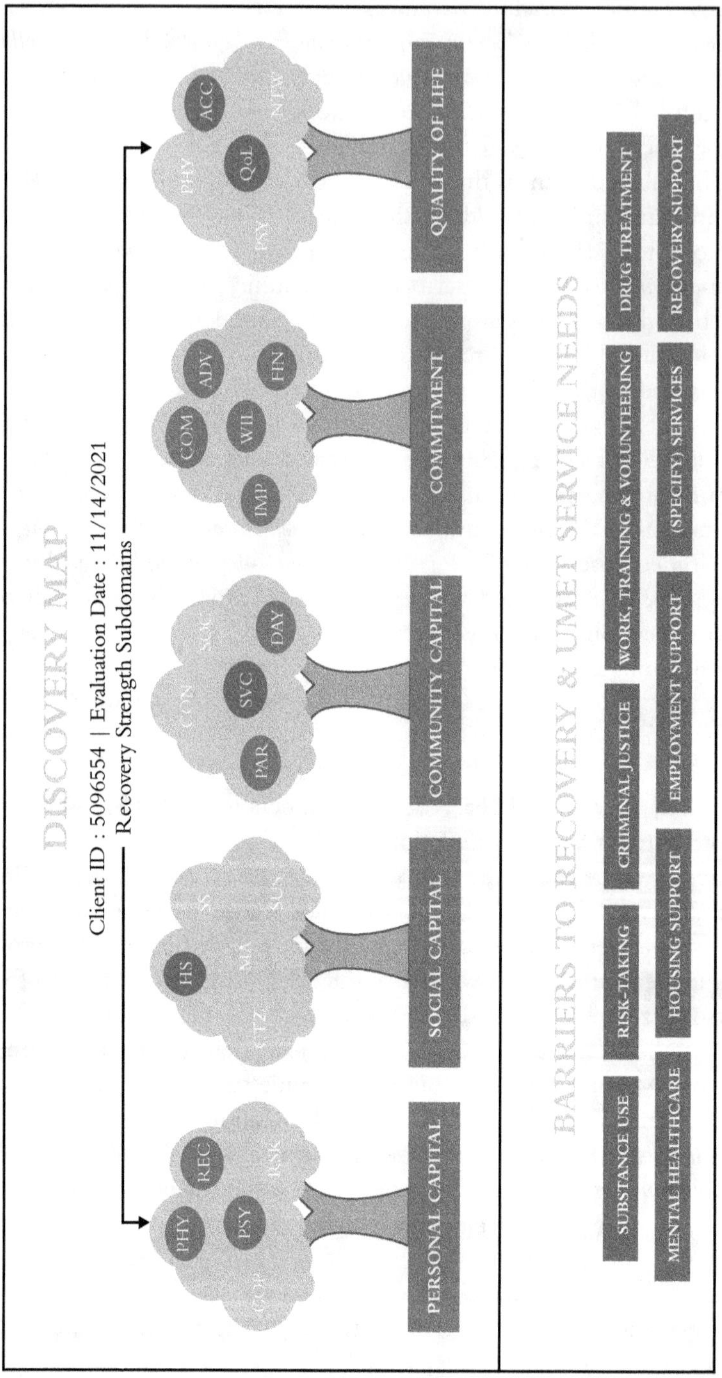

shared that to grow healthy apple trees, focus is directed to the 'soil' (see 10.4). The soil entails barriers to recovery and unmet service needs identified by the REC-CAP assessment.

Claudia celebrates being a certified peer recovery specialist who uses the MPE process in her role. Her journey began as a participant of the programme, where she used the REC-CAP to guide her own recovery planning. She understands what it is like from a lived-experience perspective and expressed that she is inspired to share similar insights with others through her role as a 'recovery navigator', which is a facilitator of the REC-CAP assessment provided with peer support. She shared that what she enjoys the most is that the REC-CAP assessment, combined with goal setting, empowers her to connect residents with essential support. '*It [MPE] has changed the culture. It is our program.*'

Final remarks and limitations

Far too long has the behavioural health space focused on deficits. This approach ignores the inherent strength of hope embedded inside each individual and within systems that influence addiction and recovery. The notion of cultivating recovery capital shifts focus from what individuals lack toward enhancing components which support the recovery journey. Personal interviews were utilized as an ethnographic approach to better identify the scope of recovery capital. Individuals among various levels of practice, within a comprehensive recovery ecosystem, supported the efficacy and usage of an instrument, the REC-CAP assessment, to measure recovery capital and inform care planning. This generates further argument for the REC-CAP as an instrument to measure the range of personal, social, and community factors associated with addiction recovery. The approach is not without limitations, including any missing and relevant information. Author and interviewee are not without bias due to associations with the VARR. However, the authorship team chose to utilize the control of scope granted by purviewing a comprehensive recovery capital network like the one among the Commonwealth of Virginia, which helped explore a concept of macro-sociological domain.

Implementing the ARMS system in Virginia took foresight and effort. Internal bias from this report is due to the personal relationships which began to cultivate recovery capital in the first place. From John Lehman to Claudia and the peers she supports, recovery capital continues to provoke discussion as to how to better advance science, technology, and infrastructure for recovery support services. This chapter encouraged sociological imagination by discussing a broad scope to better understand components that inform standardization to practice(s). The authorship team suggests several steps to enhance policy development as an outcome of this procedure.

The allocation of resources to support the development of recovery capital involves integration and synchronization of various components which helps communities function. Allocating resources to support recovery involves funding domains of education, employment, prevention, treatment, harm reduction, judicial, law enforcement, and most importantly: recovery support. Actively involving the community in processes of integration encourages stability of the system. Community collaboration with recovering individuals to assist with policy development fosters a sense of ownership and empowerment which better supports the adoption of practices. Initiatives must continue toward reducing stigma associated with addiction. The influence of recovery capital among governments and organizations demands extension to health parity laws, addiction treatment funding, and initiatives aimed at reducing health disparities.

Policies developed by utilization of the REC-CAP assessment emphasize prevention and early intervention, and with any positive effect, they build individual, community, and social resilience against harms associated with the global addiction crisis. Utilizing this tool to both cultivate recovery capital and measure its impact over time enhances the propensity by which recovery thrives. Finally, as more individuals join the tens of millions of recovering voices, the means constrained by policies will only become more germane to focus on equity. The many faces and voices of recovery highlight the need to include as many as possible at the decision-making table. This chapter highlighted how equitable decision making played a major role even in the early stages of government intervention and discussed many areas which warrant the need for infrastructure development. How individuals and organizations cultivate recovery capital varies in a multitudinous amount of ways and captures the essence of complexity which comes with discussions about how society operates. How recovery capital is applied on an individual basis is vastly different but clearly associated with how it is applied by community groups. Recalling that the relationship between micro- and meso-components is continuous; how communities respond to the demands of needs by individuals associated with addiction and recovery will continue to be of significant interest. The means to develop policies which support *all* people appears to be enabled by one explicit and indistinguishable component: *hope*.

Glossary

Accrued recovery capital: the physical or metaphysical accumulation of recovery capital and recovery related resources, particularly, but not necessarily, over time among different levels of social enterprise which lead to sustained recovery.

Applied recovery capital:	delineates practitioners or organizational elements which use or experience recovery capital theories and methods to produce positive recovery capital transformation.
Applied Sociology:	direct social interventions, as informed by sociological concepts and theories, to answer research questions/social problems.
Certified recovery residence:	a housing facility that is certified by a governing authority in accordance with regulations adopted by the associative board and provides alcohol-free and illicit-drug-free housing to individuals with substance use challenges.
Micro/ meso/ macro analysis:	sociological metatheory used as framework to analyse, observe, report, and scale theoretical phenomena involved between the dual poles of sociology (micro versus macro) with intent to permanently mobilize sociological imagination, grasp multi-paradigmatic concepts, adhere to a heuristic interdisciplinarity, and to foster reflexivity among all social levels.
REC-CAP assessment:	an evidence-based recovery capital instrument demonstrated to assist with action planning.

References

Ashford, R.D., Brown, A.M., Ryding, R., and Curtis, B. (2020) 'Building recovery ready communities: The recovery ready ecosystem model and community framework', *Addiction Research & Theory*, 28(1): 1–11.

Best, D., Sondhi, A., Best, J., Lehman, J., Grimes, A., Conner, M., and DeTriquet, R. (2023) 'Using recovery capital to predict retention and change in recovery residences in Virginia, USA', *Alcoholism Treatment Quarterly*, 41(2): 250–62.

Best, D., Sondhi, A., Hoffman, L., Best, J., Leidi, A., Grimes, A., et al (2024) 'Bridging the gap: Building and sustaining recovery capital in the transition from prison to recovery residences', *Journal of Offender Rehabilitation*, 63(1): 21–36.

Birgel, V., Decker, L., Röding, D., and Walter, U. (2023) 'Community capacity for prevention and health promotion: A scoping review on underlying domains and assessment methods', *Systematic Reviews,* 12, 147, DOI: https://doi.org/10.1186/s13643-023-02314-1.

Bruhn, J.G. (1999) 'Introductory statement: Philosophy and future direction', *Sociological Practice,* 1: 1–2.

Byrne, K.A., Mericle, A.A., and Litwin, A.H. (2023) 'Development and initial findings from the Peer Recovery Coach (PRC) checklist: A new tool to assess the nature of peer recovery coaching service delivery', *The American Journal of Drug and Alcohol Abuse,* 49(2): 159–69.

Cano, I., Best, D., Edwards, M., and Lehman, J. (2017) 'Recovery capital pathways: Modelling the components of recovery wellbeing', *Drug and Alcohol Dependence,* 181: 11–19.

Groshkova, T., Best, D., and White, W. (2012) 'The Assessment of Recovery Capital: Properties and psychometrics of a measure of addiction recovery strengths', *Drug and Alcohol Review,* 32(2): 187–94.

National Alliance of Recovery Residences (2018) 'NARR National Standard 3.0 Compendium', *The National Alliance of Recovery Residences* [online], Available from: https://narronline.org/wp-content/uploads/2018/11/NARR_Standard_V.3.0_release_11-2018.pdf

Pouille, A., Bellaert, L., Vander Laenen, F., and Vanderplasschen, W. (2021) 'Recovery capital among migrants and ethnic minorities in recovery from problem substance use: An analysis of lived experiences', *International Journal of Environmental Research and Public Health,* 18(24), 13025, DOI: https://doi.org/10.3390/ijerph182413025.

Rampini, A.A. (2019) 'Financing durable assets', *The American Economic Review,* 109(2): 664–701.

Reif, S., Braude, L., Lyman, D.R., Dougherty, R.H., Daniels, A.S., Ghose, S.S., et al (2014) 'Peer recovery support for individuals with substance use disorders: Assessing the evidence', *Psychiatric Services,* 65(7): 853–61.

Serpa, S. and Ferreira, C.M. (2019) 'Micro, meso and macro levels of social analysis', *International Journal of Social Science Studies,* 7(3): 120–4.

Steele, S.F. and Price, J. (2007) *Applied Sociology: Terms, Topics, Tools and Tasks* (2nd edn), Belmont: Thomson Wadsworth Publishing.

White, W. and Cloud, W. (2008) 'Recovery capital: A primer for addictions professionals', *Counselor,* 9(5): 22–7.

11

Justice Capital: Delivering Equitable Outcomes for Indigenous Children in State Care

Sharynne Hamilton and Lorana Bartels

Overview

Globally, Indigenous peoples have suffered the effects of the invasion and colonization by foreign countries that has detrimentally affected the long-term health and well-being of peoples and communities. In Australia, there are high numbers of Aboriginal and Torres Strait Islander families who have been deeply affected by the historical circumstances surrounding the British invasion and subsequent colonization, the harms of which continue to reverberate across communities (Dale et al, 2023). There is a need to pay attention to recovery for Indigenous children involved with state care systems, namely, child protection and youth justice. The removal of children to the child protection system, and repeated incarceration, now span multiple generations of Aboriginal and Torres Strait Islander communities, and the intersection between the two systems for Indigenous children is a significant problem (Bala et al, 2015; Malvaso et al, 2019; Keddell et al, 2022).

As discussed elsewhere in this book, and by Hamilton et al (2020b), the concept of 'recovery capital' was initially developed as a strengths-based model, in the context of recovery from substance use (Granfield and Cloud, 2001). Hamilton et al (2020b) extended this model by introducing the concept of 'justice capital', as a way to explore recovery capital in the justice context, specifically, the positive and negative assets of children and young people living in state care, to ensure equitable access to care and support, that sustains recovery and enhances well-being and positive life outcomes. Drawing on interviews with 38 young people in detention (most of whom identified as Indigenous), Hamilton et al suggested that 'the application of a recovery-focused model of assessment that explores the personal, social and community capital assets possessed by justice-involved youth provides a way to understand and respond to their neurodevelopmental needs, build on their skills and assist them to plan pathways to achieve their goals' (2020b, 31).

In this chapter, we extend the recovery capital scale scholarship (White, 2009) and the concept of justice capital, describing the development of an Australian Aboriginal Elder-led and codesigned justice capital assets scale (Farrant et al, 2019). We discuss elements of institutional justice capital that will be required to support the personal justice capital assets of children and young people living away from their families and communities in state care. We argue that investing in culturally secure, Indigenous community-led and driven approaches to the care of children will positively impact individual and community well-being. Further, considering the collective nature of Indigenous communities, this could deliver a contagion of hope (Best and de Alwis, 2017) and positive well-being outcomes for children in state care.

Background

The health and well-being of individuals and populations is determined by physical and biological factors that are closely intertwined with the social, economic, and political structures in which we live and work (Commission on the Social Determinants of Health, 2007). These structures are operationalized through governments and policies as well as the societal values that collectively shape our place in the world as individuals, and as a population (Solar and Irwin, 2010). As such, it is these structures that can impact, positively and negatively, on the conditions in which we live, the behaviours and attitudes of a population, and the health and well-being of communities (Solar and Irwin, 2010). There is a plethora of literature that discusses the harms of colonization to Indigenous peoples in Western countries, including Australia (Dockery, 2010; Blagg, 2016; Fogarty et al, 2018; Staines and Scott, 2020; Hamilton et al, 2021; Holland et al, 2023), New Zealand (Cunneen and Tauri, 2019; Moewaka Barnes and McCreanor, 2019; Smith, 2021; Deckert et al, 2023), and North America (Evans-Campbell, 2008; Menon and McCarter, 2021; Robinson et al, 2023). For Indigenous populations, colonization brought with it the undue use of incarceration and the forced removal of children from communities to missions and residential schools (Human Rights and Equal Opportunities Commission, 1997; Tsosie, 2023). These, often violent, practices have significantly contributed to contemporary health, social, political, and economic disparities for Indigenous peoples compared to dominant populations (Taylor and Habibis, 2020; Melro et al, 2023).

For Aboriginal and Torres Strait Islander peoples, the social and cultural determinants of health that advance resilience and well-being are upheld through 'traditional cultural practice, kinship, connection to land and Country, art, song and ceremony, dance, healing, spirituality, empowerment, ancestry, belonging and self-determination' (Department of Health, 2017). Traditionally, Aboriginal and Torres Strait Islander communities comprised an organized and complex web of relationships that involved reciprocal obligations of giving and receiving, continually reinforcing kinship and community connections. These webs of connectedness were crucial to cultural identity and place in community (Human Rights and Equal Opportunities Commission, 1997). When many children are removed, such as happened with colonization, this complex social fabric breaks down, threatening social order and cultural survival (Human Rights and Equal Opportunities Commission, 1997). The impact of forced child removal policies has caused significant social and health harms for Aboriginal and Torres Strait Islander families and communities across multiple generations. The transfer of intergenerational trauma has led to excessive levels of contemporary involvement with state child protection and youth justice systems (Malvaso et al, 2019; O'Donnell et al, 2019; Hamilton et al, 2022; Baidawi and Ball, 2023).

Colonized Western countries report high numbers of Indigenous children involved with both the child protection and youth justice systems. This has been documented in Australia (Malvaso et al, 2019; Hamilton et al, 2020a, 2020b; Baidawi and Ball, 2023), New Zealand (Keddell, 2022; Keddell et al, 2022), and North America (Bala et al, 2015; Baglivio et al, 2016; Flores et al, 2018). These countries' youth justice systems are littered with examples of state child protection system failures, and discriminatory policies that both influence and perpetuate an intergenerational transmission of trauma and inequalities for Indigenous peoples (Porter and Cunneen, 2021; United Nations, 2022; McCausland and Baldry, 2023).

Australian state care systems

Across Australia, Aboriginal and Torres Strait Islander children are admitted to state care at over ten times the rate of their non-Indigenous peers (Australian Institute of Health and Welfare, 2022a) and are twice as likely as their non-Indigenous peers to experience poorer outcomes, particularly in relation to mental health and long-term well-being, and longer times in care on permanent orders and through adoption. Reunification rates are low and many children are in long-term care with no identified reunification goals (Liddle et al, 2022). Once in care, Aboriginal and Torres Strait Islander children are equally likely as their non-Indigenous peers to experience neglect, and twice as likely to suffer physical, sexual, or emotional abuse (Liddle et al, 2022). The Aboriginal and Torres Strait Islander Child Placement Principle (Secretariat of National Aboriginal and Islander Child

Care – SNAICC, 2017) provides structured guidance for the placement of children removed from their families. The aim is to ensure, wherever possible, that children are placed with immediate family or extended kin, or with an Aboriginal or Torres Strait Islander carer. However, in 2020, 58 per cent of Aboriginal and Torres Strait Islander children were placed in non-Indigenous care arrangements (Australian Institute of Health and Welfare, 2022a), with little tangible change to these statistics over the last five years (O'Donnell et al, 2019; Hamilton et al, 2022). Consistently, Australian systems of government have failed children in state care, evidenced in more than 50 reports and inquiries into child protection services over the last 50 years. These include a Royal Commission into the sexual abuse of children in institutions and foster care (Australian Government, 2017); a Senate inquiry into forced adoptions (Senate Affairs Reference Committee, 2004); and an extensive inquiry by the Human Rights and Equal Opportunities Commission (1997) into the policies of forced removal of Aboriginal and Torres Strait Islander children from their kin, countries, and communities.

The long-term health and well-being outcomes for Aboriginal and Torres Strait Islander young people in child protection care are poor, with youth detention and adult prisons an inevitable trajectory for many (Malvaso et al, 2019; Hamilton et al, 2020b; Baidawi and Ball, 2023). Aboriginal and Torres Strait Islander young people make up more than half of the youth detention population (Australian Institute of Health and Welfare, 2022b), despite only accounting for 5 per cent of Australia's children and young people. Australia has come under significant recent international scrutiny for its treatment of young people engaged with the youth justice system (McLachlan et al, 2019; Cakal, 2023). An extensive report by the Australian Institute of Criminology discussed the results and themes from more than 20 inquiries into youth detention centres around the country over the last five years (Lin et al, 2020). The review identified common themes across the inquiries as reasons for poor outcomes for children and young people in detention, including their complex needs; high exposure to the child protection system and foster care; and the failure of governments to adhere to the principle of last resort when detaining young people. The review also highlighted a need for cultural training and supporting staff across a range of therapeutic service provision (Lin et al, 2020).

From as young as ten, Australian children who commit crimes can be subject to imprisonment, and for children and young people aged 14 or over, full criminal responsibility is applied (Crofts, 2023). Neurodisability is clearly identified and understood as a risk factor for individual involvement in criminal activity and the criminal justice system (Houston and Butler, 2019). Individuals can have poor judgement, memory impairments, and their ability to pay attention and to plan can be compromised (Bower et al, 2018; Mutch et al, 2022). They may find it difficult to comprehend what is being said to them (Bowen, 2019) and communicate responses (Kippin et al, 2018; Snow et al, 2018). They are likely to be impulsive, lack empathy, or fail to understand cause and effect. They are often impaired in cognition, and many have an IQ below 70 (Bower et al, 2018; Mutch et al, 2022; McCausland and Baldry, 2023). These types of disabilities are not always evident and are understood as 'invisible disabilities' (Moriña, 2022). In the only Fetal Alcohol Spectrum Disorder prevalence study of its kind in Australia, Bower and colleagues (2018) assessed 100 children and young people incarcerated in Banksia Hill Detention Centre in Western Australia, with 36 per cent receiving a diagnosis for Fetal Alcohol Spectrum Disorder, and 89 per cent found to be living with more than one severe neurodevelopmental impairment. Concerningly, 75 per cent were Aboriginal children and young people (Bower et al, 2018).

There is an imperative to significantly restructure the way youth justice and child protection services operate in the Aboriginal and Torres Strait Islander community (Blagg, 2016; Staines and Scott, 2020; Hamilton and Maslen, 2022; Hamilton et al, 2022). Recovery, in the context of these systems, involves redressing the harm from the policies of forced removal from kin, country, and culture (Cunneen and Rowe, 2014; Fogarty et al, 2018). We have long advocated for the needs of children and young people involved with these systems, investigating recovery capital, and developing the concept of justice capital to assist with understanding the assets and needs of these children in the context of state care systems.

Justice capital

The idea of justice capital was originally conceptualized from the Banksia Hill qualitative study (Hamilton et al, 2019; 2020a; 2020b). Justice capital draws attention to the assets children and young people in state care possess and what they need to participate equitably in all aspects of their care. High levels of unrecognized and undiagnosed neurodisability, despite involvement in multiple systems, is evidence of the deleterious effects of systemic disadvantage and failures to address the adversity Aboriginal and Torres Strait Islander children experience (McCausland and Baldry, 2023).

The data from the Banksia Hill qualitative study were explored to identify aspects of negative and positive justice capital (Table 11.1) (Hamilton et al, 2020b). Unrecognized neurodisability was identified as negative justice capital. Ensuring access to clinical assessments and ensuring specific supports related to neurodisability are provided were identified as positive justice capital. There were many aspects of care and support that suggested the participants in this study were often excluded from community assets that could support their well-being (Hamilton et al, 2020b). This included access to disability services and individualized support for education, health, and well-being

Table 11.1: Examples of negative and positive justice capital

Negative justice capital	Positive justice capital
Undiagnosed neurodisability	Access to clinical assessments, disability services and support, education support, legal representation, advocacy and interpreters and plain language explanations
Lack of opportunity for engagement with community organizations or recreation and social exclusion from community assets	Access to organizations that embrace strengths and use optimistic language, support individuals' hopes and future aspirations and provide support for goal setting and skill development, as well as opportunities to engage with community assets that support recreation or employment goals
Intergenerational trauma	
Denial of cultural activity, language use	
Disconnection from country	Peer support and positive mentoring
Fractured cultural identity	Recovery and healing services
	Commitment to culture, community, and country
	Opportunity for cultural activity
	Strong cultural identity

Source: Hamilton et al, 2020b.

(Hamilton et al, 2020a). The second aspect of justice capital was related to culture. In addition to 75 per cent of the children and young people in the Banksia Hill prevalence study being Aboriginal, another 10 per cent were from other cultures (Bower et al, 2018). These participants' stories centred around family, community, and home country, reflecting similar traditional worldviews to the Aboriginal participants (Hamilton et al, 2020a; 2020b).

Of the prevalence study participants, 13 per cent were in state child protection care immediately prior to detention (Bower et al, 2018) and almost all of the Aboriginal young people in the qualitative study spoke of child protection involvement at some point in their lives (Hamilton et al, 2020b). Intergenerational trauma featured in the stories of the Aboriginal young people at Banksia Hill. One participant, removed from his family and community as a young baby, 'grew himself up', had never met his biological family, and did not know where he came from. Concerningly, he described his future as being 'in the big house across the road', referring to the adult men's prison where he knew many of his male relatives were incarcerated (Hamilton et al, 2020a; 2020b). This somewhat normalized journey through the child protection system, into the youth justice system, and onto adult prisons influenced the conceptualization of justice capital. Cultural support plans in relation to Aboriginal children involved in child protection services have been found to have important cultural omissions about family and connections, and inaccuracies that negatively impact their long-term health and well-being (SNAICC, 2017; Krakouer, 2023).

The collective and relational nature of Indigenous societies means that when an Indigenous child is removed from a family through state-sanctioned child protection or youth justice interventions, the entire community grieves. For colonized countries, this complex intersection between the child welfare and youth justice system for Indigenous children calls for attention to the harm that has been incurred and to the reparation of that harm (Baglivio et al, 2016; Malvaso et al, 2019; Hamilton et al, 2020b, 2022; Keddell et al, 2022; Baidawi and Ball, 2023). The child protection and criminal justice systems for Aboriginal and Torres Strait Islander children and young people are inextricably linked. Fifth generation child removal has been identified in some Aboriginal and Torres Strait Islander families. Ensuring connection to kin, culture, traditional lands, and their community when children are removed is critical to interrupting the intergenerational cycles of harm evident in statutory systems (Paradies, 2016; Hinkson and Anthony, 2019) beginning with child protection interventions (Hamilton et al, 2022).

Within the recovery capital literature that the concept of justice capital extends, personal, family/social, and community capital are viewed as resources that individuals may draw on and can positively or negatively influence recovery (Cloud and Granfield, 2008). Recovery capital provides a potential framework for assessing hope, strength, and community development throughout the recovery journey for individuals and communities (Best and de Alwis, 2017). Recovery capital describes the range and depth of resources, both internal and external, that can be drawn upon to initiate and sustain recovery. Within these spheres there exist four main capital components: social, physical, human, and cultural capital (Granfield and Cloud, 2001; Cloud and Granfield, 2008). In the context of recovery capital, social capital allows for the identification of intimate relationships, family networks, and broader social relationships, and constitutes the availability of culturally prescribed pathways that resonate with particular individuals and families, including models for Indigenous peoples (Coyhis and Simonelli, 2008). It supports data collection and analysis of the willingness and capacity of family members to participate in recovery treatments, identify opportunities and access to prosocial activities, and interpersonal connections to others in institutions such as school, work, and community organizations (Cloud and Granfield, 2008; Best and Laudet, 2010).

Recovery capital provides a dynamic and interactive framework with which to assess personal, family/social, and community growth. The purpose of conceptualizing justice capital is to address the discrepancies that have resulted from previous and contemporary state policies and practices, that continue to be imposed on Aboriginal and Torres Strait Islander peoples with the same devastating results. This does not suggest two separate ways of working, but rather, finding ways to build relationships, rebuild community trust, and promote justice capital as a framework for how this can be achieved. Acknowledging that Indigenous societies do not hold one particular philosophy or belief system, there are fundamental differences between Western European and Indigenous belief systems that are embedded in different perceptions of relationships between individuals, their environment, and the universe (Morrissette et al, 1993), or in Australia, the 'Dreamtime' (Wolfe, 1991). Traditionally, community roles were everybody's responsibility and there was a collective understanding of responsibilities to other community members for the benefit and survival of the group (Morrissette et al, 1993). For Indigenous peoples, the concept of disability is foreign and there are very different cultural understandings of health and illness (Wandji, 2019; Hamilton et al, 2020c). This was evident in the Banksia Hill study, which found that Aboriginal caregivers of young people who were assessed did not use terminology such as 'fetal alcohol spectrum disorder'. Instead, they commonly referred to a clinical diagnosis as 'that thing in his head' (Hamilton et al, 2020c). Further, a diagnosis was not necessarily seen as a disability, because some Western Australian Aboriginal communities have the highest prevalence rates of Fetal Alcohol Spectrum disorder globally and the challenges for children have become normalized in communities (Hamilton et al, 2021; Doyle et al, 2023). The study also found that, for most of the caregivers, diagnosis did not reveal anything new about their children. They valued the potential for diagnosis to provide treatments and strategies to manage their children's challenges, however, for children from remote and regional areas, basic services and clinical treatments were a whole other world away (Hamilton et al, 2020c).

Measuring justice capital assets

Exploration of what constitutes justice capital has been undertaken since 2020, as part of consultations with Aboriginal Elders and the Perth community (Farrant et al, 2019), where Banksia Hill Detention Centre is located. Given the culturally different understandings of disability, we did not focus on a justice capital data collection tool to establish whether neurodevelopmental problems might exist for an individual or for detecting the need for clinical assessment and diagnosis. Rather, given the intersection for these children with the child protection system, we assume that it is highly likely that children's neurodevelopment will be affected by the trauma of removal from their families and communities. An Indigenous justice capital assets scale (Table 11.2) has been developed as part of an Aboriginal Elder and community-led study that is investigating the cultural connections, activities, and resources that are available or needed for Aboriginal children in the care of mainstream out-of-home care agencies and living in non-Indigenous care arrangements (Hamilton et al, 2024).

For Indigenous peoples, a complete appreciation of the challenges and support needs of children and young people in state care requires the consideration of recovery capital in relation to the historical context of

Table 11.2: Justice Capital Assets Scale[1]

Response options: 5. Strongly Agree; 4. Agree; 3. Sometimes; 2. Disagree; 1. Strongly Disagree; 0. Does Not Apply

1. ___ I have a community Elder that I trust.
2. ___ My Elders tell me cultural stories.
3. ___ I have a cultural mentor that I trust.
4. ___ I have cultural peer advocacy that can help me if I need it.
5. ___ I have cultural peer support to help me reach my goals.
6. ___ My people take me out on country.
7. ___ I participate in caring for country.
8. ___ I participate in cultural ceremonies.
9. ___ I go fishing or hunting with my people.
10. ___ I do art with my people.
11. ___ I participate in cultural dances.
12. ___ I eat traditional food.
13. ___ I can listen to or watch cultural stories on my phone.
14. ___ I read cultural stories.
15. ___ I play in a sporting team for my community.
16. ___ I live with an Indigenous foster carer.
17. ___ I have contact with one of my parents.
18. ___ I go to an Indigenous health service.
19. ___ I have an Indigenous doctor.
20. ___ I have an Indigenous teacher.
21. ___ I learn Indigenous and non-Indigenous subjects at school.
22. ___ I can talk to an Indigenous support person at school.
23. ___ I speak an Indigenous language.
24. ___ I speak more than one Indigenous language.
25. ___ I have access to an Indigenous language interpreter.
26. ___ I can get information I need in a language I understand.
27. ___ I can get resources I need in a language I understand.
28. ___ I have access to an Indigenous police support worker.
29. ___ I have an Indigenous lawyer.
30. ___ I have an Indigenous community organisation I can go to that can help me achieve my goals.

Possible Maximum Score: 150 My Score: ____

colonization and policies that have caused harm, alongside the cultural assets that promote the social and cultural determinants of health and well-being (Department of Health, 2017). Using approaches complementary to asset-based community engagement (Collinson and Best, 2019), we have developed statements (Table 11.2) informed by approaches and pathways that resonate with recovery for Indigenous peoples (Coyhis and Simonelli, 2008; Moore and Coyhis, 2010). Statements 1–16 collect the justice capital assets related to social recovery capital that have cultural importance for well-being, while statements 17–30 collect information about community capital assets (Cloud and Granfield, 2008; Best and Laudet, 2010), access to a visible and diverse range of peers and positive role models (Nash et al, 2019), and for providing comprehensive resources drawing on community assets (Collinson and Best, 2019; Nash et al, 2019). Where domains of neurodisability had the potential to impact cultural identity or knowledge-sharing, we included statements to address any gaps in access for Indigenous children. Memory impairments, for example, endanger the transfer of cultural knowledge. Indigenous societies transfer knowledge through oral storytelling and memory impairments affect the accurate transfer of cultural stories that have been passed on through generations for thousands of years (Hewlett et al, 2023). We therefore explored new and innovative ways to capture assets, such as cultural stories, through a variety of media that can assist to maintain this important cultural practice (statements 2, 13, 14), in addition to contributing to the well-being of Indigenous children living away from their families and communities. Further research and codesign with youth for developing the justice capital assets scale scoring and ways to interpret the information collected is required, as well as establishing cultural understanding and age-appropriate wording for the scale.

Personal and community justice capital can be realized at the level of both government and non-government institutions. Ultimately, at this level, institutional justice capital is the extent of belief in good outcomes for all and the embodiment of that belief in the way interventions or relationships encourage and promote, or impede, positive change (Best et al, 2021). The first step is in recognizing that if the systems that govern our lives, and the policies that shape them, do not take care of personal justice capital assets relating to culture for Indigenous children in state care systems, then the health and well-being of children and communities will not change. Moreover, efforts will be time and resource consuming, and there is a risk of even further entrenched marginalization (Hamilton and Maslen, 2022). Statements 17–30 collect information about the assets that Indigenous children possess to enable benefits from service interactions to be realized. Access to Indigenous community-controlled organizations for culturally relevant services is important. When involved with mainstream services delivered by agencies or by governments, receiving information in a language that is understood and explained and available in a variety of formats is important and also cares for children's developmental needs (Hamilton et al, 2020a).

To ensure consideration of literacy issues, or neurodisability that may not be evident, justice capital assets should be completed with a support worker. The scale provides a way to collect the sum of justice capital assets and identify the cultural needs of children living away from their families and communities in state care systems. The higher the score, the more likely their recovery journey will involve culturally relevant and meaningful opportunities for successful and happy lives. When Indigenous children are connected with their communities, achieve success and are strong, the entire community celebrates, enabling a social and community contagion of hope (Best and de Alwis, 2017). By contrast, the continual removal of Aboriginal children to state care systems does not allow this contagion to gain traction. How well institutions are utilizing justice capital assets for the benefit of Indigenous children will be significantly influenced by the institutions and organizations that children and families are involved with (Best et al, 2021).

Institutional justice capital

It is important to consider how institutions support the personal justice capital assets or meet the needs of Indigenous children and young people, as identified in the justice capital assets scale (Table 11.2). We consider elements of negative and positive institutional justice capital (Table 11.3) in two areas. First, connection and relationships and, second, service delivery and administration, including systemic factors. Many aspects of negative justice capital (Table 11.1) identified in the Banksia Hill study were underpinned by an absence of key professional relationships (Hamilton et al, 2019; 2020b). Participants disengaged from school early and did not discuss relationships with teachers or educators. They also did not discuss relationships with child protection case workers, police, or their community or social support workers. Yet they spoke extensively about their families. These aspects of negative social and community recovery capital (Granfield and Cloud, 2001; Best et al, 2017) could largely be attributed to the colonial history and subsequent distrust previously discussed (Human Rights and Equal Opportunities Commission, 1997; Hamilton et al, 2022), particularly given that almost all services for Aboriginal and Torres Strait Islander peoples are delivered by non-Indigenous staff who have limited access to the training required to bring about culturally responsive statutory systems (Cunneen and Rowe, 2014; Walker et al, 2014). Relationships and networks must be built on principles of mutual obligation and trust for recovery initiatives to be successful (Cloud and Granfield, 2008; Best and de Alwis, 2017). Culturally insecure mainstream services have been identified as an element of negative institutional justice capital. Building trust between Indigenous communities and mainstream services is essential for building on the justice capital assets of children and young people. Finding ways to work well together as allies toward recovery, particularly as the Aboriginal and Torres Strait Islander community-controlled professional sector continues to grow, will be critical for success.

Providing opportunities for cultural competency training for non-Indigenous staff, increasing Indigenous staffing levels in mainstream organizations, and providing training and development will be essential elements for supporting the building of personal justice capital assets, and

Table 11.3: Elements of negative and positive institutional justice capital that support personal justice capital

NEGATIVE INSTITUTIONAL JUSTICE CAPITAL	POSITIVE INSTITUTIONAL JUSTICE CAPITAL
Connections and relationships	**Connections and relationships**
Poor facilitation for connecting children with: • family and kin • traditional country • cultural resources • cultural activities • community-controlled organizations • community assets Absence of relationships with: • children's family and kin • the Indigenous community • community-controlled organizations Limited access to forums that support Indigenous decision-making and community input Lack of commitment to harm reparation	Engaging professional Indigenous family connection services to establish information about children Commitment to provide opportunities for connection to: • family and kin • Indigenous Elders, cultural peer support, cultural mentors • traditional country and cultural knowledge • Indigenous services, cultural activity and resources Facilitating opportunities for Indigenous knowledge-sharing Elder and community-led decision making. Providing forums that facilitate and support relationships with Indigenous communities Commitment to recovery for Indigenous children, families, and communities Adoption of strength-based recovery narratives and language
Service delivery and administration	**Service delivery and administration**
Removal of children from their families and communities to non-Indigenous care arrangements and off country detention facilities Inadequate and misinformed cultural care planning Culturally insecure service delivery Placement instability Un(der) trained staff Siloed mainstream service delivery Mainstream health messaging Western Biomedical interventions Mainstream schooling and curriculums	Commitment and adherence to removing children from their families and communities as a principle of last resort (United Nations, 2022) Commitment to searching for and finding Indigenous family and carers Resourcing place-based alternatives to detention Cultural awareness and competency training Focus on increasing Indigenous staff across all levels of service operation Facilitating forums for Indigenous knowledge sharing circles Facilitating opportunities for working together Working with Indigenous language experts Development of community codesigned social and health messaging Distribution of plain language community health and social information Community codesigned recovery messaging Community codesigned curriculums Child and family-led learning plans

increasing positive institutional justice capital. Similarly, creating a community of cultural mentors and a range of role models and peers (Collinson and Best, 2019; Nash et al, 2019) that can be drawn on to support children and young people in state care represents elements of institutional justice capital. Moreover, providing pathways that support the training and development of peer support services will increase the potential for providing culturally secure care to children and young people. We will explore through Elder and community codesign, developing a checklist for institutional justice capital to support organizations to track their progress and build awareness of organizational cultural training needs.

Moving toward recovery, asset-based community development approaches (Kretzmann, 1995) are comprised of key steps, beginning with identifying the levels of engagement with recovery and associated initiatives through asset mapping and then exploring these assets for negative and positive social and community recovery capital to identify barriers to community and professional engagement, such as access or affordability (Best et al, 2017). This then allows for exploration of the goals and hopes of community members and for the engagement of community connectors, or cultural mentors, to undertake assertive linkage (Manning et al, 2012) to available assets and resources in communities. Assertive linkage is important for Indigenous communities as it allows for assets, resources, and services to be developed and shared in a way suitable for communities (Best et al, 2017). The next step in moving toward recovery is drawing together the assets in communities to connect the strengths, assets, resources, and connections that can be linked with children living away from their families in state care (Best et al, 2017; Collinson and Best, 2019).

Positive institutional justice capital requires a mutual commitment to recovery from all stakeholders – government services, mainstream, and community-controlled organizations, and industry (Best et al, 2017). There are significant capital assets in the networks of the Aboriginal and Torres Strait Islander community and the community-controlled sector that could be drawn on and cohesively brought together (Pearson et al, 2020). Moreover, it is well established that the most successful outcomes for children are when they are delivered by Aboriginal community-controlled organizations because of their alignment with culture and community. Their success is attributed to having a well-defined service delivery region, flexibility, and a focus on community solutions (Pearson et al, 2020). Gathering the information discussed in this chapter (Tables 11.2 and 11.3) will be an important element of positive institutional justice capital for children in state care as a source of linking capital (Best et al, 2017). Attending to children's connections and cultural needs, drawing on and supporting community members as cultural or peer mentors and support, providing opportunities for prosocial and cultural activity, and providing for culturally relevant services and community-controlled organizations will be essential for building personal justice capital assets and promoting well-being (Pearson et al, 2020).

Conclusion

The ideas in this book are strongly linked to building credible recovery science, and this chapter conceptualizes justice capital in the context of Aboriginal and Torres Strait Islander children in Australia removed from their families and living in state care. This adds a significant dimension to domains that have been designed to assist recovery and will have broader application in other Western colonized countries, as well as for peoples of other traditional cultures. The justice capital assets scale was developed with, for, and by the Aboriginal community in Perth, itself an element of positive justice capital! It was developed with an Indigenous worldview (Dockery, 2010; Hewlett et al, 2023), for adaptation according to place-based cultural and language-specific needs, for children and families from other Indigenous cultures. Paying attention to recovery, and the personal justice capital assets that Indigenous children possess or need, linking community assets and support with Indigenous children living away from their families, and considering the role of negative and positive institutional justice capital assets, has the potential to initiate recovery processes and create a social contagion of hope (Best and de Alwis, 2017). A contagion that could lead to children and young people living in flourishing communities, where interventions are decided, led, and delivered by Indigenous communities, for Indigenous communities, supported by strong relationships with non-Indigenous community allies and services.

Note

[1] This name was developed in consultation with Indigenous Elders (Hamilton et al, 2024), and is a strengths-based framework. We recognize that its development cannot be viewed independently from the negative impacts of colonization on Indigenous peoples in Australia, as in other colonized countries.

References

Australian Government (2017) *Royal Commission into Institutional Responses to Child Sexual Abuse. Final Report*, Canberra: Australian Government.

Australian Institute of Health and Welfare (2022a) *Child Protection Australia 2020–2021*, Canberra: Australian Institute of Health and Welfare.

Australian Institute of Health and Welfare (2022b) *Youth Detention Population in Australia 2022*, Canberra: Australian Institute of Health and Welfare.

Baglivio, M.T., Wolff, K.T., Piquero, A.R., Bilchik, S., Jackowski, K., Greenwald, M.A., and Epps, N. (2016) 'Maltreatment, child welfare, and recidivism in a sample of deep-end crossover youth', *Journal of Youth and Adolescence*, 45(4): 625–54.

Baidawi, S. and Ball, R. (2023) 'Child protection and youth offending: Differences in youth criminal court-involved children by dual system involvement', *Children and Youth Services Review*, 144, 106736.

Bala, N., Finlay, J., De Filippis, R., and Hunter, K. (2015) 'Child welfare adolescents & the youth justice system: Failing to respond effectively to crossover youth', *Canadian Criminal Law Review*, 19(1): 129–51.

Best, D. and Laudet, A. (2010) *The Potential of Recovery Capital*, London: RSA.

Best, D. and De Alwis, S. (2017) 'Community recovery as a public health intervention: The contagion of hope', *Alcoholism Treatment Quarterly*, 35(3): 187–99.

Best, D., Hamilton, S., Hall, L. and Bartels, L. (2021) 'Justice capital: A model for reconciling structural and agentic determinants of desistance', *Probation Journal*, 68(2): 206–23.

Best, D., Irving, J., Collinson, B., Andersson, C., and Edwards, M. (2017) 'Recovery networks and community connections: Identifying connection needs and community linkage opportunities in early recovery populations', *Alcoholism Treatment Quarterly*, 35(1): 2–15.

Blagg, H. (2016) *Crime, Aboriginality and the Decolonisation of Justice*, Sydney: Hawkins Press.

Bowen, A. (2019) '"You don't have to say anything": Modality and consequences in conversations about the right to silence in the Northern Territory', *Australian Journal of Linguistics*, 39(3): 347–74.

Bower, C., Watkins, R.E., Mutch, R.C., Marriott, R., Freeman, J., Kippin, N.R., et al (2018) 'Fetal alcohol spectrum disorder and youth justice: a prevalence study among young people sentenced to detention in Western Australia', *BMJ Open*, 8, e019605, DOI: 10.1136/bmjopen-2017-019605.

Cakal, E. (2023) 'Isolating children in detention: Cautioning international comparisons', *Alternative Law Journal*, 48(3): 166–71.

Cloud, W. and Granfield, R. (2008) 'Conceptualizing recovery capital: Expansion of a theoretical construct', *Substance Use & Misuse*, 43(12–13): 1971–86.

Collinson, B. and Best, D. (2019) 'Promoting recovery from substance misuse through engagement with community assets: Asset based community engagement', *Substance Abuse: Research and Treatment*, 13, DOI: 10.1177/1178221819876575.

Commission On The Social Determinants Of Health (2007) *Achieving Health Equity: From Root Causes to Fair Outcomes. Interim Statement from the Commission*, Geneva: World Health Organisation.

Coyhis, D. and Simonelli, R. (2008) 'The Native American healing experience', *Substance Use & Misuse*, 43(12–13): 1927–49.

Crofts, T. (2023) 'Act now: Raise the minimum age of criminal responsibility', *Current Issues in Criminal Justice*, 35(1): 118–38.

Cunneen, C. and Rowe, S. (2014) 'Changing narratives: Colonised peoples, criminology and social work', *International Journal for Crime, Justice and Social Democracy,* 3(1): 49–67.

Cunneen, C. and Tauri, J.M. (2019) 'Indigenous peoples, criminology, and criminal justice', *Annual Review of Criminology,* 2: 359–81.

Dale, P.R., Meurk, C., Williams, M., Watson, M., Steele, M.L., Wittenhagen, L., et al (2023) 'Our Ways, Your Ways, Both Ways – A multi-disciplinary collaboration to develop, embed and evaluate a model of social and emotional wellbeing care for Aboriginal and Torres Strait Islander young people who experience detention–Phase 1', *Frontiers in Psychiatry,* 14, 1207103, DOI: 10.3389/fpsyt.2023.1207103.

Deckert, A., Busby-Pukeiti, W.T.G., and Tauri, J. (2023) '"Young Brown Men Being Brutish": How Police Ten 7 Portrays Māori and Pacifica People as Violent and Criminal in Aotearoa New Zealand', *Journal of Global Indigeneity,* 7(1), DOI: https://doi.org/10.54760/001c.77757.

Department of Health (2017) *My Life, My Lead – Opportunities for Strengthening Approaches to the Social Determinants and Cultural Determinants of Indigenous Health: Report on the National Consultations,* Canberra: Australian Government.

Dockery, A.M. (2010) 'Culture and wellbeing: The case of Indigenous Australians', *Social Indicators Research,* 99(2): 315–32.

Doyle, M.F., Perry, J., Bower, C., Conigrave, K.M. and Hamilton, S. (2023) 'Fetal alcohol spectrum disorder and Aboriginal and Torres Strait Islander men: A discussion to be had', *Drug and Alcohol Review,* 42(7): 1601–05.

Evans-Campbell, T. (2008) 'Historical trauma in American Indian/Native Alaska communities: A multilevel framework for exploring impacts on individuals, families, and communities', *Journal of Interpersonal Violence,* 23(3): 316–38.

Farrant, B.M., Shepherd, C.C.J., Michie, C., Scrine, C., Wright, M., Ilich, N., et al (2019) 'Delivering Elder- and community-led Aboriginal early childhood development research: Lessons from the Ngulluk Koolunga Ngulluk Koort Project', *Children (Basel),* 6(10), 106, DOI: 10.3390/children6100106.

Flores, J., Hawes, J., Westbrooks, A., and Henderson, C. (2018) 'Crossover youth and gender: What are the challenges of girls involved in both the foster care and juvenile justice systems?', *Children and Youth Services Review,* 91: 149–55.

Fogarty, W., Lovell, M., Langenberg, J., and Heron, M.-J. (2018) *Deficit Discourse and Strengths-based Approaches: Changing the Narrative of Aboriginal and Torres Strait Islander Health and Wellbeing,* Victoria, Australia: Lowitja Institute.

Granfield, R. and Cloud, W. (2001) 'Social context and "natural recovery": The role of social capital in the resolution of drug-associated problems', *Substance Use & Misuse,* 36(11): 1543–70.

Hamilton, S.L. and Maslen, S. (2022) 'Redressing "unwinnable battles": Towards institutional justice capital in Australian child protection', *Journal of Sociology,* 58(4): 535–53.

Hamilton, S., Doyle, M., and Bower, C. (2021) 'Review of fetal alcohol spectrum disorder (FASD) among Aboriginal and Torres Strait Islander people', *Australian Indigenous HealthBulletin,* 2(1).

Hamilton, S.L., Maslen, S., Farrant, B., Ilich, N., and Michie, C. (2022) '"We don't want you to come in and make a decision for us": Traversing cultural authority and responsive regulation in Australian child protection systems', *Australian Journal of Social Issues,* 57(2): 236–51.

Hamilton, S.L., Reibel, T., Watkins, R., Mutch, R.C., Kippin, N.R., Freeman, J., et al (2019) '"He has problems; he is not the problem …" A qualitative study of non-custodial staff providing services for young offenders assessed for foetal alcohol spectrum disorder in an Australian youth detention centre', *Youth Justice,* 19(2): 137–57.

Hamilton, S., Reibel, T., Maslen, S., Watkins, R., Jacinta, F., Passmore, H., et al (2020a) 'Disability "in-justice": The benefits and challenges of "yarning" with young people undergoing diagnostic assessment for fetal alcohol spectrum disorder in a youth detention center', *Qualitative Health Research,* 30(2): 314–27.

Hamilton, S.L., Maslen, S., Best, D., Freeman, J., O'Donnell, M., Reibel, T., et al (2020b) 'Putting "justice" in recovery capital: Yarning about hopes and futures with young people in detention', *International Journal for Crime, Justice and Social Democracy,* 9(2): 20–36.

Hamilton, S.L., Maslen, S., Watkins, R., Conigrave, K., Freeman, J., O'Donnell, M., et al (2020c) '"That thing in his head": Aboriginal and non-Aboriginal Australian caregiver responses to neurodevelopmental disability diagnoses', *Sociology of Health & Illness,* 42(7): 1581–96.

Hamilton, S., Jones, L., Penny, M., Pell, C., Ilich, N., Michie, C., et al (2024) '*Ngulluk Moort, Ngulluk Boodja, Ngulluk Wirin (Our Family Our Country Our Spirit):* An Aboriginal participatory action research study protocol', *PLOS One,* 19(7): e0301237.

Hewlett, N., Hayes, L., Williams, R., Hamilton, S., Holland, L., Gall, A., et al (2023) 'Development of an Australian FASD Indigenous framework: Aboriginal healing-informed and strengths-based ways of knowing, being and doing', *International Journal of Environmental Research and Public Health,* 20(6): 5215.

Hinkson, M. and Anthony, T. (2019) 'Three shots', *Arena Magazine* (Fitzroy, Vic), 163: 16–21.

Holland, L., Reid, N., Hewlett, N., Toombs, M., Elisara, T., Thomson, A., et al (2023) 'Alcohol use in Australia: Countering harm with healing', *The Lancet Regional Health–Western Pacific,* 37, 100774.

Houston, S. And Butler, M. (2019) 'More than just a number: Meeting the needs of those with mental illness, learning, speech and language difficulties in the criminal justice system', *Irish Probation Journal,* 16(1): 22–41.

Human Rights and Equal Opportunities Commission (1997) *Bringing them Home: Report of the National Inquiry into the Separation of Aboriginal and Torres Strait Islander Children from their Families*, Canberra: Australian Government.

Keddell, E. (2022) 'Mechanisms of inequity: The impact of instrumental biases in the child protection system', *Societies,* 12(3): 83.

Keddell, E., Fitzmaurice, L., Cleaver, K., and Exeter, D. (2022) 'A fight for legitimacy: Reflections on child protection reform, the reduction of baby removals, and child protection decision-making in Aotearoa New Zealand', *Kōtuitui: New Zealand Journal of Social Sciences Online,* 17(3): 378–404.

Kippin, N.R., Leitão, S., Watkins, R., Finlay-Jones, A., Condon, C., Marriott, R., et al (2018) 'Language diversity, language disorder, and fetal alcohol spectrum disorder among youth sentenced to detention in Western Australia', *International Journal of Law and Psychiatry,* 61: 40–9.

Krakouer, J. (2023) 'Journeys of culturally connecting: Aboriginal young people's experiences of cultural connection in and beyond out of home care', *Child & Family Social Work,* 28(3): 822–32.

Kretzmann, J. (1995) 'Building communities from the inside out', *CHAC Review,* 23: 4–7.

Liddle, C., Gray, P., Burton, J., Kumar, R., Tunny, T., Prideaux, C., et al (2022) *The Family Matters Report 2022,* Melbourne: Secretariat National Aboriginal and Islander Child Care.

Lin, B., Clancey, G. and Wang, S. (2020) 'Youth justice in Australia: Themes from recent inquiries', *Trends and Issues in Crime and Criminal Justice,* 605, DOI: https://doi.org/10.52922/ti04725.

Malvaso, C.G., Delfabbro, P.H., Day, A., and Nobes, G. (2019) 'Young people under youth justice supervision with varying child protection histories: An analysis of group differences', *International Journal of Offender Therapy and Comparative criminology,* 63(2): 159–78.

Manning, V., Best, D., Faulkner, N., Titherington, E., Morinan, A., Keaney, F., et al (2012) 'Does active referral by a doctor or 12-step peer improve 12-step meeting attendance? Results from a pilot randomised control trial', *Drug and Alcohol Dependence,* 126(1–2): 131–7.

McCausland, R. and Baldry, E. (2023) 'Who does Australia lock up? The social determinants of justice', *International Journal for Crime, Justice and Social Democracy,* 12(3): 37–53.

McLachlan, K., McNeil, A., Pei, J., Brain, U., Andrew, G., and Oberlander, T.F. (2019) 'Prevalence and characteristics of adults with fetal alcohol spectrum disorder in corrections: A Canadian case ascertainment study', *BMC Public Health,* 19(43), DOI: https://doi.org/10.1186/s12889-018-6292-x.

Melro, C.M., Landry, J., and Matheson, K. (2023) 'A scoping review of frameworks utilized in the design and evaluation of courses in health professional programs to address the role of historical and ongoing colonialism in the health outcomes of Indigenous Peoples', *Advances in Health Sciences Education*, 28: 1311–31.

Menon, S.E. and McCarter, S.A. (2021) 'Make juvenile justice more just: Raise-the-age to 20 years old', *Journal of Policy Practice and Research*, 2: 119–39.

Moewaka Barnes, H. and McCreanor, T. (2019) 'Colonisation, hauora and whenua in Aotearoa', *Journal of the Royal Society of New Zealand*, 49(Supplement 1): 19–33.

Moore, D. and Coyhis, D. (2010) 'The multicultural wellbriety peer recovery support program: Two decades of community-based recovery', *Alcoholism Treatment Quarterly*, 28(3): 273–92.

Moriña, A. (2022) 'When what is unseen does not exist: Disclosure, barriers and supports for students with invisible disabilities in higher education', *Disability & Society*, 39(4): 914–32.

Morrissette, V., McKenzie, B., and Morrissette, L. (1993) 'Towards an Aboriginal model of social work practice: Cultural knowledge and traditional practices', *Canadian Social Work Review / Revue canadienne de service social*, 10(1): 91–108.

Mutch, R., Freeman, J., Kippin, N., Safe, B., Pestell, C., Passmore, H., et al (2022) 'Comprehensive clinical paediatric assessment of children and adolescents sentenced to detention in Western Australia', *Journal of Fetal Alcohol Spectrum Disorder*, 4(1), DOI: https://doi.org/10.22374/jfasd.v4i1.2.

Nash, A.J., Hennessy, E.A., and Collier, C. (2019) 'Exploring recovery capital among adolescents in an alternative peer group', *Drug and Alcohol Dependence*, 199: 136–43.

O'Donnell, M., Taplin, S., Marriott, R., Lima, F., and Stanley, F.J. (2019) 'Infant removals: The need to address the over-representation of Aboriginal infants and community concerns of another "stolen generation"', *Child Abuse & Neglect*, 90: 88–98.

Paradies, Y. (2016) 'Colonisation, racism and indigenous health', *Journal of Population Research*, 33: 83–96.

Pearson, O., Schwartzkopff, K., Dawson, A., Hagger, C., Karagi, A., Davy, C., et al (2020) 'Aboriginal community controlled health organisations address health equity through action on the social determinants of health of Aboriginal and Torres Strait Islander peoples in Australia', *BMC Public Health*, 20, 1859, DOI: https://doi.org/10.1186/s12889-020-09943-4.

Porter, A. and Cunneen, C. (2021) 'Policing settler colonial societies', in P. Birch, M. Kennedy, and E. Kruger (eds) *Australian Policing: Critical Issues in 21st Century Practice*, London: Routledge, pp 397–412.

Robinson, P., Small, T., Chen, A., and Irving, M. (2023) 'Over-representation of Indigenous persons in adult provincial custody, *Statistics Canada* [online], Available from: https://www150.statcan.gc.ca/n1/pub/85-002-x/2023001/article/00004-eng.htm

Senate Affairs Reference Committee (2004) *Forgotten Australians: A Report on Australians who Experienced Institutional or Out-of-Home Care as Children*, Canberra: Australian Government.

Smith, L.T. (2021) *Decolonizing Methodologies: Research and Indigenous Peoples*, London, Zed Books.

SNAICC (2017) *Understanding and Applying the Aboriginal and Torres Strait Islander Child Placement Principle*, Melbourne: SNAICC.

Snow, P.C., Bagley, K., and White, D. (2018) 'Speech-language pathology intervention in a youth justice setting: Benefits perceived by staff extend beyond communication', *International Journal of Speech-Language Pathology*, 20(4): 458–67.

Solar, O. and Irwin, A. (2010) *A Conceptual Framework for Action on the Social Determinants of Health*, World Health Organization Document Production Services.

Staines, Z. and Scott, J. (2020) 'Crime and colonisation in Australia's Torres Strait Islands', *Australian & New Zealand Journal of Criminology*, 53(1): 25–43.

Taylor, P.S. And Habibis, D. (2020) 'Widening the gap: White ignorance, race relations and the consequences for Aboriginal people in Australia', *Australian Journal of Social Issues*, 55(3): 354–71.

Tsosie, R. (2023) 'Accountability for the harms of Indigenous boarding schools: The challenge of "healing the persisting wounds" of "historic injustice"', *Southwestern Law Review*, 52(1): 20–39.

United Nations (2022) 'Immediately end the practice of solitary confinement for children across all jurisdictions', 38(d), in *United Nations Committee Against Torture, Concluding Observations on the Sixth Periodic Report of Australia*, UN Doc CAT/C/AUS/CO6.

Walker, R., Schultz, C., and Sonn, C. (2014) 'Cultural competence – Transforming policy, services, programs and practice', in P. Dudgeon, H. Milroy, and R. Walker (eds) *Working Together: Aboriginal and Torres Strait Islander Mental Health and Wellbeing Principles and Practices* (2nd edn), Canberra: Commonwealth of Australia, pp 195–220.

Wandji, D. (2019) 'Rethinking the time and space of resilience beyond the West: An example of the post-colonial border', *Resilience*, 7(3): 288–303.

White, W. (2009) 'Recovery capital scale', *William White Papers* [online], Available from: https://www.chestnut.org/william-white-papers/

Wolfe, P. (1991) 'On being woken up: The dreamtime in anthropology and in Australian settler culture', *Comparative Studies in Society and History*, 33(2): 197–224.

12

Conclusion: Generating a Robust Science of Applied Recovery Capital

David Best, Maike Klein, and Phil Hodgson

1. Review of the contributions

It is not our intention in this section to summarize the contributions we have received as much as to explore the structure and logic of the book and how that has evolved as it has been written.

We start with two largely historical chapters outlining first the genesis of the term and the underlying model and principles (contributed by Granfield and Cloud); and second the subsequent translation of the concept into operationalization and measurement. One of the fascinating aspects of the chapter from Granfield and Cloud (Chapter 2) is the lack of traction resulting from the original presentation of the ideas. We discover in this chapter that it was not until around ten years later, with the initial involvement of William White – as recovery capital was linked to emerging ideas of Recovery-Oriented Systems of Care (ROSC) – that momentum began to build around the potential of the recovery capital concept.

This transition helped to elevate the term into both academic and policy domains. The input from William White also helped to transition the term into the consciousness of much of the US recovery community itself, an essential process particularly for a movement that is characterized by self-determination and empowerment. This expansion, however, was accelerated by the process of operationalization and the emergence of several instruments, starting with the Recovery Capital Scale (White, 2009), the Recovery Group Participation Scale (Groshkova, Best, and White, 2013, and the Assessment of Recovery Capital (Groshkova, Best, and White, 2012).

Not only did this provide a new set of publications in journals building on the foundations of the emerging recovery science movement, but it also provided a metric for monitoring self-growth and change and, at an organizational and institutional level, offered the opportunity for strengths-based outcome monitoring and performance management within addiction and recovery, a move away from the deficit-focused models of the past.

The final chapter in the book's first section, Chapter 4, written by Bunaciu and colleagues, builds on a systematic review (Bunaciu et al, 2023) of the range of methods of measuring recovery capital (including but not restricted to self-report) and of examining their scientific credentials. The review examines the 11 instruments that have peer-reviewed journal papers linked to them as well as additional methods such as social network analysis and social identity mapping. Bunaciu and colleagues point out that the 11 instruments address a total of 41 different domains of recovery capital, suggesting that there remains considerable variation in the interpretation and operationalization of the concept. This can be seen as either a strength (offering selection opportunities to users based on what they want to measure) or a weakness in our ability to reach consensus about what is included.

The second section opens with Chapter 5 by Hennessy and colleagues addressing key questions around dimensionality of the recovery capital concept (ranging from three to five possible domains) and the challenges associated with conceptualizing and measuring 'negative recovery capital'. This chapter is also illustrated with a case study that examines the application of recovery capital measurement across stakeholders and its translation into recovery-oriented interventions.

The following chapter by Bowen and Hennessy offers a critique of the conceptual development of the recovery capital model, including a review of the concept of negative recovery capital (Cloud and Granfield, 2008). The fundamental question is whether a 'capital' measure can have a negative component, particularly given that the rhetoric of recovery has at its core the transition from a deficit to a strengths-based approach. However, as White (2009) has argued, recovery is not a linear journey, and the discussion may primarily be around language and the gradual transition to an approach predicated on barriers rather than negative capital. In the same chapter, Bowen and Hennessy also recognize the limitations of the existing populations that have been studied in recovery capital research to date, with consideration given to the paucity of research in this area on women, people of colour, those who identify as LGBTQIA+, young people, and to underlying issues of cultural factors.

The issue of the role of culture and its underpinning assumptions in the writing of Bourdieu (2021) also arises in the contribution from Best, Collinson, and Patton about community capital (Chapter 7). Their argument is that context plays a role through creating the conditions in which recovery can take place, which in turn necessitates a switch in research, policy, and practice from exclusive focus on the individual to consideration of the environmental factors that both facilitate or alternatively hinder individual attempts at recovery. This suggestion for an alternative lens is also promoted by Leighton in Chapter 8 who discusses some of the philosophy of science assumptions made in existing recovery capital research designs and argues for more diverse research methods, championing the use of a realist evaluation model in advancing the knowledge foundations of recovery capital.

In the third main section of the book, the focus switches to application and implementation. Vanderplasschen and colleagues reviewed the evidence around the translation of recovery capital approaches and measurement techniques to specialist addiction treatment settings, concluding that there are clear benefits in deploying strengths-based recovery capital measures even in acute clinical settings. Similarly, in Chapter 10, Yearwood, Best, and Mericle use a case study approach to examine the application and implementation of one recovery capital measurement method, the REC-CAP, in recovery housing in the US state of Virginia. This chapter involves original interviews with some of the key players in the implementation process and reviews some of the emerging evidence about iterative process, coproduction, and organizational learning. Finally, in Chapter 11, Hamilton and Bartels discuss the translation of the recovery capital model and measurement approach to youth justice with the elaboration on the concept of justice capital. This approach opens the door to a particular form of translation for recovery capital – where the tools will be radically different, but where the underlying assumptions about strength building, empowerment, and social justice are retained.

In the following section, we will discuss key emerging themes and debates from the substantive chapters of the book.

2. Areas of common ground where consensus emerges among the contributors

Broadening the scope of application is a common theme across the chapters with potential application to other populations (including young people and focusing on various specific populations) and to other settings (the focus of Chapter 11 is on criminal justice and youth, but could be applied across a range of vulnerable populations and characteristics). This is a part of a generally positive conclusion and interpretation about the viability of the concept of recovery capital, its utility, and its potential for creating both a dedicated metric for peer-based and recovery-focused approaches and a strengths-based model in acute treatment settings (as outlined by Vanderplasschen and colleagues in Chapter 9). The latter point is critically important and reverses a trend where deficits measures had failed to provide adequate assessment of sustainable growth and well-being, but suggests the benefits of deploying a strengths-based approach across a diverse array of settings.

However, this optimism is predicated within a wider theme of caution about the current state of theory, measurement, and metrics and implementation in practice. Leighton, in particular, has expressed concern about the challenge of 'reification' – the danger that we assume what we count is in some way measuring a 'real thing', where (as Hennessy and colleagues point out) we are continuing to build the monuments to recovery capital on the sands of contested definitions of recovery. And, as Bunaciu and colleagues call attention to, this is reflected in the 41 different domains assessed in the first 11 published measures of recovery capital.

This links to the limitations pointed out in both the Bunaciu and colleagues and Bowen and Hennessy chapters about the assumptions of uni- or multidimensionality of the recovery capital metrics and how much they would be expected to vary according to the population assessed and the context in which the measurement takes place. There is general consensus that this is not simply an empirical issue but also a conceptual concern that relates to underlying questions of what recovery is and how recovery capital as a concept translates those frameworks into strengths (and by doing so identifies potential barriers) that can be specified within a coherent conceptual framework.

3. Areas of contention provoking further discussion and investigation

The first area of concern is around the use of self-complete questionnaires to assess recovery capital, with three chapters addressing this concern albeit from different perspectives. While Bunaciu and colleagues adopt an optimistic and 'positivist' position in suggesting that recovery capital tools can be supplemented with other kinds of measurement (such as social network approaches to capture more nuanced detail about a domain), Leighton's criticism of the use of self-report questionnaires within the uncritical logical positivism model of natural sciences is a more fundamental question about what kind of thing we are attempting to count and whether the assumptions of empirical science are either necessary or sufficient. Best, Collinson, and Patton argue against the sufficiency of individual self-report by suggesting that contextual factors must be addressed to adequately explain the variance in outcomes. In this argument, individual recovery capital is viewed as a dynamic interplay between individual capability to maximize resources and the conditions that create the resources, relationships, and networks which in turn determine the limits of individual growth.

The second area of contention is around what might be termed the primacy of science versus the primacy of practice. As the historical chapters by Granfield and Cloud, and then Best, White, and Hoffman suggest, the concept originated from an attempt to make sense of empirical research data (outlined in the book *Coming Clean*), but the explosion of interest in the term really derived from the White and Cloud (2008) paper where recovery capital was put to work in intervention and treatment planning using a quadrant model that categorized the resource needs of particular individuals and groups. This distinction persists to this day with the ARC, BARC-10, SABRS, and MIRC examples of traditional research tools (Best, Vanderplasschen, and Nisic, 2020; Bowen et al, 2023; Vilsaint et al, 2017), while the REC-CAP and RCI are examples of tools that attempt to capture (and develop) recovery capital in practice. The latter process has been accelerated by the latter tools' inclusion in online packages where instant scoring and feedback allow for planning and action to be undertaken during the same session, thereby also increasing their appeal to practitioners, including peer recovery workers.

As Bowen and Hennessy point out, there is also a debate about the kind of things that should be counted, with the suggestion that the MIRC is more behaviourally focussed and also includes practical barriers in contrast to, for example, the ARC, which is all about strengths and is also exclusively predicated on perceptions and beliefs. This aspect of the measurement of recovery capital has not had sufficient consideration and it will be important moving forward to link the predictive power of recovery capital tools to measurement of affect, behaviour, and cognition. This also provokes the question of validation (that will be addressed in more detail in the next section) but for the moment the key question that emerges is what criteria should be used to validate recovery capital measurement tools. To some extent, this leads directly back to the issue of how we choose to define recovery – thus, it could be argued (using the Betty Ford Consensus document; Betty Ford Institute, 2007) that recovery capital tools should be used to predict abstinence from the primary substance, global health and well-being, and active citizenship. This key question of 'what work do we want recovery capital science to do?' remains largely unanswered.

4. Implications for research and practice

Research on recovery capital is still lacking. This applies particularly to the testing of research instruments. At present, with the exception of the Assessment of Recovery Capital, for most of the tools described by Bunaciu and colleagues, what few empirical papers there are have largely been written by the authors of the tool and generally only in one setting or context. Although it is important to note that recovery capital research remains a new kid on the block (just over 20 years at the time of writing), both Hennessy (2017) and Best and Hennessy (2022) are right to be cautious about recovery capital research as a body of work and knowledge.

Furthermore, almost none of the research using recovery capital as an outcome or a marker of other outcomes has been prospective or has involved any kind of comparison group (even through a quasi-experimental design that may be more appropriate for the kinds of interventions typically used in recovery research). Thus, given that the main longitudinal research has been done in studies using the ARC and the REC-CAP as measures of recovery capital, but without either a control group or an intention to treat design, it is difficult to draw conclusions about impact. There is more encouraging evidence in Vanderplasschen and colleagues' chapter about the use of recovery capital tools as outcome measures and this will also help to expand the research into populations who would not necessarily describe themselves as being in recovery. The notion of increased diversification of populations is going to be particularly important moving forward, something which almost all our authors have also identified; either the need for increased focus on particular populations (by age, gender, sexual orientation, location, or culture, and combinations of these factors) or particular settings. Thus, the work of Hamilton and Bartels is particularly welcome in focusing on an under-researched and marginalized group (Aboriginal youth) in a specific context (youth justice). And as both Bunaciu and colleagues and Leighton have asserted, there is a need for both complementary methods and alternative research paradigms in testing and triangulating the flow of data that is now coming out of the quantitative self-report tools.

Yearwood, Best, and Mericle provide an important and illustrative case study about effective implementation in one setting (recovery housing) in one US state (Virginia), with important lessons for generating evidence-based practice, improving the skills of the peer workforce, and providing a model that can improve client retention and recovery capital growth. However, there is almost no research on implementation science around recovery capital and the resulting implications for training, service delivery, and professional development, and this is a major gap that will need to be addressed moving forwards.

5. Implications for theory

At its most fundamental, the book has illustrated the translation of an established sociological concept (social capital) to addiction recovery, initially to explain empirical findings relating to a group of individuals who experienced what has been referred to as 'natural recovery' (Granfield and Cloud, 1999). Thus, many of the challenges arising from the concept as articulated by Bourdieu (1985) and more recently by Putnam (2000) around its availability to consciousness (particularly for cultural capital) and its tractability remain. Further, as outlined earlier, this challenge of what we mean by 'capital' (manifest in the debate about whether capital can be negative) is compounded by questions around what we mean by 'recovery'.

This in turn provokes the underlying challenge of Leighton's chapter which is the argument that just because we can measure something, does not mean that something is what we want to measure. Not only do we assume that recovery capital is something that can go up (and go down), but we assume that there are things we can do to influence that process and, as Best, Collinson, and Patton argue, that is not simply at the level of individuals but also at the level of community. Clarity around what we see as the key mechanisms of action will be essential not only to improve the measures and methods but also to test and enhance our conceptual frameworks.

The question of mechanisms also provokes the question of action. In other words, if we have testable theories around how recovery capital changes (ideally grows), we then move to the development of interventions that will allow us to influence and shape that process. These should not be pale shadows of traditional treatment models, but recovery-oriented and embedded within a peer-driven, community-based, and strengths-based model of capital building, all of which will then allow the testing of the dimensionality of recovery capital (for example, should there be categories separately for cultural capital or physical capital), as articulated by Hennessy and colleagues. The issue of cultural capital is particularly important here in two different senses – first, the extent to which cultural capital reflects unchanging learning principles and processes based on family and community in childhood; and second, in the more localized sense that specific cultural groups (such as the Aboriginal youth that Hamilton and Bartels have focused on) have a sense of collective identity, morals, and practices that are both separate from social networks and intrinsic to the recovery journey.

This also provokes a further conceptual question about the universalizability of operational recovery capital measures. If Best, Collinson, and Patton are correct to assume that community level factors are intrinsic to recovery capital, then it does not follow that there will be a single set of recovery capital factors that can be applied regardless of setting and context. Whether this is the case, and if so whether it fundamentally challenges the viability of a singular recovery capital science requires both conceptual and empirical testing.

Conclusion

Ultimately the questions for recovery capital research and practice are 'does it work?' and 'does it matter?', in the sense of internal coherence ('does it work?') and value in applied settings ('does it matter?'). Huge strides have been made in less than 20 years to translate the work of Granfield and Cloud into a meaningful body of recovery capital research, with strong implications for the wider recovery science endeavour. Nonetheless, it is not yet clear how widely this has positively impacted on the lives of people in recovery. While Yearwood, Best, and Mericle offer a positive example of effective implementation linked to clear markers of growth, this needs to be replicated across multiple locations and with multiple populations before we can confidently assert that recovery capital can be more than a new way of collecting data. More science is needed; science which is coproduced and owned by those who will implement and mobilize this knowledge.

References

Best, D. and Hennessy, E.A. (2022) 'The science of recovery capital: Where do we go from here?', *Addiction*, 117(4): 1139–45.

Best, D., Vanderplasschen, W., and Nisic, M. (2020) 'Measuring capital in active addiction and recovery: The development of the strengths and barriers recovery scale (SABRS)', *Substance Abuse: Treatment, Prevention, and Policy*, 15, 40, DOI: https://doi.org/10.1186/s13011-020-00281-7.

Betty Ford Institute Consensus Panel (2007) 'What is recovery? A working definition from the Betty Ford Institute', *Journal of Substance Abuse Treatment*, 33(3): 221–8.

Bourdieu, P. (2021) *Forms of Capital: General Sociology, Volume 3 Lectures at the Collège de France 1983–1984*, Cambridge: Polity Press.

Bourdieu, P. (1985) 'The social space and the genesis of groups', *Social Science Information*, 24(2): 195–220.

Bowen, E., Irish, A., Wilding, G., LaBarre, C., Capozziello, N., Nochajski, T., et al (2023) 'Development and psychometric properties of the Multidimensional Inventory of Recovery Capital (MIRC)', *Drug and Alcohol Dependence*, 247, 109875, DOI: 10.1016/j.drugalcdep.2023.109875.

Bunaciu, A., Bliuc, A.M., Best, D., Hennessy, E.A., Belanger, M.J., and Benwell, C.S.Y. (2023) 'Measuring recovery capital for people recovering from alcohol and drug addiction: A systematic review', *Addiction Research & Theory*, 32(3): 225–36.

Cloud, W. and Granfield, R. (2008) 'Conceptualizing recovery capital: Expansion of a theoretical construct', *Substance Use & Misuse*, 43(12–13): 1971–86.

Granfield, R. and Cloud, W. (1999) *Coming Clean: Overcoming Addiction without Treatment*, New York: New York University Press.

Groshkova, T., Best, D., and White, W. (2012) 'The Assessment of Recovery Capital: Properties and psychometrics of a measure of addiction recovery strengths', *Drug and Alcohol Review*, 32(2): 187–94.

Groshkova, T., Best, D., and White, W. (2013) 'Recovery Group Participation Scale (RGPS): Factor structure in alcohol and heroin recovery populations', in Jeffrey D. Roth and David Best (eds) *Addiction and Recovery in the UK*, Oxford, UK: Routledge, pp 87–103.

Hennessy, E.A. (2017) 'Recovery capital: A systematic review of the literature', *Addiction Research and Theory*, 25(5): 349–60.

Putnam, R. (2000) *Bowling Alone: The Collapse and Revival of American Community*, New York: Simon & Schuster.

Vilsaint, C.L., Kelly, J.F., Bergman, B.G., Groshkova, T., Best, D., and White, W. (2017) 'Development and validation of a Brief Assessment of Recovery Capital (BARC-10) for alcohol and drug use disorder', *Drug and Alcohol Dependence*, 177(May): 71–6.

White W. 2009. *Recovery Capital Scale*. https://www.chestnut.org/william-white-papers/

White, W. and Cloud, W. (2008) 'Recovery capital: A primer for addictions professionals', *Counselor*, 9(5): 22–7.

Index

References to tables appear in **bold** type. References to figures are in *italic* type. References to endnotes show both the page number and the note number (231n3).

A
ABCD *see* Asset Based Community Development (ABCD)
ABCE *see* Asset Based Community Engagement (ABCE) Mapping
Aboriginal and Torres Straight Islander peoples
  children, state care systems for 213–14
  colonization on, impact of 211, 213
  intergenerational trauma 216–17
  webs of connectedness of 212–13, 223
  youth justice system 214–15
  see also Indigenous peoples
abstinence 55, 61, 65–6, 89, 146, 148, 171, 172
Achenbach Self Report 60
addiction xv, 169–70 *see also* disease model framework; recovery; treatment
addiction recovery *see* recovery
Addiction Recovery Management (Kelly and White) 36, 134
Addiction Severity Index (ASI) 39, 52, 54
Addiction Technology Transfer Center (ATTC) 34, 35
addiction treatment *see* treatment
adolescents/youth
  community recovery capital for 125–6
  Indigenous children 213–14
  neurodisability and 214, 215, **216**, 220–1
  recovery capital for 66, 104–6
  youth justice system 214–15
Adult Health Capital Scale (AHCS) 53, 60, 67n1
Advanced Recovery Management System (ARMS) 196–7, *198*, 202–3, 204, 207
AHCS *see* Adult Health Capital Scale (AHCS)
AI (artificial intelligence) 26–7
Albright, Lonnetta 35
alcohol 12, 111

alcohol and other drug (AOD) problems xiv, xv–xvi, 111–12 *see also specific drugs (e.g., opioids, methamphetamines)*
Alcohol Expectancies Questionnaire 60
Alcoholics Anonymous (AA) 13, 145, 149, 169
altruism *see* reciprocal altruism
American Society of Addiction Medicine 78
AOD *see* alcohol and other drug (AOD) problems
applied recovery capital 195, 197, 198–9, 201
applied sociology 195
ARC *see* Assessment of Recovery Capital (ARC)
Archer, Margaret 153–4, **154**, 155, 158, 163–4
ARMS *see* Advanced Recovery Management System (ARMS)
Arndt, S. 54
artificial intelligence (AI) 26–7
ASI *see* Addiction Severity Index (ASI)
assertive linkage 125, 127–8, **128**, *128*, 157, 223
Assessment of Recovery Capital (ARC)
  author's overview of 41, 53–4, 67
  comparison with other tools 55, 56
  development of 40, 53
  domains/subdomains of 62, *63*, 67n4, 102
  and other questionnaires 56, 60, 61
  and recovery capital 147, 173–4, 175
  strengths-based focus of 104
assessments *see* measurement of recovery capital
Asset Based Community Development (ABCD) 123–7, 128, 132–3, 137
Asset Based Community Engagement (ABCE) Mapping 64–5, 129, *130*, 130–2, 132–3, 137

INDEX

ATTC (Addiction Technology Transfer Center) 34, 35
autonomous reflexivity **154**

B

BAHCS–10 *see* Brief Adult Health Capital Scale (BAHCS–10)
Baldwin, H. 180
Banksia Hill Detention Centre 215, 216, 218, 221
BARC–10 *see* Brief Assessment of Recovery Capital (BARC–10)
barriers to recovery *see* negative recovery capital; structural barriers
Bartels, Lorana 4, 8, 233, 236
Behavioral Health Recovery Management (BHRM) project 33–4, 35
Behavioural Risk Factor Surveillance System Questionnaire 57
Belanger, M.J. 176
Best, David
  Asset Based Community Development (ABCD) 125, 126
  Asset Based Community Engagement (ABCE) 64–5
  and measurement of recovery capital 39–41, 156–7, 233, 237
  REC-CAP assessment 195–6
  recovery capital model 100, 121–2
  on recovery capital research 151
  recovery pathways 170
  research on recovery capital 37, 148, 175, 176, 232–3
Best, Jessica 233, 236
Betty Ford Institute 38, 88, **90**
BHRM (Behavioral Health Recovery Management) project 33–4, 35
Bliuc, A.M. 64
Block, P. 124
Blount, T.N. 107
Bormann, N.L. 174–5
Bourdieu, Pierre 3, 4, 10, 17, 151, 153, 157, 232, 236
Bowen, Elizabeth 54, 61, 110, 232, 234, 235
Bower, C. 215
Bowling Alone (Putnam) 3
Braithwaite, John 4
Brief Adult Health Capital Scale (BAHCS–10) 60–1, 67n3
Brief Assessment of Recovery Capital (BARC–10)
  author's overview of 42–3, 55–6, 235
  domains/subdomains of 62, *63*, 67n4
  and other questionnaires 59, 61
  research using 177
  strengths-based focus of 104
Bronfenbrenner, U. 97–8
Bunaciu, A. 232, 234, 235, 236

Bunge, M. 153
Burns, J. 55

C

Canada 23–4, 38
capital 3–5, 91–2 see also *specific types (e.g., community recovery capital, justice recovery capital)*
Center for Substance Abuse Treatment (CSAT) 146
certified recovery residences (CRRs) 195–6
Cheney, A.M. 109
children *see* adolescents/youth
Cloud, William
  challenges with measurement tools 81
  on cultural recovery capital 151–2
  impact of recovery capital concept xiv, xvi–xvii
  on long-term recovery 1
  on measurement of recovery capital 76
  and natural recovery 143–4
  on negative recovery capital 5
  on recovery capital concept 13–15, 121
  recovery capital model 98, 99, 100, 122, 170
  recovery experiences xv
  research on recovery capital 34–5, 104, 145, 147, 234–5
  scores to activities/actions, linking 41, 43
Coleman, J. 3, 16, 17, 121, 152, 153
Collinson, B. 64–5, 131, 232–3, 234, 237
colonization 211, 212–13, 217, 219, 224n1
Coming Clean (Grandfield and Cloud) 14, 15, 44, 144
Commitment to Sobriety Scale 56
communicative reflexivity **154**
communities
  adolescent/young adults, support for 106
  grassroots recovery community organizations 22, 23–4, 36, 40–1
  online 26–7, 64
community connectors 124, 125–6, 127, 223
community recovery capital
  assertive linkage 125, 127–8, **128**, *128*, 157, 223
  author's overview of xvi, *99*, 100
  cultural recovery capital and 122, 152
  as domain of recovery capital 121–2, 147
  importance of 120–1, 136–7, 146, 185
  for Indigenous peoples **219**, 219–20, 221–2
  measurement of 41, 55, 61, 64–5
  research on 125–7, 128
  social recovery capital and 133
  and strengths-based approach 2, 124–5
  see also Asset Based Community Development (ABCD); Asset Based Community Engagement (ABCE) Mapping; Recovery-Oriented System of Care (ROSC)

241

connection 78, *78*, 217, 221, **222**
Conner, Matthew 202–4
constructivism 157–8
corporate actors 152, 155–7
criminal legal system-involved people 85, 110–11, 179, 214–15
critical realism 142–3, 150, 158, 163–4
  see also realist research
CRRs (certified recovery residences) 195–6
CSAT (Center for Substance Abuse Treatment) 146
cultural recovery capital
  author's overview of 98, *99*, 100, 232–3
  community recovery capital and 122, 152
  existing research on 151–3
  as population-specific 104
cultural trauma 109
culture of recovery xvi

D

Dalkin, S.M. 163
Davidson, L. 172
Dawes, William 25
deficit management approach 1–2
De Maeyer, J. 160, 162
discovery maps 205, *206*, 207
disease model framework 11, 12–13, 144–5, 148, 149, 169, 193–4
distrust 178–9, 221
domains (of recovery capital framework/model)
  author's overview of 97–8, *99*, 121–2
  four-domain model 34, 46n1, 55, 101
  measurement of 62, *63*, 67n4, 86–7, *87*, 232
  multi-domain engagement 132
  research on 102–3
  three-domain model 99, *99*, 100, 101, 121–2
drugs 111–12 see also *specific drugs (e.g., opioids, methamphetamines)*
Duffy, P. 180
Dunlop, Robert 13

E

Ecological Systems Theory (Bronfenbrenner) 97–8
employment 85, *87*, 177–8
empowerment 78, 78–9, **90**, 91–2, 130, 131
Evans, Arthur 36

F

families
  future research areas for 93, 107
  intergenerational trauma 213, 216–17
  recovery capital, roles of in 44, 106
Fernandez, D.E.R. 177
Fetal Alcohol Spectrum Disorder 215, 218
financial recovery capital 4, 98, *99*, 155, 164
Flaherty, Mike 35
Fleming, Alexander 10–11

Foucault, Michel 15
four-domain recovery capital model 34, 46n1, 55, 101
fractured reflexivity **154**
Francis, M.W. 60
funding 20–1, 39, 83, 149, 156, 199, 201–2, 208

G

Galanter, Mark 149
G–CHIME framework 78, 78–9
gender 66, 107, 132, 180, 183
General Well-Being Schedule 57
Gilbert, P.A. 107
Gilbert, W.C. 174
Gladwell, Malcolm 25
Granfield, Robert
  on cultural recovery capital 151
  impact of recovery capital concept xiv, xvi–xvii
  and natural recovery 143–4
  on negative recovery capital 5
  on recovery capital concept 13–15, 121
  recovery capital model 98, *99*, 100, 171
  recovery experiences xv
  research on recovery capital 104, 145, 147, 234–5, 237
grassroots recovery community organizations 22, 23–4, 36, 40–1
Greene, M.C. 163
Grimes, Anthony 197, 199, 201–2
Groshkova, Teodora 39, 173
groups/populations see *specific groups (e.g. adolescents, women, LGBTQIA+)*
growth 78, *78*, 87–8, 91, 92–3
growth recovery capital 98, *99*

H

habitus 3, 151, 153, 156
Hamilton, Sharynne 4, 8, 211–12, 233, 236
Hanauer, M. 59, 61, 67n1
Hassles and Uplifts scale 60
Headid, R.J. 176–7, 178
health inequalities 85
Hennessy, Emily
  on existing recovery capital research 3, 151, 232, 234, 235
  recovery capital research by 42, 105, 179
heroin 107, 111, 148, 160–1
Hispanic people 85
Hoeppner, B. 41–2
hope 78, *78*, 86, 133, 207, 208, 224
human recovery capital 98, *99*, 100, 105, 107, 121, 145, 151

I

identity 78, *78*
Important People and Activities (IPA) instrument 60

INDEX

incarcerated people *see* criminal legal system-involved people
Inclusive Recovery Cities (IRC) model 123, 136, 137
Indigenous peoples
 colonization on, impact of 212–13
 on disability 218
 justice capital assets scale 218, **219**, 219–21, 224n1
 see also Aboriginal and Torres Straight Islander peoples
individuals in recovery
 case studies of 79–81
 recovery capital, assessment of **77**, 78–9
 research on 173–6, 180–3
 treatment retention and completion 176–8
 see also recovery; treatment
institutional justice capital 221, **222**, 223–4
intergenerational trauma 213, 216–17
intersectionality 107, 108–9, 109–10, 112, 113
IPA (Important People and Activities) instrument 60
IRC *see* Inclusive Recovery Cities (IRC) model
Ivers, J.H. 157

J

Jellinek, E.M. 13
jobs *see* employment
justice recovery capital
 assets scale for Indigenous peoples 218, **219**, 219–21, 224n1
 author's overview of 4, 215
 examples of negative/positive **216**
 for Indigenous peoples 217–18
 institutional justice capital 221, **222**, 223–4
 neurodisability and 214, 215, 220–1

K

Karlsson, Jan 164
Kelly, John 37, 41–3, 87, 145, 163
Kelly, P.J. 179
Kirk, Thomas 36
Krentzman, Amy 38
Kretzmann, J. 124
Kuhn, Thomas 10

L

Last Door Recovery Society (LDRS) 23–4
Latino people 85, 110
Laudet, Alexandre 36, 39–40, 100, 121–2
LDRS (Last Door Recovery Society) 23–4
LEAP (Lothians and Edinburgh Abstinence Project) 40–1
Lehman, John 195–6, 197, 200
Leighton, Tim 233, 234, 236, 237
LEROs *see* Lived Experience Recovery Organisations (LEROs)

Levy, S. 163
LGBTQIA+ people 108
Life in Recovery (LiR) surveys 59
Likert scales 55, 56, 58, 59, 60, 61
Linguistic Inquiry and Word Count (LIWC) 64
Link, B.G. 108–9
linkage *see* assertive linkage
LiR (Life in Recovery) surveys 59
Lived Experience Recovery Organisations (LEROs) 149, 156, 162
LIWC (Linguistic Inquiry and Word Count) 64
Lothians and Edinburgh Abstinence Project (LEAP) 40–1
lower-income people 109–10

M

MacDonald, A. 175
macro level of recovery capital analysis 15, 85, 130, 194, 197, 201
maintained recovery 148
Mann, Marty 13
MAP *see* Maudsley Addiction Profile (MAP)
Martinelli, T.F. 174
Marx, K. 147
Matamonasa-Bennett, A. 109
Matlack, M. 163
Maudsley Addiction Profile (MAP) 39, 56
McKnight, J. 124
meaning (in life) 78, *78*, 91, 144, 159, 161
Measure, Plan, and Engage (MPE) model 196, 197, 203, 204–5, 207
measurement of recovery capital
 access to tools for 44
 author's overview of 33–6, *35*, 37–8
 author's review of 65–7, 152
 challenges with 41, 81, 83–4, 84–6, 156–7, 202–3
 development of tools for 39–41, 50–1
 domains/subdomains 62, *63*, 67n4, 86–7, *87*
 future steps for 44–5, 92–3
 gaps in, current 45
 interpretation of results 86–7, *87*
 of justice capital 218, **219**, 219–21, **222**, 223–4
 online mechanisms for 43
 reasons for 76, **77**
 for research/programme evaluation 81–5
 strengths-based approach to 40, 78, 172–3
 for treatment planning/intervention 76, **77**–9, 79–81
 see also domains (of recovery capital framework/model); *specific tools (e.g., Assessment of Recovery Capital, REC-CAP)*
mechanisms
 author's overview of 150
 context and 156–7

243

realist approach and 159–60
  for recovery 145
  research on 153
men 107, 109
Mericle, Amy 236, 238
meso level of recovery capital analysis 130, 152, 194, 202, 208
meta-reflexivity **154**
methadone 148, 160–1
methamphetamines 111, 175
metrics *see* measurement of recovery capital
micro level of recovery capital analysis 15, 85, 130, 152, 194, 202, 208
minority groups 108, 147, 201
MIRC *see* Multidimensional Inventory of Recovery Capital (MIRC)
moral theories of addiction 12–13, 148, 169
Morton, S. 180–1
MPE *see* Measure, Plan, and Engage (MPE) model
Multidimensional Inventory of Recovery Capital (MIRC) 61–2, *63*, 67n4, 102, 104, 235
mutual aid groups 121, 127, 143–4, 146, 155, 174, 176, 181

N

National Alliance of Recovery Residences (NARR) 199
National Institute on Alcohol Abuse and Alcoholism 13
National Institute on Alcohol and Alcohol Use 89
National Recovery Study 85, 108
Native American people 109, 110 *see also* Indigenous peoples
natural recovery 13, 14–15, 15–17, 143–5, 170
navigators *see* recovery navigators
Neale, J. 107, 111
negative recovery capital
  author's overview of 5, 18–20, 98, 99, 171–2, 194
  challenges with 103–4, 232
  continuum 98–100, *100*
  as dynamic 87–8, 172
  examples of **216**
  institutional justice capital **222**, 223
  neurodisability as, undiagnosed 215, **216**
  population-specific examples 107, 110–11
  in recovery capital assessments 59, 61, 84–5
  research on 181–2, 183, *198*
negative social capital 20, 145
neurodisability 214, 215, **216**, 220–1
NIAAA 90

O

opioids 54, 85, 111, 148, 175, 177

Osborne, B. 179
outcomes 39, 89, 91

P

parents *see* families
Parlier-Ahmad, A.B. 177
pathways *see* recovery pathways
Patient Health Questionnaire (PHQ-9) 61
Patton, David 103, 181, 232–3, 234, 237
Pawson, Ray 159, 161, 162
Peele, Stanton 14
Peer Recovery Specialists (PRS) 124, 195, 205, 207
peers *see* recovery navigators
penicillin 10–11
people *see* specific groups (e.g., adolescents, women, LGBTQIA+)
people of colour 108–9
Peters, B. 177
The Phoenix 135
PHQ-9 (Patient Health Questionnaire) 61
physical recovery capital 98, *99*, 110, 179, 180
Polcin, D.L. 53
populations/groups *see* specific groups (e.g. adolescents, women, LGBTQIA+)
Portes, A. 147, 152
positive recovery capital
  author's overview of 5, 18–20, *100*
  continuum 98–100, *100*
  examples of **216**
  institutional justice capital **222**, 223
professionals *see* service providers
programme evaluations 81–5, 86
progress, recovery capital as 89, 91
prohibition 12
Project MATCH 145
PRS *see* Peer Recovery Specialists (PRS)
PTSD Checklist – Civilian Versions 57
Putnam, R.D. 3, 4, 236

Q

qualitative research
  author's overview of 157–8
  on justice capital 215, 216, 218, 221
  on natural recovery 14
  population-specific 104, 107, 108, 111–12
  on recovery capital 102, 162, 173, 180, 181, 182
quality of life, assessment of 56, 57, 174, *198*, 206 *see also* WHOQOL-BREF
Quality of Life, Spirituality, Religiousness, and Personal Beliefs Questionnaire (WHO) 57
quantitative research 81, 86, 157, 162, 163, 173

R

racial health inequalities 85
RCAM (Recovery Capital for Adolescents Model) 42, 105

INDEX

RCI *see* Recovery Capital Index (RCI)
RCQ *see* Recovery Capital Questionnaire (RCQ)
RCS *see* Recovery Capital Scale (RCS) (Sterling et al); Recovery Capital Scale (RCS) (White's)
realism
  critical realism 142–3, 150, 158, 163–4
  scientific realism 150
realist research
  author's overview of 158–60
  benefits of 160–1
  future possibilities for 161–2
  see also reflexivity
REC–CAP
  Advanced Recovery Management System (ARMS) 196–7, *198*, 202–3, 204, 207
  author's overview of 195–7
  benefits of 81, 158–9, 235
  development of 53, 56–7, 193, 195–6
  discovery maps 205, *206*, 207
  domains/subdomains of 62, *63*, 67n4, 102–3
  Measure, Plan, & Engage (MPE) model 196, 197, 203, 204–5, 207
  and negative recovery capital 104, 196
  online support for 66, 235
  research using, recovery capital 174, 175, 176, 179, 197–201
  service providers on 202–5, 207
  strengths-based approach of 84–5
reciprocal altruism 123, 136
Reciprocal Community Development 126, 133
recovery
  communities for 123
  definitions of 65–6, 88–9, **90**, 120, 146
  G–CHIME framework for *78*, 78–9
  history of xv
  as a lived experience 27
  mechanisms for 145
  methadone 148, 160–1
  models of 41–3
  natural recovery 13, 14–15, 15–17, 143–5, 170
  as nonlinear 89, 91, 170, 232
  predictors of long-term 1, 35
  programmes, evaluation of 81–5, 86
  as progress 89, 91
  recovery capital and xvi, 20, 25
  recovery pathways 170–1, 181, 183
  see also negative recovery capital; treatment
recovery capital
  addiction treatment, impact of on xiv
  applied recovery capital 195, 197, 198–9, 201
  author's overview of xv, xvi
  concept of 12–13, 14–15, 17–20, 121, 144, 194–5
  from disease model to 147–9
  future steps for 92–3, 113
  institutionalization of theory 20–5, 26
  as progress 89, 91
  as variable 87–8
  see also measurement of recovery capital; recovery capital framework/model; reflexivity; research; *specific types (e.g., community recovery capital, justice recovery capital)*
Recovery Capital for Adolescents Model (RCAM) 42, 105
recovery capital framework/model
  author's overview of 11, 182–3
  challenges with 84–6
  definitions of recovery and 65–6, 88–9, **90**
  research on 36–7
  see also domains (of recovery capital framework/model)
Recovery Capital Index (RCI) 57–8, 62, *63*, 66, 67n4, 81, 235
Recovery Capital Questionnaire (RCQ) 54–5, 61, 62, *63*, 67n4
Recovery Capital Scale (RCS) (Sterling et al) 52, 62, *63*, 67n4
Recovery Capital Scale (RCS) (White's) 37, 48–9, 52–3, 59, 67n3
recovery carriers/champions xvi, 43
recovery cascades xvi, 43
recovery coaches xvi, 79, 181
recovery contagion 40, 43, 44
Recovery Group Participation Scale (RGPS) 40, 41, 56
recovery identity xvii, 78, 92, 132
recovery movement 40, 146, 170
recovery navigators 65, 79, 80–1, 196, 202, 204, 205, 207
Recovery-Oriented System of Care (ROSC) 21–2, 34, 35–6, 78, 134–5, 137, 231
recovery paradigm xiv, 43, 148
recovery pathways 170–1, 181, 183
Recovery Research Institute 37, 42, 88, **90**
Recovery Science Research Collaborative 89
Recovery Strengths Questionnaire (RSQ) 58, 62, *63*, 67n4
recovery transmission 43, 44
REC–PATH study 170, 174
reflexivity 153–4, **154**, 155, 156, 159–60, 161, 162–3, 209
remission xv, 42, 84, 88–9, **90**, 143 *see also* natural recovery
research
  on community recovery capital 125–7, 128
  cultural capital, existing research on 151–3
  on domains of recovery capital 102–3
  future research suggestions by authors 44–5, 92–3, 107, 113, 161–2, 183–5, 235–6
  with an intersectional lens 112

245

on justice capital 218, **219**, 219–21, **222**, 223–4
on measurement of recovery capital 197, *198*, 198–9, 200–1
population-specific 104–11, 147, 200–1
quantitative research 81, 86, 157, 162, 163, 173
realist research 157–60
recovery capital, existing research on 150–1
on recovery capital 36–8, 39–41, 42, 158–9, 173–6
recovery capital assessments in 81–5
on recovery management 34–6
on recovery pathways 170
on service providers 178–80
on service users' experiences 180–3
substance-specific 111–12
theory-driven interviews 162–3
on treatment effectiveness 170–1, 176–8
see also qualitative research; realist research
retraditionalization 109
Revere, Paul 25
RGPS *see* Recovery Group Participation Scale (RGPS)
ROSC *see* Recovery-Oriented System of Care (ROSC)
RSQ *see* Recovery Strengths Questionnaire (RSQ)
RSRC 90

S

SABRS *see* Strengths and Barriers Recovery Scale (SABRS)
salutogenesis 44
SAMHSA (Substance Abuse and Mental Health Services Administration) 34, 35, **90**, 120
Savic, M. 125
scales *see* measurement of recovery capital
scientific realism 150
service providers 178–80, 201–2, 202–5, 207
service users *see* individuals in recovery
sexual minorities 108
Sheedy, C.K. 134
Short Recovery Capital Scale (SRCS–10) 59, 67n4
SIM–AR *see* Social Identity Mapping in Addiction Recovery (SIM–AR)
Skogens, L. 180, 182
SNA *see* Social Network Analysis (SNA)
social identities 64, 106, 121, 132
Social Identity Mapping in Addiction Recovery (SIM–AR) 63–4, 66
Social Network Analysis (SNA) 64, 65, 232
social recovery capital
for adolescents/young adults 105–6
author's overview of 3–4, 98, *99*
building of 45, 80, 156, 181, 182, 184–5
community recovery capital and 133
continuum *100*
as domain of recovery capital 55, 57, 58, 61, 98, 102, 121
for Indigenous peoples 217, 219, **219**
measuring of 63–4
natural recovery and 16–18
negative social capital 20, 145
in online settings 64
research on 41, 42
as resources 152
Social Recovery Capital (SRC–IPA) questionnaire 59–60, 62, *63*, 67n4
Social Support Scale 56, 62
spontaneous remission *see* natural recovery
SRC–IPA *see* Social Recovery Capital (SRC–IPA) questionnaire
SRCS–10 *see* Short Recovery Capital Scale (SRCS–10)
stakeholders *see* individuals in recovery
Sterling, 52, 67n4
Strengths and Barriers Recovery Scale (SABRS) 59, 62, *63*, 67n4, 235
strengths-based approaches
actions for transition to 1–2
challenges with 84–5
for communities 2, 124–5
and measurement of recovery capital 40, 78, 104, 172–3
structural barriers 84–5
Subica, A.M. 108–9
Substance Abuse and Mental Health Services Administration (SAMHSA) 34, 35, 88, **90**, 120
Surgeon General's Report on Alcohol, Drugs, and Health (US) 171

T

technologies of the self 15
theory-driven interviews 162–3
three-domain recovery capital model 99, *99*, 100, 101, 121–2
The Tipping Point (Gladwell) 25
tools *see* measurement of recovery capital
transmission of recovery 43, 44
trauma 103, 107, 109, 213, 216–17
treatment
history of xv, xvi
mutual aid groups 121, 127, 143–4, 146, 155, 174, 176, 181
pathology focus of xiv, xv
planning and intervention 76, 78–81
recommendations for 184–5
retention and completion of 176–8
as a tool 27
see also individuals in recovery; recovery; research
True Recovery RVA 204–5

INDEX

U

United Kingdom
  Drugs Strategies 148
  Lived Experience Recovery Organisations (LEROs) 156
  recovery communities in 149
  recovery movement in 40, 146
United States
  health disparities in 85
  people of colour in 109, 110

V

Vanderplasschen, W. 170, 233, 236
VARR *see* Virginia Association of Recovery Residences (VARR)
Vilsaint, C.L. 56
Virginia Association of Recovery Residences (VARR) 197, 199, *200*, 200–3
von Greiff, N. 180, 182

W

Wacquant, L. 17
Waugh, Chris 204–5
White, William
  challenges with measurement tools 81
  on community 120
  on cultural recovery capital 152
  impact of 22–3, 231, 235
  on long-term recovery 1
  on measurement of recovery capital 33–6, 37, 38, 76
  on recovery 146, 172, 232
  on recovery capital concept 18, 147–8
  recovery capital model 100, 122
  Recovery Capital Scale (RCS) 37, 48–9, **51**, 52–3, 59, 67n3
  Recovery-Oriented System of Care (ROSC) 134
  scores to activities/actions, linking 41, 43
  on social capital 16
White people 85
Whitesock, D. 58
Whitter, M. 134
WHOQOL–BREF 54, 55, 62
women 107, 132
work *see* employment
Wrong, Dennis 158

Y

Yates, R. 55
Yearwood, Reed 236, 238
young adults 66, 104–6
youth *see* adolescents/youth

Z

Zemore, S.E. 163

www.ingramcontent.com/pod-product-compliance
Lightning Source LLC
Chambersburg PA
CBHW051534020426
42333CB00016B/1917